Blueprint
CROCHET
SWEATERS

Blueprint
CROCHET
SWEATERS

techniques for custom construction

ROBYN CHACHULA

INTERWEAVE.
interweave.com

EDITOR Wendy Williams

TECHNICAL EDITOR Marty Miller

PHOTOGRAPHER Joe Hancock

STYLIST Emily Choi

HAIR AND MAKEUP Kathy MacKay

ART DIRECTOR Liz Quan

COVER AND INTERIOR DESIGN Karla Baker

PRODUCTION DESIGNER Katherine Jackson

Interweave Press LLC
A division of F+W Media Inc
201 East Fourth Street
Loveland, Colorado 80537
interweave.com

Printed in China by Asia Pacific Offset
Ltd.

Library of Congress
Cataloging-in-Publication Data

Chachula, Robyn, 1978-
Blueprint crochet sweaters : techniques
for custom construction / Robyn
Chachula.
   p. cm.
   Includes index
ISBN 978-1-59668-828-5 (pbk.)
1. Crocheting--Patterns. 2. Sweaters. I.
Title.
TT825.C3783 2013
746.43'4--dc23

2012034027

10 9 8 7 6 5 4 3 2 1

I dedicate this book to my fellow crochet designers. Your passion inspires me every day to keep learning and exploring our craft.

Acknowledgments

I am deeply grateful for this opportunity to share my quite analytical, visually based, engineer's approach to crochet design—especially because it's not directed at houses, but fashionable sweaters.

All the yarns used in the book were graciously donated by the yarn companies: Blue Sky Alpacas, Caron International, Cascade Yarns, Lion Brand, Tahki Stacy Charles, and Universal Yarn. I thank them for the support and quick responses to my requests. I truly appreciate all that they've given me.

Thank you to everyone at Interweave, especially Wendy Williams and Marty Miller, for making the ramblings of a sleep-deprived mom sound intelligent. I also thank Megan Granholm, Rebecca DeSensi, Diane Halpern, and Virginia Boundy for helping with several of the sweaters as I focused on writing.

Most importantly, I thank my family and friends for their ongoing love and support as I take on each new challenge. And, as always, I especially thank my husband, Mark, for his unwavering love. Without his encouragement and help, this book would not have been possible.

Lastly, I thank you, the readers, for enjoying what I love to do so much. Please know that your enthusiasm for crochet keeps me energized to create and share my designs!

CONTENTS

INTRODUCTION

Like many crocheters, you might be intimidated by the idea of making sweaters, let alone designing your own. I wrote *Blueprint Crochet Sweaters* to take the mystery out of stitching sweaters and give you the confidence to create your beautiful sweaters. The book breaks sweater construction down into four types: classic construction created by crocheting panels and seaming them, top-down (or in the round) construction, granny motif, and unique construction methods. The designs in each chapter are variations on each type of construction, and sidebars illuminate various aspects of construction.

Before we get into the projects, I'll let you in on the mammoth secret crochet designers harbor about how we create our best projects. We cheat! One key to my designs lies in my mistakes. I'm not talking about just dropping a stitch here and there, but about a neckline that suddenly falls off your shoulders or buttonholes not even close to being equally spaced. When I make mistakes, they are sumo-sized, and because I re-crochet only as a last resort, I have amassed quite an assortment of fixes.

This is not to say that the basics aren't valid; they are. Yes, you need to match gauge, and, yes, you need to use the same fiber content as shown on the pattern, and, yes, you need to know your body shape. These basics are essential. So let's review each of them briefly.

GAUGE

We all know we need it. It's the size of your stitch pattern (or motif) in both width and height. But you'll need to experiment to get it right. I always start with the hook and yarn weight (the yarn thickness) recommended in the pattern. I chain enough to make a 6" (15 cm) swatch so there is plenty of space to measure the gauge. After about 4" (10 cm), I'll measure the width and check it against the gauge. Waiting to measure your gauge is important; often stitch patterns can either tighten or loosen after a few rows. When you swatch for gauge, if your hook size hits exactly for the width but not the height, you can probably go with it. You can either crochet an extra row to make up the difference or stretch the garment to the measurements you need when you block it. One trick to getting the right measurements is to never measure the whole swatch. Only measure stitch repeat to stitch repeat inside of the swatch. Including the edges can sometimes add or subtract from your actual gauge measurement.

FIBER CONTENT

Why is fiber content important? Why not use wool even though the pattern calls for cotton? All fibers behave differently when you stitch them, and they do so most noticeably in crochet. When you crochet, you loop one strand around another over and over, almost like making Velcro with hooks and loops. Therefore, when you have fibers that are naturally sleek (such as bamboo, cotton, and silk), the loops won't lock into place as tightly, and you'll have a naturally draping garment. Animal fibers (such as wool, alpaca, and cashmere) naturally want to tangle and will have less drape. Even more important, sleek yarns are usually significantly heavier than animal fibers. If a pattern calls for wool and you use cotton, your bustline might fall to your waist because of the weight alone. If you're concerned about a wool allergy and can't substitute another animal fiber, try acrylic. Acrylic can work well if you know how to block it (think steam).

FIT

Knowing your size is more than just knowing you're a standard Large. You do need to know your bust, waist, and hip circumference, but you'll need go further to get a great fit. In my yarn notebook, I record my torso length, back width (from shoulder to shoulder), neck width, and armhole depth of my favorite sweater. Taking those measurements directly from a favorite sweater lets you know how to get exactly the fit you want from schematics. Taking the guesswork out of a sweater's fit will fix a number of concerns you might have with the pattern. When all else fails, I make a mock-up of the schematic in a cheap felt fabric (something thick to mimic the crochet fabric) to test the style on my body before I pick up a hook.

The best way to learn how to do something is by doing it, so jump in and start crocheting the sweaters that follow. I hope you'll take what you learn from making them and apply it to your own designs. This is just a blueprint!

Top 10 Tips for Mastering Your Crochet Design

Suppose you're getting the gauge called for in the pattern, using the recommended fiber content in your yarn, and happy with the schematic size for your body type—but you're unhappy with the results. At this point, you can turn from crafter to professional in a heartbeat. You might need to block the garment more aggressively to get it to drape correctly. Or you might need to add a larger edging to smooth rough edges. Or you might simply need to sew in some ribbon to tighten the neckline. Below is a list of some of my favorite fixes for jams I seem to constantly get into as I crochet. The list begins with the start of a project and goes to the finish. Also, be warned: Some fixes are not for the faint of heart! Be sure to test any that you think might work on a swatch first. If you want to see any of these tips in action before you give them a go, be sure to check out my workshop DVD, *Crochet Sweater Studio*, from Interweave.

1 USING SPECIAL STITCHES

A variation on a common stitch, foundation crochet stitches have their foundation chain built in. Learn these stitches! They're extremely helpful for tight-chain crocheters. Foundation stitches are looser than the typical foundation chain and make a great start for sweaters and dresses crocheted from the bottom up. They're also fantastic when you realize you should have chained one or two more for the foundation. Instead of ripping out to the foundation, you can add the needed stitches to the beginning of the foundation. To see some foundation stitches, look at the Magnolia Tank (page 54) and Burnt Plaid Dress (page 40) projects.

2 SYMBOL SHAPING

Symbols are not just for visual learners like me; they're incredibly helpful tools. Have you ever read a stitch pattern and thought, huh? Symbol diagrams can help guide your hook to the correct stitch. (For information about reading diagrams, see Symbol Crochet Basics on page 152.) Symbols make it easy to test shaping without having to crochet and re-crochet until you get it right. Symbol shaping lets you take your stitch pattern and mark the line of shaping you want in color. When you follow the pattern, crochet everything up to the colored

line and leave the rest of the pattern unworked. Then turn your work and use your symbols to get you back to your stitch pattern.

If you're at the start of a row, use slip stitches and chains to get you going again. At the end of a row, use standard stitches to finish it. I like to sketch directly on the stitch pattern to guess at the shaping. You may have to assume, for example, that a double crochet or a treble will work in a certain spot, knowing that a single crochet will be too short. Look at the sample shaping for the Berry Lace stitch pattern (page 8).

As you see, this shaping cuts off the bottom corner and helps create a curve in the sweater. The first diagram shows the stitch pattern with the red line that I used to create the shaping in the second diagram. If you look at the end of Row 1 of the Bottom Edge Shaping, you can see that the real stitch in the pattern that ended right before the red line was a chain. The chain would not work for turning. Replacing it with a double crochet as tall as the stitch next to it was a perfect switch. Although replacing and adding stitches involves an educated guess, it cuts down on the amount of re-crocheting you need to do when you just want to change, for example, a neckline.

3 MODIFYING MOTIFS

Motifs make fantastic fabric but can be confusing to modify. I have a simple technique for working out shapes: sticky notes. I designate a sticky note as a motif, then place each note where the motif is located in the layout drawings. I cut the note in half vertically or diagonally to represent a partial motif. Knowing my shape, I can tell if a neckline will be too wide or low by counting the sticky notes. If it will be, I use folded notes to gauge how to fill in space as needed. Using the partial motifs already worked out in the pattern, I can cobble together other motifs by taking the beginning of one and meshing it with the end of another to get the perfect fit.

4 CHANGING HOOK SIZE

Although you definitely need to get gauge, some projects like to creep and stretch. Hook size changes can help you make simple adjustments. For collars that want to wing out, I drop a hook size to pull them in closer. When

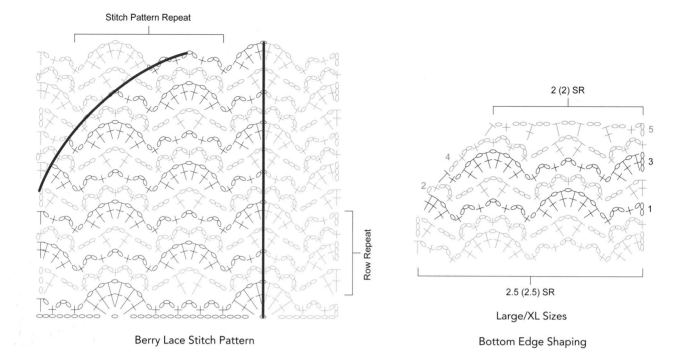

Stitch Pattern Repeat

Row Repeat

Berry Lace Stitch Pattern

2 (2) SR

2.5 (2.5) SR

Large/XL Sizes

Bottom Edge Shaping

I don't want a project to highlight my tummy but float more around it, I sometimes go up a hook size. Harvest Cowl Shift (page 84) uses these quick hook tricks for all its shaping.

5 TIDYING EDGES

I never think a project (even a scarf) is finished until the row ends are covered with at least one row of single crochet edging. Hiding the bumps elevates your work and makes everything look nice and tidy. Large edgings can be really helpful to smooth harsh angles into smooth lines. Look at the Calypso Kimono (page 107) project for an example.

6 MOVING BUTTONHOLES

Have you ever crocheted buttonholes into an edging only to see later that they've been placed incorrectly? A little know-how and scissors can help you avoid re-crocheting. For a helpful, carefully photographed tutorial that shows the following steps, go to crochetbyfaye.blogspot.com/2007/07/wait-how-did-that-buttonhole-get-there.html. For a video demonstration of this technique, check out my *Crochet Sweater Studio* workshop DVD, available from Interweave at interweavestore.com.

STEP 1. Mark the correct buttonhole location.

STEP 2. On the RS of the buttonhole row, at the last stitch before the new buttonhole, join yarn with a slip stitch. Chain to the desired buttonhole length, remove the hook. With a smaller-sized hook (I use a hook 3 sizes smaller), thread the hook through the legs of the stitches on the row above that you want to sit on the chain space. Place the last loop of the chain on the end of the hook.

STEP 3. Pull the chain and hook through those stitches. Pull the loose end of the yarn through the stitches as well. Secure the chain with a slip stitch around the first stitch after the buttonhole.

STEP 4. Now, cut the stitches out of your buttonhole. Cut through one strand of any stitch in the middle of the buttonhole. Unwind the stitches to the left, secure by weaving the ends in. Unwind stitches to the right, slowing down as you get close to the last stitch. Because this is your working side (the side that wants to frog easily), you'll need to secure the working loop (or the loose loop) of the last stitch you unwind. To do so, pull the yarn end through the working loop (loose loop) with a yarn needle and weave in the ends.

STEP 5. Join the yarn at the top of the last stitch of the previous buttonhole with a slip stitch (on the RS of the buttonhole row), and remove the hook. Thread the hook through one stitch on the row above and place the slip stitch loop onto the hook. Pull through the stitch. Complete the stitch as usual, removing the hook after the finished stitch.

STEP 6. Thread the hook through the next stitch on the row above. Place the working loop on the hook and pull through stitch. Complete stitch as normal. Remove hook. Continue to end.

STEP 7. Secure the yarn with a slip stitch around the next stitch. Fasten off and weave in ends. Optionally, you can cut the chain out of the stitches above if the chain is too bulky in the fabric.

You can also use this technique for repairing old crochet projects.

7 BLOCKING

I never think any project is finished until it has its edging and has been blocked. Of the many ways of blocking, here are three that I find helpful. I first test my blocking on my project swatch. If one method doesn't work well, I try a different one.

Option 1: Pin your pieces to schematic size, spray them with water, and allow them to dry. I use this method most often on bamboo, silk, acrylic, and wool-blend projects.

Option 2: Pin your pieces to schematic size and steam them with an iron, holding the iron at least an inch above the fabric (and being careful never to let the iron touch it). I use this method most often on acrylic and superwash wool projects.

Option 3: Submerge your project in a cool gentle-wash bath, gently towel it dry, and pin it to schematic size. I use this method most often on animal-fiber (wool, alpaca, mohair) and linen projects.

8 FELTING AND LINING

If your project has a part that has significantly drooped or stretched, one of these two fixes may help. If you've used an animal fiber, try gently felting it. You would be surprised what a quick felting—rubbing your project under hot water—can do for crochet. You can usually tighten up any wayward collar unnoticeably. For a project in a sleek fiber, consider a lining. The Stormy Lace Tunic on page 130 really benefited from lining; the lining helped the lace fabric hold up the rest of the skirt.

9 SEAMING

All seams are not equal. Whipstitched seams may be easy, but they're also the most noticeable. Slip-stitched shoulder seams are sturdy and can hold up heavy garments. Basketweave or woven seams can make joined panels on the sides nearly invisible. You can see illustrations of these in the Glossary.

10 FINISHING WITH RIBBON

On heavily worn garments, ribbon helps keep collars from stretching out. The neckline of the Structured Cardigan (page 74) uses ribbon to keep the neck from falling off the shoulders. Ribbon also keeps hook-and-eye closures from leaving marks on the front panels.

Classic
CONSTRUCTION

"Classic" means tried and true—in our case, tried and true to fit and shape beautifully. Classic construction is a method for making a garment from blocked panels that are sewn together. The garment could be a raglan vest seamed only at the shoulders, as in the Summer Sky Vest (page 22), or a cardigan with seams on each side, at the shoulders, and under the arms, as in the Foliage Shrug (page 31). This construction method creates garments that fit well, with body panels that fit the curve of the body and sleeve panels with minimal excess bulk in the arms—whether you have raglan, cap-shaping, or side-saddle sleeves, as in the Burnt Plaid Dress (page 41). And whatever the project—simple or complex—using symbols helps ensure that the shaping will go from a jumble of letters to a garment that fits well, as you'll see in the Cranberry Cardigan (page 12). Truly understanding the classic construction will make all other variations easier to understand.

cranberry
CARDIGAN

With its classic and easy-to-wear style, this cardigan can be a go-to sweater year-round. But behind the style lies a quick lesson on crochet symbols. The two-row stitch pattern is easily repeatable. However, even though the pattern is easy, and the shaping for each size is simple, written directions for six sizes become quite long. *Diagrams A–H are located at the back of the book, on pages 158–163.*

Materials

YARN

DK weight (#3 Light)

SHOWN: Cascade Ultra Pima (100% pima cotton; 220 yd [200 m]/3.5 oz [100 g]): #3701 Cranberry, 4 (4, 5, 5, 6, 6) hanks.

HOOK

Size G/7 (4.5 mm) or hook needed to obtain gauge.

NOTIONS

Tapestry needle for weaving in ends; two ⅞" (22 mm) buttons; spray bottle with water; straight pins for blocking

Gauge

21 sts by 8 rows = 4¼" × 4" (11 × 10 cm) in alternating rows of linked double treble and single crochet.

5 SR by 9 rows = 4¼" × 4⅛" (11 × 10.5 cm) in diamond lattice stitch pattern.

Note: 10 rows of lower body pattern repeat = 4" (10 cm).

Finished Size

Bust measurement is 32½ (36, 39¼, 44½", 47¾", 51¼") (82.5 [91.5, 99.5, 113, 121.5, 130] cm). Sized for X-Small (Small, Medium, Large, X-Large, 2X). Size shown is Small.

Notes

Turning ch of linked stitches does not count as a stitch.

Special Stitches

LINKED DOUBLE TREBLE CROCHET (LDTR)

SET-UP STITCH: Ch 5, insert hook into the 2nd ch from hook, yo, pull up lp, insert hook into 3rd ch from hook, yo, pull up lp, insert hook into 4th ch from hook, yo, pull up lp, insert hook into next st, yo, pull up lp (5 lps on hook), [yo, draw through 2 lps on hook] 3 times, yo, draw through last 2 lps (first stitch made).

NEXT STITCHES: Insert hook into upper horizontal bar of previous stitch from top to bottom (the first bar is found below the stitch's top 2 lps), yo, pull up lp, insert hook into middle horizontal bar, yo, pull up lp, insert hook into lower horizontal bar, yo, pull up lp, insert hook into next st, yo, pull up lp, (5 lps on hook), [yo, draw through 2 lps on hook] 3 times, yo, draw through last 2 lps.

DCTRTOG

Yo, insert hook into st indicated, pull up a lp, yo pull through 2 lps on hook, yo twice, insert hook into st indicated, pull up a lp, yo pull through 2 lps on hook twice, yo, pull through remaining lps on hook.

LINKED TREBLE CROCHET (LTR)

SET-UP STITCH: Ch 4, insert hook into the 2nd ch from hook, yo, pull up lp, insert hook into 3rd ch from hook, yo, pull up lp, iinsert hook into next st, yo, pull up lp (4 lps on hook), [yo, draw through 2 lps on hook] 2 times, yo, draw through last 2 lps (first stitch made).

NEXT STITCHES: Insert hook into upper horizontal bar of previous stitch from top to bottom (the first bar is found below the stitch's top 2 lps), yo, pull up lp, insert hook into middle horizontal bar, yo, pull up lp, insert hook into next st, yo, pull up lp, (4 lps on hook), [yo, draw through 2 lps on hook] 2 times, yo, draw through last 2 lps.

DIAMOND LATTICE STITCH PATTERN

See Diamond Lattice Stitch Pattern diagram (page 14) for assistance.

Ch a multiple of 4 plus 2.

ROW 1 (RS): Sc in 2nd ch from hook, *ch 2, dc2tog in same ch and ch 4 chs away (sk 3 chs), ch 2, sc in same ch as dc2tog, rep from * across, turn.

ROW 2: Ch 4 (counts as tr), dc in next dc2tog, ch 2, sc around previous dc2tog (bet posts of dc), *ch 2, dc2tog in previous and next dc2tog, ch 2, sc around same dc2tog, rep from * across to last dc2tog, ch 2, dctrtog in previous dc2tog and sc, turn.

ROW 3: Ch 1, sc in dctrtog, *ch 2, dc2tog in previous st and next dc2tog, ch 2, sc around dc2tog (bet posts of dc), rep from * across to end, turn.

Rep Rows 2–3 to desired length.

Lower Body

Note: Diagrams A–H are located at the back of the book, on pages 158–163.

See Diagram A (page 158) for assistance. Ch 146 (162, 178, 202, 218, 234).

ROW 1 (WS): Sc in 2nd ch from hook, sc in each ch across, turn—145 (161, 177, 201, 217, 233) sts.

ROW 2: Ch 5 (does not count as a st), LDTR in 2nd, 3rd, 4th ch and next st, LDTR in each remaining sc across, turn.

ROW 3: Ch 1, sc in each LDTR across, turn.

ROW 4: Ch 1, sc in first sc, *ch 2, dc2tog in same sc and sc 4 sts away (sk 3 sc), ch 2, sc in same sc as dc2tog, rep from * across, turn—36 (40, 44, 50, 54, 58] dc2tog.

ROW 5: Cont in Row 2 of diamond lattice stitch pattern across, turn.

ROW 6: Cont in Row 3 of diamond lattice stitch pattern across, turn.

ROWS 7–8: Rep Rows 5–6.

ROW 9: Rep Row 5.

ROW 10: Ch 1, sc in dctrtog, *ch 3, sc around dc2tog (bet posts of dc), rep from * across to end, turn.

ROW 11: Ch 1, sc in first sc, *3 sc in next ch-3 sp, sc in next sc, rep from * across, turn.

ROWS 12–31: Rep Rows 2–11 twice more.

ROWS 32–37: Rep Rows 2–7 once.

FRONT PANEL

See Diagram B (page 158).

ROW 1 (RS): Ch 1, sc in dctrtog, *ch 2, dc2tog in previous st and next dc2tog, ch 2, sc around dc2tog (bet posts of dc), rep from * 7 (8, 8, 9, 10, 10) times total, ch 2, dc2tog in previous st and next dc2tog, leave remaining sts unworked, turn—8 (9, 9, 10, 11, 11] dc2tog.

ROW 2: Ch 1, sc in dc2tog, *ch 2, dc2tog in previous st and next dc2tog, ch 2, sc around dc2tog (bet posts of dc), rep from * across to last dc2tog, ch 2, dctrtog in previous dc2tog and sc, turn.

ROW 3: Ch 1, sc in dctrtog, *ch 3, sc around dc2tog (bet posts of dc), rep from * across to last dc2tog, (XS, S, M, L) ch 1, hdc in last sc, turn.

ROW 4: Ch 1, (XS, S, M, L) sc in hdc, sc in ch-1 sp, (ALL) sc in next sc, *3 sc in next ch-3 sp, sc in next sc, rep from * across, turn—31 (35, 35, 39, 41, 41) sc.

ROW 5: Ch 5 (does not count as a st), LDTR in 2nd, 3rd, 4th ch and next st, LDTR in each remaining sc across, turn.

ROW 6: Ch 1, sc in each LDTR across, turn.

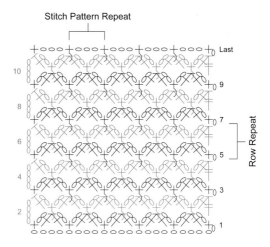

Diamond Lattice Stitch Pattern

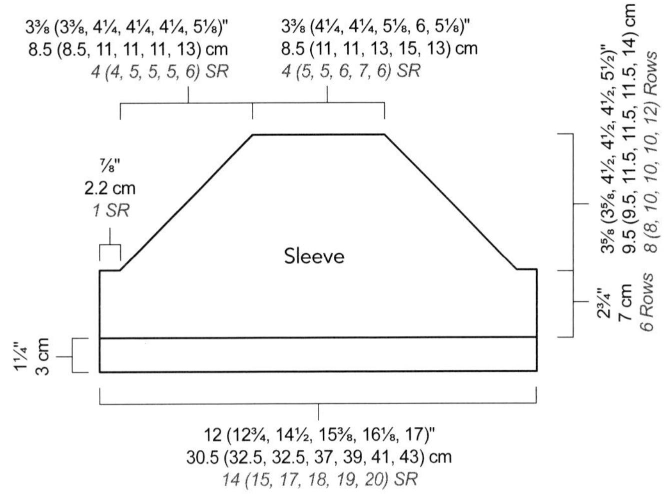
3⅜ (3⅜, 4¼, 4¼, 4¼, 5⅛)"
8.5 (8.5, 11, 11, 11, 13) cm
4 (4, 5, 5, 5, 6) SR
3⅜ (4¼, 4¼, 5⅛, 6, 5⅛)"
8.5 (11, 11, 13, 15, 13) cm
4 (5, 5, 6, 7, 6) SR
⅞"
2.2 cm
1 SR
Sleeve
3⅝ (3⅝, 4½, 4½, 4½, 5½)"
9.5 (9.5, 11.5, 11.5, 11.5, 14) cm
8 (8, 10, 10, 10, 12) Rows
2¾"
7 cm
6 Rows
1¼"
3 cm
12 (12¾, 14½, 15⅜, 16⅛, 17)"
30.5 (32.5, 32.5, 37, 39, 41, 43) cm
14 (15, 17, 18, 19, 20) SR

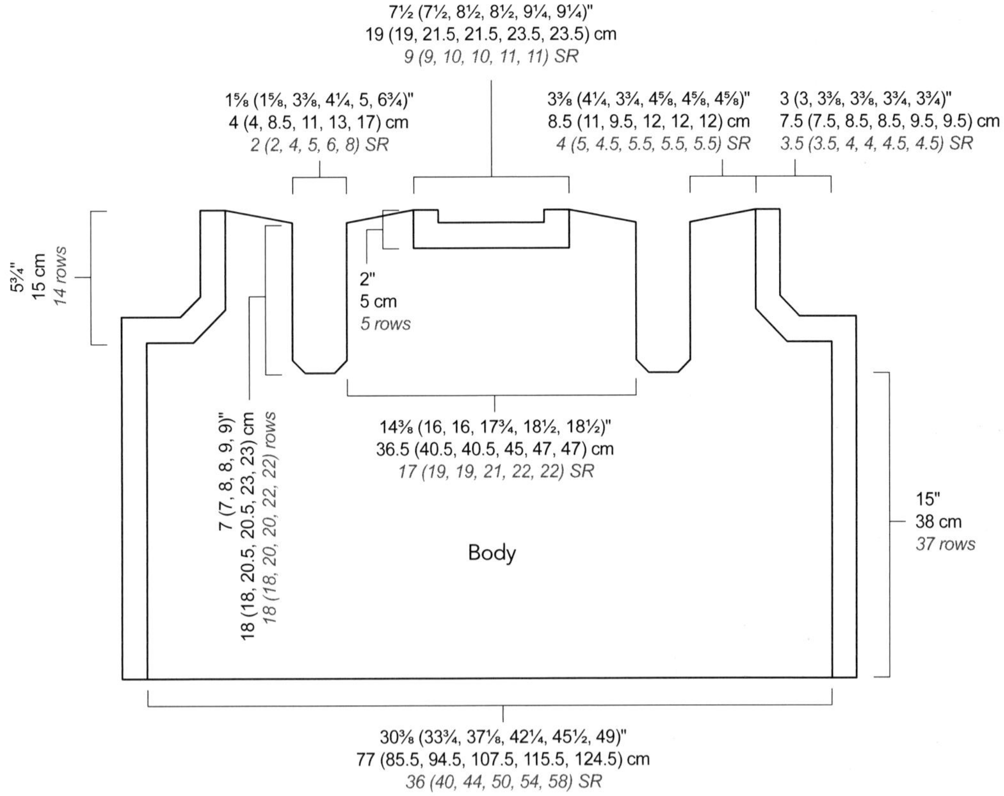
7½ (7½, 8½, 8½, 9¼, 9¼)"
19 (19, 21.5, 21.5, 23.5, 23.5) cm
9 (9, 10, 10, 11, 11) SR
1⅝ (1⅝, 3⅜, 4¼, 5, 6¾)"
4 (4, 8.5, 11, 13, 17) cm
2 (2, 4, 5, 6, 8) SR
3⅜ (4¼, 3¾, 4⅝, 4⅝, 4⅝)"
8.5 (11, 9.5, 12, 12, 12) cm
4 (5, 4.5, 5.5, 5.5, 5.5) SR
3 (3, 3⅜, 3⅜, 3¾, 3¾)"
7.5 (7.5, 8.5, 8.5, 9.5, 9.5) cm
3.5 (3.5, 4, 4, 4.5, 4.5) SR
5¾"
15 cm
14 rows
2"
5 cm
5 rows
7 (7, 8, 8, 9, 9)"
18 (18, 20.5, 20.5, 23, 23) cm
18 (18, 20, 20, 22, 22) rows
14⅜ (16, 16, 17¾, 18½, 18½)"
36.5 (40.5, 40.5, 45, 47, 47) cm
17 (19, 19, 21, 22, 22) SR
Body
15"
38 cm
37 rows
30⅜ (33¾, 37⅛, 42¼, 45½, 49)"
77 (85.5, 94.5, 107.5, 115.5, 124.5) cm
36 (40, 44, 50, 54, 58) SR

ROW 3: Ch 1, sc in dc2tog, *ch 2, dc2tog in previous st and next dc2tog, ch 2, sc around dc2tog (bet posts of dc), rep from * across to last dc2tog, ch 2, dctrtog in previous dc2tog and last sc, turn—4 (5) dc2tog.

ROW 3: Ch 1, sc in dc2tog, *ch 2, dc2tog in previous st and next dc2tog, ch 2, sc around dc2tog (bet posts of dc), rep from * across to last dc2tog, ch 2, dctrtog in previous dc2tog and last sc, turn—4 (5) dc2tog.

ROW 4: Rep Row 3 of diamond lattice stitch pattern.

ROWS 5–6: Rep Rows 2–3 of diamond lattice stitch pattern.

ROW 7: Ch 3 (counts as hdc, ch-1 sp), sc around dc2tog (bet posts of dc), *ch 3, sc around next dc2tog, rep from * across to last sc, ch 1, hdc in last sc, turn—3 (4) ch-3 sps.

ROW 8: Ch 1, sc in hdc, sc in ch-1 sp, *sc in next sc, 3 sc in ch-3 sp, rep from * across to last sc, sc in last sc, 2 sc in tch sp, turn—17 (21) sc.

ROW 9: Ch 5 (does not count as a st), LDTR in 2nd, 3rd, 4th ch and next st, LDTR in each remaining sc across, turn.

ROW 10: Ch 1, sc in each LDTR across, turn.

ROW 11: Rep Row 3 of diamond lattice stitch pattern.

ROW 12: Rep Row 2 of diamond lattice stitch pattern—4 (5) dc2tog.

(M/L)

ROW 1 (RS): Ch 1, sc in dctrtog, [ch 3, sc around next dc2tog] twice, *ch 2, dc2tog in previous st and next dc2tog, ch 2, sc around dc2tog (bet posts of dc), rep from * across to last sc, ch 2, dctrtog over previous st and last sc, turn—6 (7) dc2tog.

ROW 2: Ch 1, sc in dctrtog, *ch 2, dc2tog in previous st and next dc2tog, ch 2, sc around dc2tog (bet posts of dc), rep from * 5 (6) times total, ch 2, dc2tog in previous st and next dc2tog, leave remaining sts unworked, turn—5 (6) dc2tog.

ROW 3: Ch 1, sc in dc2tog, *ch 2, dc2tog in previous st and next dc2tog, ch 2, sc around dc2tog (bet posts of dc), rep from * across to last dc2tog, ch 2, dctrtog in previous dc2tog and last sc, turn—4 (5) dc2tog.

ROW 4: Ch 1, sc in dctrtog, *ch 2, dc2tog in previous st and next dc2tog, ch 2, sc around dc2tog (bet posts of dc), rep from * 4 (5) times total, ch 2, dc2tog in previous st and next dc2tog, leave remaining sts unworked, turn—5 (6) dc2tog.

ROW 5: Ch 1, sc around dc2tog (bet posts of dc), *ch 3, sc around next dc2tog, rep from * across to last sc, ch 1, hdc in last sc, turn—4 (5) ch-3 sp.

ROW 6: Ch 1, sc in hdc, sc in ch-1 sp, *sc in next sc, 3 sc in ch-3 sp, rep from * across to last sc, sc in last sc, turn—19 (23) sc.

ROW 7: Ch 5 (does not count as a st), LDTR in 2nd, 3rd, 4th ch and next st, LDTR in each remaining sc across, turn.

ROW 8: Ch 1, sc in each LDTR across, turn.

ROW 9: Ch 3, sk 2 sc, dc in next sc, ch 2, sc in same sc, *ch 2, dc2tog in same sc and sc 4 sts away (sk 3 sc), ch 2, sc in same sc as dc2tog, rep from * across, turn—4 (5) dc2tog.

(M/L)

ROW 7: Ch 1, sc in first sc, *ch 2, dc2tog in same sc and sc 4 sts away (sk 3 sc), ch 2, sc in same sc as dc2tog, rep from * across to last 2 sc, ch 2, dctrtog in previous and last sc, turn—8 (9) dc2tog.

ROW 8: Ch 1, sc in dctrtog, *ch 2, dc2tog in previous st and next dc2tog, ch 2, sc around dc2tog (bet posts of dc), rep from * across to last sc, ch 2, dctrtog in previous and last sc, turn.

(XL/2X)

ROW 7: Ch 1, sc in first sc, *ch 2, dc2tog in same sc and sc 4 sts away (sk 3 sc), ch 2, sc in same sc as dc2tog, rep from * across, turn—10 (10) dc2tog.

ROWS 8–9: Rep Rows 2–3 of diamond lattice stitch pattern.

ROW 10: Rep Row 2 of diamond lattice stitch pattern.

FRONT-PANEL NECK OPENING

See Diagram B (page 158).

(XS/S)

ROW 1 (RS): Sk 7 sc, join yarn with sl st to next sc, sc in next sc, *ch 2, dc2tog in same sc and sc 4 sts away (sk 3 sc), ch 2, sc in same sc as dc2tog, rep from * across to last 2 sc, ch 2, dctrtog over previous st and last sc, turn—5 (6) dc2tog.

ROW 2: Ch 1, sc in dctrtog, *ch 2, dc2tog in previous st and next dc2tog, ch 2, sc around dc2tog (bet posts of dc), rep from * 4 (5) times total, ch 2, dc2tog in previous st and next dc2tog, leave remaining sts unworked, turn—5 (6) dc2tog.

ROW 10: Ch 4, dc in first dc2tog, ch 2, sc around dc2tog, *ch 2, dc2tog in previous st and next dc2tog, ch 2, sc around dc2tog (bet posts of dc), rep from * across, turn.

ROWS 11–12: Rep Row 10 twice.

(XL/2X)

ROW 1 (RS): Ch 1, sc in dctrtog, [ch 3, sc around next dc2tog] 3 times, *ch 2, dc2tog in previous st and next dc2tog, ch 2, sc around dc2tog (bet posts of dc), rep from * across end, turn—7 (7) dc2tog.

ROW 2: Ch 4, dc in first dc2tog, ch 2, sc around next dc2tog, *ch 2, dc2tog in previous st and next dc2tog, ch 2, sc around dc2tog (bet posts of dc), rep from * 5 times total, ch 2, dc2tog in previous st and last dc2tog, leave remaining sts unworked, turn—6 (6) dc2tog.

ROW 3: Ch 1, sc around dc2tog (bet posts of dc), *ch 3, sc around next dc2tog, rep from * across, turn—6 (6) ch-3 sp.

ROW 4: Ch 1, *sc in next sc, 3 sc in ch-3 sp, rep from * across to last ch-3 sp, sc in next sc, 2 sc in next ch-3 sp, sc2tog in ch-3 sp and last sc, turn—24 (24) sc.

ROW 5: Ch 5 (does not count as a st), LDTR in 2nd, 3rd, 4th ch and next sc (sk sc2tog), LDTR in each remaining sc across, turn—23 (23) LDTR.

ROW 6: Ch 1, sc in each LDTR across, turn.

ROW 7: Ch 3, sk 2 sc, dc in next sc, ch 2, sc in same sc, *ch 2, dc2tog in same sc and sc 4 sts away (sk 3 sc), ch 2, sc in same sc as dc2tog, rep from * across, turn—5 (5) dc2tog.

ROW 8: Ch 4, dc in first dc2tog, ch 2, sc around dc2tog, *ch 2, dc2tog in previous st and next dc2tog, ch 2, sc around dc2tog (bet posts of dc), rep from * across, turn.

ROWS 9–12: Rep Row 8 four times.

SHOULDER FRONT PANEL

See Diagram C (page 159).

(XS, S, XL, 2X)

ROW 1: Ch 1, sc in dctrtog, *ch 2, dc2tog in previous st and next dc2tog, ch 2, sc around dc2tog (bet posts of dc), rep from * zero (once, once, once) more, ch 2, dc2tog in previous st and next dc2tog, ch 1, hdc around dc2tog, ch 4, sc around dc2tog, ch 3, sl st to last dc, fasten off, turn.

ROW 2: (XS) Join yarn with sl st to ch-1 sp, (S, XL, 2X) Join yarn with sl st to first dc2tog, ch 3, (ALL) sc around dc2tog, ch 4, hdc around dc2tog, ch 1, dctrtog in previous st and last sc, fasten off.

(M, L)

ROW 1: Ch 4, dc in first dc2tog, ch 2, *sc around dc2tog, ch 2, dc2tog in previous st and next dc2tog, ch 2, rep from * (zero, once) more, sc around dc2tog (bet posts of dc), ch 2, dc2tog in previous st and next dc2tog, ch 1, hdc around dc2tog, ch 4, sc around dc2tog, ch 3, sl st to dc, fasten off, turn.

ROW 2: (M) Join yarn with sl st to ch-1 sp. (L) Join yarn with sl st to first dc2tog, ch 3, (ALL) sc around next dc2tog, ch 4, hdc around dc2tog, ch 1, dc2tog in previous dc2tog and last dc, ch 1, dc in top of tch, fasten off.

BACK PANEL

See Diagram D (page 159)).

ROW 1 (RS): Join yarn with sl st in same st as last dc2tog on Row 1 of front panel, sc around same st as join, [ch 3, sc around next dc2tog] 1 (1, 4, 5, 4, 6) times, *ch 2, dc2tog in previous st and next dc2tog, ch 2, sc around dc2tog (bet posts of dc), rep from * 17 (19, 19, 21, 23, 23) times total, ch 2, dc2tog in previous st and next dc2tog, leave remaining sts unworked, turn—18 (20, 20, 22, 24, 24) dc2tog.

ROW 2: Ch 1, sc in dc2tog, *ch 2, dc2tog in previous st and next dc2tog, ch 2, sc around dc2tog (bet posts of dc), rep from * across to last 2 dc2tog, ch 2, dc2tog in previous st and next dc2tog, (XS, S, M, L) ch 2, sc around dc2tog (bet posts of dc), turn.

ROW 3: (XS, S, M, L) Ch 3 (counts as hdc, ch-1 sp), (XL, 2X) ch 1, (ALL) sc around first dc2tog, *ch 3, sc around dc2tog (bet posts of dc), rep from * across to last dc2tog, (XS, S, M, L) ch 1, hdc in last sc, turn—16 (18, 18, 20, 22, 22] ch-3 sp.

ROW 4: Ch 1, (XS, S, M, L) sc in hdc, sc in ch-1 sp, (ALL) sc in next sc, *3 sc in next ch-3 sp, sc in next sc, rep from * across, (XS, S, M, L) 2 sc in tch sp, turn—69 (77, 77, 85, 89, 89) sc.

ROWS 5–6: Rep Rows 2–3 of lower body.

(XS, S, M, L)

ROWS 7–14: Rep Rows 4–11 of lower body once.

ROW 15: Rep Row 2 of lower body once.

(M, L)

ROWS 15–16: Rep Rows 3–4 of lower body.

(XL, 2X)

ROW 7: Ch 3, sk 2 sc, dc in next sc, ch 2, sc in same sc, *ch 2, dc2tog in same sc and sc 4 sts away (sk 3 sc), ch 2, sc in same sc as dc2tog, rep from * across, ch 2, dctrtog in previous st and last sc, turn—21 (21) dc2tog.

ROW 8: Ch 1, sc in dctrtog, *ch 2, dc2tog in previous st and next dc2tog, ch 2, sc around dc2tog (bet posts of dc), rep from * across to end, turn.

ROW 9: Ch 4 (counts as tr), dc in next dc2tog, ch 2, sc around previous dc2tog (bet posts of dc), *ch 2, dc2tog in previous and next dc2tog, ch 2, sc around same dc2tog, rep from * across to last dc2tog, ch 2, dctrtog in previous dc2tog and sc, turn.

ROWS 10–11: Rep Rows 8–9.

ROW 12: Rep Row 8.

ROW 13: Ch 3 (counts as hdc in ch-1 sp), sc around first dc2tog, *ch 3, sc around dc2tog (bet posts of dc), rep from * across to last dc2tog, ch 1, hdc in last sc, turn—21 (21) ch-3 sp.

ROW 14: Ch 1, sc in hdc, sc in ch-1 sp, sc in next sc, *3 sc in next ch-3 sp, sc in next sc, rep from * across, 2 sc in tch sp, turn—89 (89) sc.

ROWS 15–16: Rep Rows 2–3 of lower body.

ROWS 17–19: Rep Rows 7–9 of back panel.

SHOULDER BACK PANEL

See Diagram E (page 160).

(XS, S)

ROW 1: Ch 1, sc in next 17 (21) LDTR, leave remaining sts unworked, turn.

ROW 2: Ch 1, sc in first sc, *ch 2, dc2tog in same sc and sc 4 sts away (sk 3 sc), ch 2, sc in same sc as dc2tog, rep from * across, turn—4 (5) dc2tog.

ROW 3: Cont in Row 2 of diamond lattice stitch pattern.

ROWS 4–5: Rep Rows 1–2 of front-panel shoulder.

Opposite Shoulder Shaping

ROW 1: Skip 34 sts from end of Row 1 of shoulder, join yarn with sl st to next st, sc in each remaining sts across, turn—17 (21) sc.

ROWS 2–3: Rep Rows 2–3 of shoulder shaping.

ROW 4: Sl st in dctrtog, ch 3, sc around next dc2tog, ch 4, hdc around next dc2tog, ch 1, dc2tog in previous and next dc2tog, ch 2, *sc around previous dc2tog, ch 2, dc2tog in previous and last dc, ch 2, rep from * (0,1) more time, sc in last dc, turn.

ROW 5: Ch 4, dc in first dc2tog, ch 1, hdc around previous dc-2tog, ch 4, sc around next dc2tog, (S) ch 3, sl st in last dc2tog, (XS) sl st in ch-sp, fasten off.

(M, L)

ROW 1: Ch 4 (counts as tr), dc in next dc2tog, ch 2, sc around previous dc2tog (bet posts of dc), *ch 2, dc2tog in previous and next dc2tog, ch 2, sc around same dc2tog*, rep from * 4 (5) times total, [ch 3, sc around next dc2tog] 10 times, rep from * to * 4 (5) times total, ch 2, dctrtog in previous dc2tog and sc, turn.

ROWS 2–3: Ch 1, sc in dctrtog, *ch 2, dc2tog in previous and next dc2tog, ch 2, sc around same dc2tog, rep from * across to last dc2tog, ch 2, dctrtog in previous dc2tog and next sc, turn.

ROW 4: Sl st in dctrtog, ch 3, sc around dc2tog, ch 4, hdc around next dc2tog, ch 1, dc2tog in previous and next dc2tog, ch 2, *sc around previous dc2tog, ch 2, dc2tog in previous and next dc2tog, ch 2, rep from * (0, 1) more time, sc around previous dc2tog, ch 2, dctrtog in previous dc2tog and last sc, turn.

ROW 5: Ch 5, dc2tog in dctrtog and next dc2tog, ch 1, hdc around previous dc2tog, ch 4, sc around next dc2tog, (M) sl st in ch-1 sp, (L) ch 3, sl st in next dc2tog, fasten off.

Opposite Shoulder Shaping

ROW 1: Skip 10 ch-3 sps from end of Row 2 of shoulder shaping, join yarn with sl st in next sc, ch 4, dc in next dc2tog, ch 2, sc around previous dc2tog (bet posts of dc), *ch 2, dc2tog in previous and next dc2tog, ch 2, sc around same dc2tog, rep from * across, turn.

ROW 2: Ch 4, dc in next dc2tog, ch 2, sc around previous dc2tog (bet posts of dc), *ch 2, dc2tog in previous and next dc2tog, ch 2, sc around same dc2tog, rep from * across, turn.

ROWS 3–4: Rep Rows 1–2 of front-panel shoulder shaping.

(XL, 2X)

ROW 1: Ch 1, sc in dctrtog, *ch 2, dc2tog in previous and next dc2tog, ch 2, sc around same dc2tog*, rep from * 6 times total, [ch 3, sc around next dc2tog] 10 times, rep from * to * 6 times total, turn.

ROWS 2–3: Ch 4, dc in next dc2tog, ch 2, sc around previous dc2tog (bet posts of dc), *ch 2, dc2tog in previous and next dc2tog, ch 2, sc around same dc2tog, rep from * across, fasten off, turn.

ROW 4: Join yarn with sl st to first dc2tog, ch 3, sc around next dc2tog, ch 4, hdc around next dc2tog, ch 1, dc2tog in previous and next dc2tog, ch 2, *sc around previous dc2tog, ch 2, dc2tog in previous and last dc, ch 2, rep from * once more, sc in last dc, turn.

ROW 5: Ch 4, dc in first dc2tog, ch 1, hdc around previous dc2tog, ch 4, sc around next dc2tog, ch 3, sl st in last dc2tog, fasten off.

Opposite Shoulder Shaping

ROW 1: Skip 10 ch-3 sps from end of Row 2 of shoulder shaping, join yarn with sl st in next dc2tog, sc around previous dc2tog (bet posts of dc), *ch 2, dc2tog in previous and next dc2tog, ch 2, sc around same dc2tog, rep from * across, ch 2, dctrtog in previous dc2tog and last sc, turn.

ROW 2: Ch 1, sc in dctrtog, *ch 2, dc2tog in previous and next dc2tog, ch 2, sc around same dc2tog, rep from * across to last dc2tog, ch 2, dctrtog in previous dc2tog and next sc, turn.

ROWS 3–4: Rep Rows 1–2 of front-panel shoulder shaping.

OPPOSITE FRONT PANEL

See Diagram F (on pages 161–162).

ROW 1 (RS): Join yarn with sl st in same st as last dc2tog on Row 1 of back panel, sc around same st as join, [ch 3, sc around next dc2tog] 1 (1, 4, 5, 4, 6) times, *ch 2, dc2tog in previous st and next dc2tog, ch 2, sc around dc2tog (bet posts of dc), rep from * 7 (8, 9, 10, 11, 11) times total, turn.

ROW 2: Ch 4, dc in first dc2tog, ch 2, sc around previous dc2tog, *ch 2, dc2tog in previous st and next dc2tog, ch 2, sc around dc2tog (bet posts of dc), rep from * across to last 2 dc2tog, ch 2, dc2tog in previous st and next dc2tog, (XS, S, M, L) ch 2, sc around dc2tog (bet posts of dc), turn.

ROW 3: (XS, S, M, L) Ch 3 (counts as hdc, ch-1 sp), (XL, 2X) ch 1, (ALL) sc around first dc2tog, *ch 3, sc around dc2tog (bet posts of dc), rep from * across to last dc2tog, turn—7 (8, 8, 9, 10, 10) ch-3 sp.

ROW 4: Ch 1, sc in next sc, *3 sc in next ch-3 sp, sc in next sc, rep from * across, (XS, S, M, L) 2 sc in tch sp, turn—31 (35, 35, 39, 41, 41) sc.

ROWS 5–6: Rep Rows 2–3 of lower body.

(M/L)

ROW 7: Ch 3, sk 2 sc, dc in next sc, ch 2, sc in same sc, *ch 2, dc2tog in same sc and sc 4 sts away (sk 3 sc), ch 2, sc in same sc as dc2tog, rep from * across, turn—8 (9) dc2tog.

ROW 8: Ch 4, dc in first dc2tog, ch 2, sc around previous dc2tog, *ch 2, dc2tog in previous st and next dc2tog, ch 2, sc around dc2tog (bet posts of dc), rep from * across, turn.

(XL/2X)

ROW 7: Ch 1, sc in first sc, *ch 2, dc2tog in same sc and sc 4 sts away (sk 3 sc), ch 2, sc in same sc as dc2tog, rep from * across, turn—10 (10) dc2tog.

ROWS 8–9: Rep Rows 2–3 of diamond lattice stitch pattern.

ROW 10: Rep Row 2 of diamond lattice stitch pattern.

OPPOSITE FRONT-PANEL NECK OPENING

See Diagram F (on pages 161–162).

(XS/S)

ROW 1 (RS): Ch 3, sk 2 sc, dc in next sc, ch 2, sc around same sc, *ch 2, dc2tog in same sc and sc 4 sts away (sk 3 sc), ch 2, sc in same sc as dc2tog, rep from * 4 (5) times total, ch 2, dc2tog in same sc and sc 4 sts away (sk 3 sc), leave remaining sts unworked, turn—5 (6) dc2tog.

ROW 2: Ch 1, sc in dc2tog, *ch 2, dc2tog in previous st and next dc2tog, ch 2, sc around dc2tog (bet posts of dc), rep from * across, turn—5 (6) dc2tog.

ROW 3: Ch 4, dc in first dc2tog, ch 2, sc around previous dc2tog, *ch 2, dc2tog in previous st and next dc2tog, ch 2, sc around dc2tog (bet posts of dc), rep from * 3 (4) times, ch 2, dc2tog in previous and next dc2tog, turn—4 (5) dc2tog.

Cont in Front-Panel Neck Opening directions to shoulder shaping.

(M/L)

ROW 1 (RS): Ch 4, dc in first dc2tog, ch 2, sc around previous dc2tog, *ch 2, dc2tog in previous st and next dc2tog, ch 2, sc around dc2tog (bet posts of dc), rep from * 6 (7) times, ch 3, sc around next dc2tog, ch 3, sc in last dc, fasten off, turn—6 (7) dc2tog.

ROW 2: Join yarn with sl st to first dc2tog, sc in same dc2tog, *ch 2, dc2tog in previous st and next dc2tog, ch 2, sc around dc2tog (bet posts of dc), rep from * across, turn—6 (7) dc2tog.

ROW 3: Ch 4, dc in first dc2tog, ch 2, sc around same dc2tog, *ch 2, dc2tog in previous st and next dc2tog, ch 2, sc around dc2tog (bet posts of dc), rep from * 4 (5) times total, ch 2, dc2tog in previous and next dc2tog, turn—4 (5) dc2tog.

ROW 4: Ch 1, sc in dc2tog, *ch 2, dc2tog in prev st and next dc2tog, ch 2, sc around dc2tog (bet posts of dc), rep from * across, turn—4 (5) dc2tog.

ROW 5: Ch 3 (counts as hdc, ch-1 sp), sc around dc2tog (bet posts of dc), *ch 3, sc around next dc2tog, rep from * across, turn—4 (5) ch-3 sp.

ROW 6: Ch 1, *sc in next sc, 3 sc in ch-3 sp, rep from * across to last sc, sc in last sc, 2 sc in tch sp, turn—19 (23) sc.

ROW 7: Ch 5 (does not count as a st), LDTR in 2nd, 3rd, 4th ch and next st, LDTR in each remaining sc across, turn.

ROW 8: Ch 1, sc in each LDTR across, turn.

Shaping with Symbols

Shaping doesn't have to work against the grain. Work with your stitch pattern. If it has a natural diagonal, as this one does, go with it. It's much easier to use the natural diagonal than to recreate an entire stitch pattern. If you do need to use another shape, draw the diagram first, then draw a line on the diagram that shows your path. Use your crochet symbols to fit true to that line. Review the basics in the introduction on page 7.

ROW 9: Ch 1, sc in first sc, *ch 2, dc2tog in same sc and sc 4 sts away (sk 3 sc), ch 2, sc in same sc as dc2tog, rep from * across to last 2 sc, ch 2, dc2tog in previous and last sc, turn—5 (6) dc2tog.

ROW 10: Ch 1, sc in first st, *ch 2, dc2tog in previous st and next dc2tog, ch 2, sc around dc2tog (bet posts of dc), rep from * across to last dc2tog, ch 2, dctrtog in previous dc2tog and last sc, turn.

ROWS 11–12: Rep Row 10 twice.

(XL/2X)

ROW 1 (RS): Ch 1, sc in dctrtog, *ch 2, dc2tog in previous st and next dc2tog, ch 2, sc around dc2tog (bet posts of dc), rep from * 7 times total, [ch 3, sc around next dc2tog] 3 times, fasten off, turn—7 (7) dc2tog.

ROW 2: Join yarn with sl st to first dc2tog, sc around same dc2tog, *ch 2, dc2tog in previous st and next dc2tog, ch 2, sc around dc2tog (bet posts of dc), rep from * to last dc2tog, ch 2, dctrtog in previous dc2tog and last sc, turn—6 (6) dc2tog.

ROW 3: Ch 1, sc in dctrtog, *ch 3, sc around next dc2tog, rep from * across, turn—6 (6) ch-3 sp.

ROW 4: Ch 1, sc2tog in sc and first ch-3 sp, 2 sc in same ch-3 sp, *sc in next sc, 3 sc in ch-3 sp, rep from * across to last sc, sc in last sc, turn—24 (24) sc.

ROW 5: Ch 5 (does not count as a st), LDTR in 2nd, 3rd, 4th ch and next sc, LDTR in each remaining sc across, sk sc2tog, turn—23 (23) LDTR.

ROW 6: Ch 1, sc in each LDTR across, turn.

ROW 7: Ch 1, sc in first sc, *ch 2, dc2tog in same sc and sc 4 sts away (sk 3 sc), ch 2, sc in same sc as dc2tog, rep from * across to last 2 sc, ch 2, dc2tog in previous and last sc, turn—6 (6) dc2tog.

ROW 8: Ch 1, sc in first st, *ch 2, dc2tog in previous st and next dc2tog, ch 2, sc around dc2tog (bet posts of dc), rep from * across to last dc2tog, ch 2, dctrtog in previous dc2tog and last sc, turn.

ROWS 9–12: Rep Row 8 four times.

OPPOSITE SHOULDER FRONT PANEL

See Diagram G (on page 163).

(XS, S, XL, 2X)

ROW 1: (XS, S) Sl st in dctrtog, (XL, 2X) join yarn to first dc2tog, (ALL) ch 3, sc around next dc2tog, ch 4, hdc around next dc2tog, ch 1, dc2tog in previous and next dc2tog, ch 2, *sc around previous dc2tog, ch 2, dc2tog in previous and last dc, ch 2, rep from * 0 (1, 1, 1,) more time sc in last dc, turn.

ROW 2: Ch 4, dc in first dc2tog, ch 1, hdc around previous dc2tog, ch 4, sc around next dc2tog, (S, XL, 2X) ch 3, sl st in last dc2tog, (XS) sl st in ch-sp, fasten off.

(M, L)

ROW 1: Sl st in dctrtog, ch 3, sc around dc2tog, ch 4, hdc around next dc2tog, ch 1, dc2tog in previous and next dc2tog, ch 2, *sc around previous dc2tog, ch 2, dc2tog in previous and next dc2tog, ch 2, rep from * 0 (1) more time, sc around previous dc2tog, ch 2, dctrtog in previous dc2tog and last sc, turn.

ROW 2: Ch 5, dc2tog in dctrtog and next dc2tog, ch 1, hdc around previous dc2tog, ch 4, sc around next dc2tog, (M) sl st in ch-1 sp, (L) ch 3, sl st in next dc2tog, fasten off.

SLEEVES

Make 2.

See Diagram H (on page 163). Ch 58 (62, 70, 74, 78, 82).

ROW 1 (RS): Sc in 2nd ch from hook, *ch 2, dc2tog in same ch and ch 4 chs away (sk 3 chs), ch 2, sc in same ch as dc2tog, rep from * across, turn—14 (15, 17, 18, 19, 20) dc2tog.

ROWS 2–5: Rep Rows 2–3 of Diamond Lattice Stitch pattern twice.

ROW 6: Rep Row 2 of diamond lattice stitch pattern once.

Cap Shaping

See Diagram H (on page 163).

ROW 1: Ch 1, sc in dctrtog, ch 3, sc around next dc2tog, *ch 2, dc2tog in previous st and next dc2tog, ch 2, sc around dc2tog (bet posts of dc), rep from * across to last dc2tog, ch 3, sc in last dc, fasten off, turn—12 (13, 15, 16, 17, 18) dc2tog.

ROW 2: Join yarn with sl st to first dc2tog, sc in same st, *ch 2, dc2tog in previous st and next dc2tog, ch 2, sc around dc2tog (bet posts of dc), rep from * across to last 2 dc2tog, ch 2, dc2tog in previous and last dc2tog, turn—11 (12, 14, 15, 16, 17) dc2tog.

ROW 3: Ch 1, sc in first st, *ch 2, dc2tog in previous st and next dc2tog, ch 2, sc around dc2tog (bet posts of dc), rep from * across to last 2 dc2tog, ch 2, dc2tog in previous and last dc2tog, turn—10 (11, 13, 14, 15, 16) dc2tog.

ROWS 4–8 (8, 10, 10, 10, 12): Rep Row 3 of cap shaping 5 (5, 7, 7, 7, 9) times—5 (6, 6, 7, 8, 7) dc2tog.

ROW 9 (9, 11, 11, 11, 13): Ch 1, sc in first dc2tog, *ch 3, sc around dc2tog, rep from * across, fasten off.

Finishing
BLOCKING AND SEAMING

Pin body and sleeves to schematic size and spray with water. Allow to dry. Pin front and back shoulders together with right sides together. Join yarn to edge with sl st, working through both front and back panels at once, sc across shoulder, fasten off, weave in ends. Pin sleeves to arm opening with right sides facing. Whipstitch sleeve to armhole opening with tapestry needle. Whipstitch sleeve together at underarm.

Collar, Front-Panel Opening, and Edging

RND 1: Join yarn to RS edge of cardigan, sc evenly up edge of cardigan, 3 sc on outside corner, turn work and sc evenly around neck, 3 sc on outside corner, turn work, sc evenly down edge of cardigan, fasten off.

RIGHT PANEL EDGE: Join yarn to RS at bottom edge, ch 5 (does not count as a st), LDTR in 2nd, 3rd, 4th ch and next st, LDTR in each remaining sc across to last 4 sc from neck line, dtr in next sc (space bet dtr and linked dtr is a buttonhole), LDTR in last 3 sts, fasten off.

LEFT PANEL EDGE: Join yarn to RS at neck edge, ch 5 (does not count as a st), LDTR in 2nd, 3rd, 4th ch and next st, LDTR in each remaining sc across, fasten off.

RIGHT NECK COLLAR: Join yarn to RS at top of right panel edge, ch 5 (does not count as a st), LDTR in 2nd, 3rd, 4th ch and next st, LDTR in next sc, dtr in next st (space bet dtr and LDTR is a buttonhole), LDTR in each remaining sc across to back neck, fasten off, leaving long tail. Whipstitch row to back neck.

LEFT NECK COLLAR: Join yarn to RS at back neck of left panel edge, ch 5 (does not count as a st), LDTR in 2nd, 3rd, 4th ch and next st, LDTR in each remaining sc across to front panel, fasten off, whipstitch chain at beginning of row to back neck.

FINAL EDGING: Join yarn to RS at bottom of back panel, sc in each st across to front-panel opening, 3 sc at outside corner, sc in each st up opening to collar, 3 sc at outside edge, sc in each st for 3 (3, 3.5, 3.5, 4, 4)" (7.5 [7.5, 9, 9, 10, 10] cm), sc3tog over next 3 sts, sc in next 2 sts, sc3tog over next 3 sts, [sc in each st to back neck edge, sc3tog over next 3 sts] twice, sc in each st to last 4 (4, 4½, 4½, 5, 5)" (10 [10, 11.5, 11.5, 14, 12.5, 12.5] cm) of neck, sc3tog over next 3 sts, sc in next 2 sts, sc3tog over next 3 sts, sc in each st to outside corner, 3 sc in outside corner of front panel, sc in each st down front panel to bottom edge, 3 sc in corner of bottom edge, sc in each st across to beginning, sl st to first sc, fasten off.

Sleeve Cuffs

RND 1: Join yarn to RS edge of sleeve, sc evenly around sleeve, sl st to first sc, do not turn.

RND 2: Ch 4 (does not count as a st), LTR in 2nd, 3rd, and next st, LTR in each remaining sc around, sl st to top of tch, do not turn.

RND 3: Ch 1, sc in each LTR around, fasten off with long tail. Whipstitch chain to last st on Rnd 2 to close hole created.

summer sky
VEST

This easy-to-wear vest highlights my favorite way to incorporate post stitches in crocheted fabric—by surrounding them with touches of lace. The raglan shaping may seem daunting, but if you follow the diagrams, you'll see how simple it is. The vest pockets are optional and can be eliminated by simply continuing the stitch pattern without interrupting the pattern for the pocket openings.

Materials

YARN

DK weight (#3 Light)

SHOWN: Cascade Yarns 220 Superwash (100% superwash wool; 220 yd [200 m]/3.5 oz [100 g]): #1910 Summer Sky, 10 (11, 12, 14, 15) balls.

HOOK

Size H/8 (5 mm) or hook needed to obtain gauge.

NOTIONS

Tapestry needle for weaving in ends; spray bottle with water; straight pins for blocking.

Gauge

3 SR by 12 rows = 4½" × 4¼" (11.5 × 11 cm) in Eugenia Stitch Pattern

Finished Size

Bust measurement is 33 (37, 40, 46, 49)" (84 [94, 101.5, 117, 124.5] cm). Sized for Small (Medium, Large, X-Large, 2X). Size shown is Medium.

Notes

The vest is worked in one piece to the neck-line. The collar joins the front and back panels together.

Special Stitches

FPtrdctog

Yo twice, insert hook around post of st indicated, pull up a lp, (yo pull through 2 lps on hook) twice, yo, insert hook into st indicated, pull up a lp, yo, pull through 2 lps on hook, yo, pull through remaining lps on hook.

EUGENIA STITCH PATTERN (ESP)

See Eugenia Stitch Pattern diagram (page 24) for assistance.

Ch 21.

ROW 1 (RS): Dc in 4th ch from hook, dc in next 4 ch, *ch 1, sk 1 ch, dc in next 5 ch, rep from * across, dc in last ch, turn—17 dc, 3 SR.

ROW 2: Ch 1, sc in first dc, *sc in next 5 dc, ch 1, sk ch-1 sp, rep from * across to last 6 dc, sc in each dc across, sc in top of tch, turn.

ROW 3: Ch 3 (counts as dc), *dc in next sc, sk 1 st, FPtr around next dc 1 row below, dc in next sc, FPtr in same dc 1 row below, sk 1 st, dc in next sc, ch 1, sk ch-1 sp, rep from * across to last 6 sc, dc in next sc, sk 1 st, FPtr around next dc 1 row below, dc in next sc, FPtr in same dc 1 row below, sk 1 st, dc in last 2 sc, turn.

ROW 4: Ch 1, sc in each st across, ch 1 over each ch-1 sp across, sc in the top of tch, turn.

Rep Rows 3–4 for pattern.

Body

See Diagram A (page 24) for assistance.

Ch 129 (141, 153, 177, 189).

ROW 1 (RS): Dc in 4th ch from hook (sk ch count as dc), dc in next 4 ch, *ch 1, sk 1 ch, dc in next 5 ch, rep from * across, dc in last ch, turn—107 (117, 127, 147, 157) dc, 21 (23, 25, 29, 31) SR.

ROW 2: Ch 1, sc in first dc, *sc in next 5 dc, ch 1, sk ch-1 sp, rep from * across to last 6 dc, sc in each dc across, sc in top of tch, turn.

ROW 3: Ch 3 (counts as dc), *dc in next sc, sk 1 st, FPtr around next dc 1 row below, dc in next sc, FPtr in same dc 1 row below, sk 1 st, dc in next sc, ch 1, sk ch-1 sp, rep from * across to last 6 sc, dc in next sc, sk 1 st, FPtr around next dc 1 row below, dc in next sc, FPtr in same dc 1 row below, sk 1 st, dc in last 2 sc, turn.

ROW 4: Ch 1, sc in each st across, ch 1 over each ch-1 sp across, sc in top of tch, turn.

ROW 5: Cont in ESP for 4 (4, 4, 5, 5) SR, dc in next 2 sc, turn.

ROW 6: Ch 1, sc in each st across, ch 1 over each ch-1 sp across, sc in top of tch, turn.

ROW 7–18: Rep Rows 5–6 six times.

ROW 19: Rep Row 5 once, fasten off.

ROW 5B: Join yarn 1 st from end of row 5 with sl st, ch 3 (counts as dc), dc in next sc, ch 1, cont in ESP to last 5 (5, 5, 6, 6) SR, dc in next 2 sc, turn.

ROW 6B: Rep Row 6.

Rep Rows 5b–6b six times, rep Row 5b once, fasten off.

ROW 5C: Join yarn 1 st from end of Row 5 with sl st, ch 3 (counts as dc), dc in next sc, ch 1, cont in ESP to end, dc in last sc, turn–4 (4, 4, 5, 5) SR.

ROW 6C: Rep Row 6.

Rep Rows 5c-6c six times. Rep Row 5c once.

ROW 20: Ch 1, sc in first st, *sc in next 5 sts, ch 1, sk ch-1 sp, rep from * 3 (3, 3, 4, 4) more times, sc in next 2 dc, ch 1, sc in next 2 dc, ch 1, sk ch-1 sp, rep from * to * across to next pocket, sc in next 2 dc, ch 1, sc in next 2 dc, rep from * to * across, sc in top of tch, turn.

ROW 21: Cont in ESP for 4 (4, 4, 5, 5) SR, dc in next 2 sc, dc in next ch-1 sp, dc in next 2 sc, cont in ESP across to last 5 (5, 5, 6, 6) SR, dc in next 2 sc, dc in next ch-1 sp, dc in next 2 sc, cont in ESP across to end.

ROW 22: Rep Row 4 once.

ROWS 23–32 (32, 32, 36, 42): Rep Rows 3–4 5 (5, 5, 7, 10) times.

ROW 33 (33, 33, 37, 43): Rep Row 3 once.

Neck Shaping

See Diagram B (pages 26–27) for assistance.

ROW 1: Ch 1, sc2tog over first 2 sts, cont in ESP across to last 2 sts, sc2tog over last 2 sc, turn.

ROW 2: Ch 3, sk first 2 sc, FPtr in next dc 2 rows below, dc in next sc, FPtr in same dc 2 rows below, sk 1 sc, dc in next sc, ch 1, sk ch-1 sp, cont in ESP across to last ch-1 sp, dc in next sc, sk next sc, FPtr in next dc 2 rows below, dc in next sc, FPtrdctog in same dc 2 rows below and last sc, turn.

ROW 3: Rep Row 1 of neck shaping (2X move to front-panel shaping).

ROW 4: Ch 4, sk 2 sc, dc in next sc, ch 1, sk ch-1 sp, cont in ESP across to last ch-1 sp, dc in next sc, tr in last sc, turn—19 (21, 23, 27, 29) SR.

ROW 5: Rep Row 1 of neck shaping.

ROW 6: Ch 4, sk ch-1 sp, dc in next sc, FPtr in next dc 2 rows below, dc in next dc, FPtr in same dc 2 rows below, sk 1 sc, dc in next sc, ch 1, sk ch-1 sp, cont in ESP across to last 2 ch-1 sps, dc in next sc, sk 1 sc, FPtr in next dc 2 rows below, dc in next sc, FPtr in

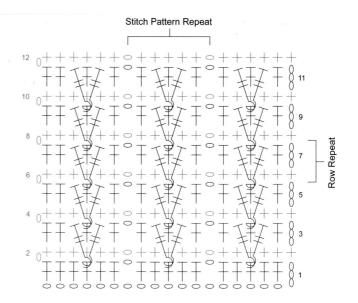

Eugenia Stitch Pattern

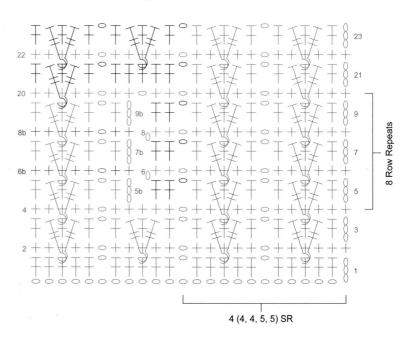

a. Pocket Diagram

same dc 2 rows below, sk 1 sc, dc in next sc, tr in last sc, turn.

ROW 7–9: Rep Rows 1–3 of neck shaping.

Front-Panel Shaping

See Diagram B (pages 26–27) for assistance.

ROW 1: Ch 4, sk 2 sc, dc in next sc, ch 1, sk ch-1 sp, cont in ESP across to 2 (2, 3, 3, 4) SR, dc in next sc, sk 1 sc, tr in next sc, turn—2 (2, 3, 3, 4) SR.

ROW 2: Rep Row 1 of neck shaping.

ROW 3: Rep Row 6 of neck shaping.

ROWS 4–6: Rep Rows 1–3 of neck shaping—6 (6, 11, 11, 16) sc, 0 (0, 1, 1, 2) SR.

(2X)

ROWS 7–12: Rep Rows 1–6 of front-panel shaping (6 sc).

(S/M/2X)

ROW 7 (7, 13): Ch 4, sk 2 sc, dc in next sc, ch 1, sk ch-1 sp, dc in next sc, sk next sc, tr in last sc, turn—5 sts.

ROW 8 (8, 14): Ch 1, sc2tog over first 2 sts, ch 1, sk ch-1 sp, sc2tog over last 2 sts, turn—3 sts.

ROW 9 (9, 15): Ch 2, dc2tog over ch-1 sp and sc, fasten off.

(L/XL)

ROWS 7–8: Rep Rows 1–2 of front-panel shaping (7 sts).

ROW 9: Ch 4, sk ch-1 sp, dc in next sc, sk 1 sc, FPtr in next dc 2 rows below, dc in next sc, FPtr in same dc 2 rows below, sk 1 sc, dc in next sc, sk ch-1 sp, tr in last sc, turn—7 sts.

ROW 10: Ch 1, sc2tog over first 2 sts, sc in next 3 sts, sc2tog over last 2 sts, turn—5 sts.

ROW 11: Ch 3, sk next sc, FPtr in next dc 2 rows below, dc in next sc, FPtrdctog in same dc 2 rows below and last sc, turn—3 sts.

ROW 12: Ch 1, sc3tog over all 3 sts, fasten off.

Back-Panel Shaping

See Diagram C (pages 26–27) for assistance.

Join yarn 6 (12, 6, 18, 24) sts from end of Row 1 of front-panel shaping with sl st.

ROW 1: Ch 4, sk 2 sc, dc in next sc, ch 1, sk ch-1 sp, cont in ESP across to 9 (9, 10, 10, 11) SR, dc in next sc, sk 1 sc, tr in next sc, turn—9 (9, 10, 10, 11) SR.

ROW 2: Rep Row 1 of neck shaping.

ROW 3: Rep Row 6 of neck shaping.

ROWS 4–6: Rep Rows 1–3 of neck shaping—7 (7, 8, 8, 9) sc.

ROWS 7–8: Rep Rows 1–2 of front-panel shaping.

(2X)

ROWS 9–14: Rep Rows 3–8 of front-panel shaping—7 SR.

(S/M/2X)

ROW 9 (9, 15): Ch 2, dc in ch-1 sp, cont in ESP across to last ch-1 sp, dc2tog over ch-1 sp and sc, fasten off.

(L/XL)

ROWS 9–12: Rep Rows 3–6, fasten off.

Opposite Front-Panel Shaping

With sl st join yarn 6 (12, 6, 18, 24) sts from end of Row 1 of back-panel shaping.

Rep directions for front-panel shaping. *Note: Shaping is exactly symmetrical so directions actually work as written for this case. Usually, opposite front-panel shaping requires that the shaping be reversed.*

Finishing
BLOCKING AND SEAMING

Pin body to schematic size and spray with water. Allow to dry.

Bottom Ribbing

Join yarn on left side at bottom edge, ch 16.

ROW 1: Hdc in 3rd ch from hook (sk ch count as hdc), hdc in each remaining ch across, sl st to bottom edge of vest twice (once to join row, once to count as turning ch), turn—15 hdc.

ROW 2: Sc in middle bar of hdc across, sc in top of tch, turn.

ROW 3: Ch 2 (counts as hdc), hdc in each sc across, sl st twice to edge of vest, turn.

ROW 4–5: Rep Rows 2–3 across bottom edge, fasten off.

Collar Ribbing

Join yarn on right side at corner of bottom ribbing, ch 12.

ROW 1: Hdc in 3rd ch from hook (sk chs count as hdc), hdc in each remaning ch across, sl st to edge of vest twice (once to join row, once to count as turning ch), turn—11 hdc.

ROW 2: Sc in middle bar of hdc across, sc in top of tch, turn.

ROW 3: Ch 2 (counts as hdc), hdc in each sc across, sl st twice to edge of vest, turn.

Rep Rows 2–3 up front edge to beginning of neck shaping.

BUTTONHOLE ROW: Ch 1, sc in the middle bar of the next 3 hdc, ch 4, sk 4 hdc, sc in the middle bar of next 4 hdc, turn (buttonhole made).

NECK ROW: Ch 2 (counts as hdc), hdc in next 4 sc, 4 hdc in ch-4 sp, hdc in next 3 sc, sl st to edge twice, turn.

Rep Rows 2–3 of collar ribbing to top edge of front panel. *Note: If your front-panel ribbing is puckering at the corner between the straight body and slanted neckline, rip out all but 2 rows before the neckline. Rep directions, but space sl st at the end of hdc rows closer together. Doing so will add rows to your ribbing and let it fan out instead of pucker.*

Sleeve Ribbing

ROW 1: Sc in middle bar of hdc across, sc in top of tch, turn.

ROW 2: Ch 2 (counts as hdc), hdc in each sc across, turn.

ROWS 3–28 (28, 36, 36, 36): Rep Rows 1–2 thirteen (13, 17, 17, 17) more times.

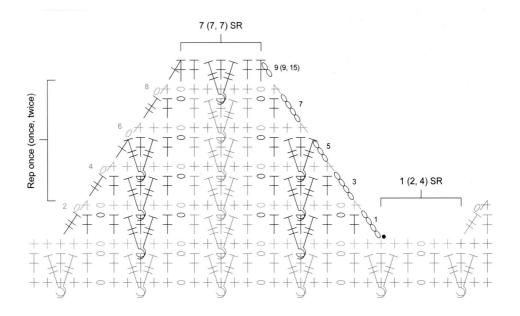

c. S/M/2X Back Panel Shaping

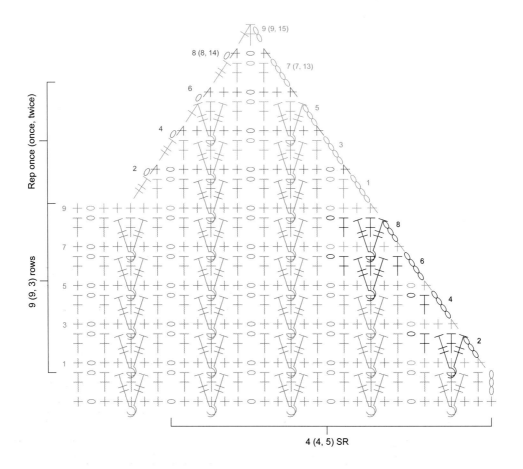

b. S/M/2X Front Panel Shaping

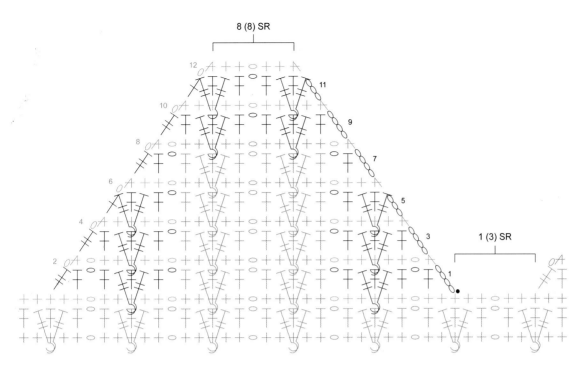

8 (8) SR

1 (3) SR

c. L/XL Back Panel Shaping

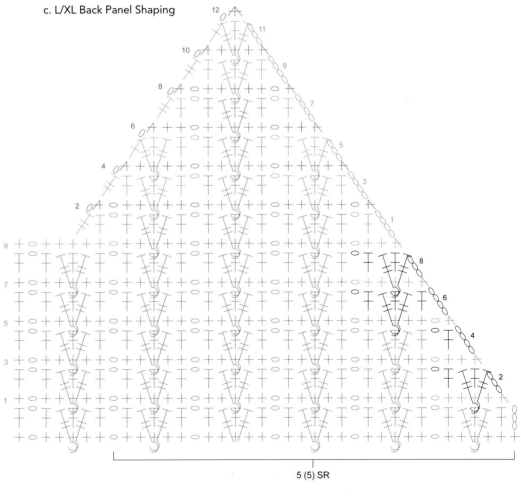

5 (5) SR

b. L/XL Front Panel Shaping

Rah Rah, Raglan!

To crocheters, raglan seams can seem mysterious. I'm convinced it's only because they're less common in crocheting than in knitting. We need to take a page from our sister stitchers' playbook. Although figuring out the shaping of raglan seams can be a challenge, the ease of seaming and fit are definitely worth it. Plus, once you figure it out for the back, you have it figured out for both front panels (because they have to match).

Raglan seams go from your armhole (usually from the back width dimension) to somewhere on your neck. The sleeves fit with a diagonal that matches the length of the diagonal edge on the front and back panels. The angles don't have to be the same, just the lengths. Steep angles on the sleeves give you a shallow cap, and shallow angles give you a wider cap. That's good to keep in mind if you have broad shoulders and might want more room in your sleeve cap.

What I also love about raglan lines is the opportunity to add another stitch pattern in the seam. Look at the Rose Quartz Pullover (page 66) for another take on raglans from the top down.

Back Neck Ribbing

Join sleeve ribbing with sl st to the back neck, turn.

ROW 1: Sc2tog in the middle bar of next 2 hdc, sc in middle bar of each hdc across to last 2, sc2tog over last 2 hdc, turn—9 sc.

ROW 2: Ch 1, sk first sc, hdc in each sc across to last 2 sc, hdc2tog over last 2 sc, sl st to back neck edge twice, turn—7 hdc.

ROWS 3–4: Rep Rows 1–2 once.

ROW 5: Sc3tog over last 3 hdc, fasten off.

Join yarn to top edge of back neck ribbing with sl st.

ROW 6: Ch 2, 10 hdc evenly down edge (working in row ends), sl st to back-panel edge twice.

ROWS 7–8: Rep Rows 2–3 of collar ribbing across to last 2" (5 cm) of back panel, fasten off.

Opposite Sleeve Ribbing

ROW 1: Join yarn on wrong side of back panel in corner of ribbing and panel with sc, sl st to edge of back neck ribbing twice, turn.

ROW 2: 3 hdc in sc, sl st twice to edge of back panel, turn.

ROW 3: 2 sc in middle bar of first hdc, sc in middle bar of each hdc across to last, 2 sc in middle bar of last hdc, sl st to edge twice, turn—5 sc.

ROW 4: 2 hdc in first sc, hdc in each sc to last, 2 hdc in last sc, sl st to edge twice, turn—7 hdc.

ROWS 5–6: Rep Rows 3–4 once—11 hdc.

ROWS 7–34 (34, 42, 42, 42): Rep Rows 1–2 of sleeve ribbing fourteen (14, 18, 18, 18) times.

Opposite Panel Ribbing

Sl st to edge of front panel.

ROWS 1–2: Rep Rows 2–3 of collar edging down front panel, fasten off.

Block ribbing by pinning it to schematic size, spraying it with water, and allowing to dry. *Note: If ribbing still curls, join yarn to the right side at the edge of the bottom ribbing. Sc evenly around the edge of ribbing in row ends around to the first sc, sl st to the first sc, and fasten off.*

Armhole Opening Edging

Join yarn on right side to the edge of the armhole. Sc evenly around the armhole, including sleeve ribbing, sl st to the first sc, and fasten off.

Pockets

Ch 24.

ROW 1: Sc in 2nd ch from hook, sc in each remaining ch across, turn—23 sc.

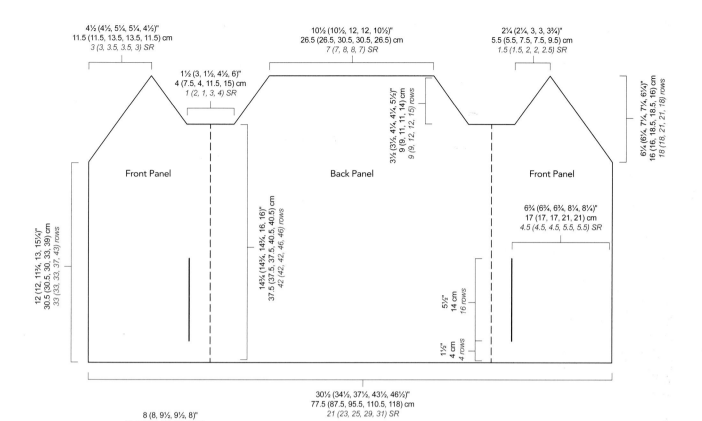

4½ (4½, 5¼, 5¼, 4½)"
11.5 (11.5, 13.5, 13.5, 11.5) cm
3 (3, 3.5, 3.5, 3) SR

1½ (3, 1½, 4½, 6)"
4 (7.5, 4, 11.5, 15) cm
1 (2, 1, 3, 4) SR

10½ (10½, 12, 12, 10½)"
26.5 (26.5, 30.5, 30.5, 26.5) cm
7 (7, 8, 8, 7) SR

2¼ (2¼, 3, 3, 3¾)"
5.5 (5.5, 7.5, 7.5, 9.5) cm
1.5 (1.5, 2, 2, 2.5) SR

6¼ (6¼, 7¼, 7¼, 6¼)"
16 (16, 18.5, 18.5, 16) cm
18 (18, 21, 21, 18) rows

Front Panel

Back Panel

Front Panel

3½ (3½, 4¼, 4¼, 5½)"
9 (9, 11, 11, 14) cm
9 (9, 12, 12, 15) rows

14¾ (14¾, 14¾, 16, 16)"
37.5 (37.5, 37.5, 40.5, 40.5) cm
42 (42, 42, 46, 46) rows

12 (12, 11¾, 13, 15¼)"
30.5 (30.5, 30, 33, 39) cm
33 (33, 33, 37, 43) rows

6¾ (6¾, 6¾, 8¼, 8¼)"
17 (17, 17, 21, 21) cm
4.5 (4.5, 4.5, 5.5, 5.5) SR

5½"
14 cm
16 rows

1½"
4 cm
4 rows

30½ (34½, 37½, 43½, 46½)"
77.5 (87.5, 95.5, 110.5, 118) cm
21 (23, 25, 29, 31) SR

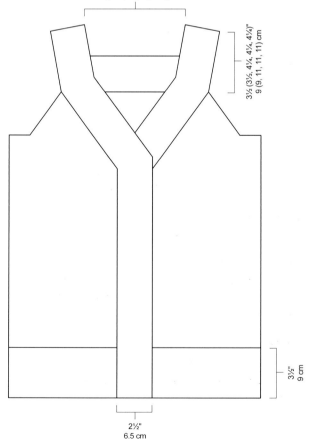

8 (8, 9½, 9½, 8)"
20.5 (20.5, 24, 24, 20.5) cm

3½ (3½, 4¼, 4¼, 4¼)"
9 (9, 11, 11, 11) cm

3½"
9 cm

2½"
6.5 cm

ROW 2: Ch 2 (counts as esc), esc in each st across, turn.

ROWS 3–17: Rep Row 2 fifteen more times.

ROW 18: Ch 1, sc in each esc across, fasten off.

Block flat if needed. Pin to the inside of the vest. Whipstitch to the pocket opening and wrong side of the vest.

Pocket Cuff

Join yarn to right side of vest at pocket opening.

ROW 1: Sc evenly across row ends, turn.

ROW 2: Ch 1, sc in each sc across.

ROWS 3–4: Repeat Row 2. At end of Row 4, fasten off.

Join yarn at the right side at the edge of the cuff, sc evenly up cuff side, working in row ends, 3 sc in first sc, turn corner, sc evenly across row, 3 sc in last sc, turn corner, sc evenly down edge, fasten off. Backstitch the cuff edges to vest.

foliage
SHRUG

This textured, classic tweed cardigan shrug, with a cable running along the front and back neck edge, is a great addition to your everyday wardrobe. Usually, having a textured stitch pattern wreaks a little havoc on shaping; however, this one is easily memorized, and you only have to concentrate on where to place your increases and decreases. Here, you increase only when you're on an increasing row and at a marker. Otherwise, you'll find it smooth sailing over the cable and body-stitch patterns.

Designed by SIMONA MERCHANT-DEST

Materials

YARN
Worsted weight (#4 Medium)

SHOWN: Caron International Naturally Caron Country (75% microdenier acrylic, 25% merino; 185yd [170m]/3 oz [85g]): #0012 Foliage, 8 (9, 10, 11, 12) balls.

HOOK
RIB: US size F/5 (3.75 mm); BODY: US size G/6 (4.0 mm) or hook needed to obtain gauge.

NOTIONS
Removable stitch markers (m); tapestry needle for weaving in ends; two 1" (25 mm) closures ("la petite" #1056); spray bottle with water, and straight pins for blocking.

Gauge
16 sts by 13 rows = 4" × 4" (10 × 10 cm) in Main Body Stitch Pattern (MBSP); 17 sts by 16 rows = 4" × 4" (10 × 10 cm) in RIB pattern; 20 sts by 12 rows = 4" × 4" (10 × 10 cm) in CABLE pattern.

Finished Size
Bust measurement is 32¼ (35¼, 38¼, 41¼, 44¼, 47¼)" (82 [89.5, 97, 105, 112.5, 120] cm). Sized for X-Small (Small, Medium, Large, X-Large, 2X). Size shown is Small.

Notes
Shrug is worked from the lower edge upward in one piece in rows to the underarms. Body is increased for bust at the side seams, then divided for fronts and back, with each piece finished separately. Sleeves are worked in joined rounds to the underarm and finished off with sleeve caps worked in rows.

Special Stitches

MAIN BODY STITCH PATTERN (MBSP)

See Main Body Stitch Pattern diagram for assistance.

Fsc multiple of 6 sts plus 5.

ROW 1 (WS): Ch 2, hdc in first st, * ch 1, sk next st, hdc in next 5 sts, rep from * to last 2 sts, ch 1, sk next st, hdc in last st, turn.

ROW 2: Ch 3, dc in first hdc, 2dc-cl in st located 1 row below ch-1 sp, * dc in next 2 hdc, ch 1, sk next st, dc in next 2 hdc, 2dc-cl in st located 1 row below ch-sp, rep from * to last st, dc in last hdc, turn.

ROW 3: Ch 2, hdc in first dc, * ch 1, sk next st, hdc in next 2 dc, 2dc-cl in st located 1 row below ch-sp, hdc in next 2 dc, rep from * to last 2 sts, ch 1, sk next dc, hdc in last dc, turn.

Rep Rows 2–3 for pattern.

CABLE STITCH PATTERN (CABLE)

See Cable Stitch diagram (opposite) for assistance.

Fsc 18.

ROW 1 (WS): Ch 2 (counts as hdc here and throughout), sk first st, BPdc in next 2 sts, hdc in next st, BPdc in next 3 sts, hdc in next 6 sts, BPdc in next 3 sts, hdc in next st, BPdc in next 2 sts, hdc in last st, turn.

ROW 2: Ch 3 (counts as hdc here and throughout), sk first st, FPdc in next 2 sts, dc in next hdc, sk next 3 sts, tr in next 3 hdc, working in front of sts just made, FPtr in 3 skipped sts, sk next 3 hdc, FPtr in next 3 hdc, working behind sts just made, tr in 3 skipped sts, dc in next hdc, FPdc in next 2 sts, dc in last st, turn.

ROW 3: Ch 2, sk first st, BPdc in next 2 sts, hdc in next 4 sts, BPdc in next 6 sts, hdc in next 4 sts, BPdc in next 2 sts, hdc in last st, turn.

ROW 4: Ch 3, sk first st, FPdc in next 2 sts, dc in next 4 hdc, sk next 3 sts, FPtr in next 3 sts, working in front of sts just made, FPtr in 3 skipped sts, dc in next 4 hdc, FPdc in next 2 dc, dc in last st, turn.

ROW 5: Rep Row 3.

ROW 6: Ch 3, sk first st, FPdc in next 2 sts, dc in next hdc, sk next 3 hdc, FPtr in next 3 sts, working behind sts just made, tr in 3 skipped sts, sk next 3 sts, tr in next 3 hdc, working in front of sts just made, FPtr in 3 skipped sts, dc in next hdc, FPdc in next 2 sts, dc in last st, turn.

ROW 7: Rep Row 1.

ROW 8: Ch 3, sk first st, FPdc in next 2 sts, dc in next hdc, FPdc in next 3 sts, dc in next 6 hdc, FPdc in next 3 sts, dc in next hdc, FPdc in next 2 sts, dc in last st, turn.

Rep Rows 1–8 for pattern.

RIB STITCH PATTERN (RIB)

Fsc multiple of 2 sts plus 1.

ROW 1 (RS): Ch 3 (counts as dc), sk first st, dc in each st across, turn.

ROW 2: Ch 2, sk first st, * BPdc in next st, FPdc in next st, rep from * to last 2 sts, BPdc in next st, hdc in last st, turn.

ROW 3: Ch 2, sk first st, * FPdc in next st, BPdc in next st, rep from * to last 2 sts, FPdc in next st, hdc in last st, turn.

Rep Rows 2–3 for pattern.

Main Body Stitch Pattern

Body

With smaller hook, fsc 121 (133, 145, 157, 169, 181).

ROW 1 (WS): Ch 3 (counts as dc here and throughout), sk first st, dc in each st across, turn—121 (133, 145, 157, 169, 181) dc.

ROW 2: Ch 3, sk first st, work Row 2 of CABLE over next 18 sts, dc in next st, * FPdc in next st, BPdc in next st, rep from * to last 21 sts, FPdc in next st, dc in next st, work Row 2 of CABLE over next 18 sts, dc in last st, turn.

ROW 3: Change to larger hook. Ch 2 (counts as hdc), sk first st, work Row 3 of CABLE over next 18 sts, hdc in next 5 (2, 5, 2, 5, 2) sts, [ch 1, sk 1 st, hdc in next 5 sts] 1 (2, 2, 3, 3, 4) times, ch 1, sk 1 st, hdc in next st, pm (left side), hdc in next st, [ch 1, sk 1 st, hdc in next 5 sts] 9 (10, 11, 12, 13, 14) times, ch 1, sk 1 st, hdc in next st, pm (right side), hdc in next st, ch 1, sk 1 st, [hdc in next 5 sts, ch 1, sk 1 st] 1 (2, 2, 3, 3, 4) times, hdc in next 5 (2, 5, 2, 5, 2) sts, work Row 3 of CABLE to last st, hdc in last st, turn.

ROW 4: Ch 3, sk first st, work Row 4 of CABLE over next 18 sts, (**XS, M, XL**) dc in next 2 hdc, ch 1, sk 1 st, (**ALL**) dc in next 2 hdc, *2dc-cl in st 1 row below ch-sp, dc in next 2 hdc, ch 1, sk next st, dc in next 2 hdc*; rep from * to 2 sts before m, 2dc-cl in st 1 row below ch-sp, dc in next hdc, pm, dc in next hdc, rep from * to * 9 (10, 11, 12, 13, 14) times, 2dc-cl in st 1 row below, dc in next hdc, pm, dc in next hdc, 2dc-cl in st 1 row below, **dc in next 2 hdc, ch 1, sk next st, dc in next 2 hdc, 2dc-cl in st 1 row below 1 (2, 2, 3, 3, 4) times, dc in next 2 hdc, (**XS, M, XL**) ch 1, sk 1 st, dc in next 2 hdc, (**ALL**) work Row 4 of CABLE to last st, dc in last st, turn.

ROW 5: Ch 2 (counts as hdc), sk first st, work Row 5 of CABLE over next 18 sts, (**XS, M, XL**) hdc in next 2 dc, 2dc-cl in st 1 row below, (**ALL**) hdc in next 2 hdc, cont in Row 3 of MBSP to 2 sts before m, ch 1, sk 1 st, hdc in next dc, pm, hdc in next dc, cont in Row 3 of MBSP to 2 sts before m, ch 1, sk 1 st, hdc in next dc, pm, hdc in next dc, ch 1, sk 1 st, cont in MBSP across to last 5 (2, 5, 2, 5, 2) sts before CABLE, hdc in next 2 dc, (**XS, M, XL**) 2 dc-cl in st 1 row below, hdc in next 2 dc, (**ALL**) work Row 3 of CABLE to last st, hdc in last st, turn.

ROWS 6–10: Repeat Rows 4 and 5 of Body twice and Row 4 once, working Rows 6–10 of CABLE chart.

Shape for Bust

INC ROW 1 (WS): Ch 2 (counts as hdc), sk first st, work Row 3 of CABLE over next 18 sts, hdc in next st, cont in MBSP to 1 st before m, 2 hdc in next st, pm (left side), 2 hdc in next st, cont in MBSP across to 1 st before m, 2 hdc in next st, pm (right side), 2 hdc in next st, work in MBSP to last 20 sts, hdc in next st, work Row 3 of CABLE to last st, hdc in last st, turn—4 sts inc'd: 2 sts inc'd for back, 1 st inc'd for each front—125 (137, 149, 161, 173, 185) sts.

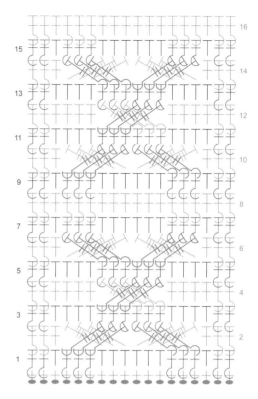

Cable Stitch Pattern

ROW 2: Ch 3, sk first st, work row 4 of CABLE over next 18 sts, dc in next st, [cont in MBSP across to m, pm] twice, work MBSP to last 20 sts, dc in next st, work in CABLE to last st, dc in last st, turn.

ROW 3: Ch 2, sk first st, work Row 5 of CABLE over next 18 sts, hdc in next st, [cont in MBSP across to m, pm] twice, work MBSP to last 20 sts, hdc in next st, work in CABLE to last st, hdc in last st, turn.

ROW 4: Rep Row 2, using Row 6 of CABLE.

INC ROW 5: Ch 2, sk first st, work Row 7 of CABLE over next 18 sts, hdc in next st, * cont in MBSP to 1 st before m, 2 hdc in next st, pm, 2 hdc in next st, rep from * once more, work MBSP to last 20 sts, hdc in next st, work CABLE to last st, hdc in last st, turn—4 sts inc'd: 2 sts inc'd for back, 1 st inc'd for each front—129 (141, 153, 165, 177, 189) sts.

ROWS 6–13: Repeat Rows 2–5 of bust shaping twice using Row 8 and Rows 1–7 of CABLE. Turn—137 (149, 161, 173, 185, 197) sts: 65 (71, 77, 83, 89, 95) sts for back; 36 (39, 42, 45, 48, 51) sts for each front.

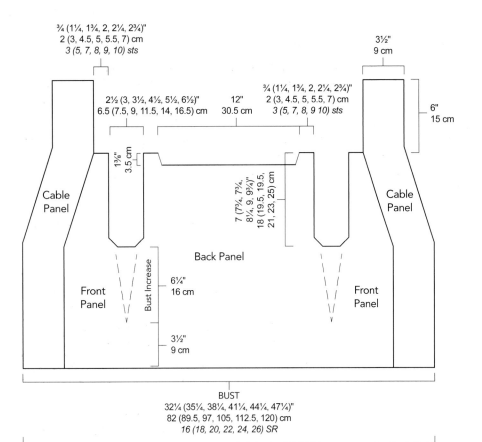

¾ (1¼, 1¾, 2, 2¼, 2¾)"
2 (3, 4.5, 5, 5.5, 7) cm
3 (5, 7, 8, 9, 10) sts

3½"
9 cm

2½ (3, 3½, 4½, 5½, 6½)"
6.5 (7.5, 9, 11.5, 14, 16.5) cm

12"
30.5 cm

¾ (1¼, 1¾, 2, 2¼, 2¾)"
2 (3, 4.5, 5, 5.5, 7) cm
3 (5, 7, 8, 9 10) sts

6"
15 cm

Cable Panel

1⅜"
3.5 cm

7 (7¾, 7¾,
8¼, 9, 9¾)"
18 (19.5, 19.5,
21, 23, 25) cm

Cable Panel

Front Panel

Bust Increase

Back Panel

6¼"
16 cm

Front Panel

3½"
9 cm

BUST
32¼ (35¼, 38¼, 41¼, 44¼, 47¼)"
82 (89.5, 97, 105, 112.5, 120) cm
16 (18, 20, 22, 24, 26) SR

WAIST
28¼ (31¼, 34¼, 37¼, 40¼, 43¼)"
72 (79.5, 87, 94.5, 102, 110) cm
13 (15, 17, 19, 21, 23) SR

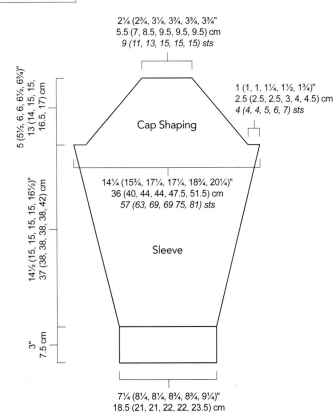

2¼ (2¾, 3¼, 3¾, 3¾, 3¾)"
5.5 (7, 8.5, 9.5, 9.5, 9.5) cm
9 (11, 13, 15, 15, 15) sts

1 (1, 1, 1¼, 1½, 1¾)"
2.5 (2.5, 2.5, 3, 4, 4.5) cm
4 (4, 4, 5, 6, 7) sts

Cap Shaping

5 (5½, 6, 6, 6½, 6¾)"
13 (14, 15, 15,
16.5, 17) cm

14¼ (15¾, 17¼, 17¼, 18¾, 20¼)"
36 (40, 44, 44, 47.5, 51.5) cm
57 (63, 69, 69 75, 81) sts

14½ (15, 15, 15, 15, 16½)"
37 (38, 38, 38, 38, 42) cm

Sleeve

3"
7.5 cm

7¼ (8¼, 8¼, 8¾, 8¾, 9¼)"
18.5 (21, 21, 22, 22, 23.5) cm
33 (37, 37, 39, 39, 41) sts

XL (2X)

ROWS 14–17: Rep Rows 2–3 of Bust Shaping using next rows CABLE as est.

(ALL)
Shape Front Neck

DEC ROW 1 (RS): Ch 3, sk first st, work next row of CABLE over next 18 sts, dc in next st, dc2tog over next 2 sts, *work next row of MBSP to m, pm, rep from * once more, work MBSP to last 22 sts, dc2tog over next 2 sts, dc in next st, work CABLE to last st, dc in last st, turn—2 sts dec'd: 1 st dec'd at each front.

ROW 2: Ch 2, sk first st, work next row of CABLE over next 18 sts, hdc in next st, * work MBSP to m, pm, rep from *, work MBSP to last 20 sts, hdc in next st, work CABLE to last st, hdc in last st, turn.

ROW 3: Ch 3, sk first st, work next row of CABLE over next 18 sts, dc in next st, * work MBSP to m, pm, rep from * once more, work MBSP to last 20 sts, dc in next st, work CABLE to last st, dc in last st, turn.

ROW 4: Rep Row 2.

(XS, S, M, L)

DEC ROW 5: Rep Dec Row 1.

ROWS 6–8: Rep Rows 2–4 of Front Neck shaping.

Shrug measures about 10" (25 cm) from beg.

Divide for front and back.

Set left and right fronts aside unworked and work over back sts only.

BACK
Shape Underarms

DEC ROW 1 (RS): With new ball of yarn, sl st into 4th (4th, 4th, 5th, 6th, 7th) st after m (right side), ch 3, dc2tog over next 2 sts, work MBSP as est to last 6 (6, 6, 7, 7, 8) sts before m, dc2tog over next 2 sts, dc in next st, leave last 3 (3, 3, 4, 4, 5) sts before next m (left side) unworked, turn—57 (63, 69, 73, 77, 81) sts.

ROW 2: Ch 2, work in MBSP as est to end, turn.

DEC ROW 3: Ch 3, dc2tog over next 2 sts, work MBSP as est to last 3 sts, dc2tog over next 2 sts, dc in last st, turn—55 (61, 67, 71, 75, 79) sts.

(S, M, L, XL, 2X)

ROWS 4–5 (7, 9, 11, 13): Rep Rows 2–3 of Armhole shaping, turn—2 (4, 6, 8, 10) sts dec'd, 59 (63, 65, 67, 69) sts rem.

(ALL)

ROWS 4 (6, 8, 10, 12, 14)–16 (18, 18, 20, 22, 22): Work in MBSP as est to end, turn.

Shape Neck
Right side

DEC ROW 1 (RS): Work in MBSP patt as est over first 4 (6, 8, 9, 10, 11) sts, dc2tog over next 2 sts, turn—5 (7, 9, 10, 11, 12) sts.

DEC ROW 2: Ch 2, sk first st, hdc2tog over next 2 sts, cont in MBSP patt as est to end, turn—4 (6, 8, 9, 10, 11) sts.

DEC ROW 3: Work in MBSP patt as est to last 2 sts, dc2tog over next 2 sts, turn—3 (5, 7, 8, 9, 10) sts.

ROW 4: Ch 2, hdc in each st across. Fasten off.

Left side

DEC ROW 1 (RS): With RS facing and new ball of yarn, sl st into 6th (8th, 10th, 11th, 12th, 13th) st before end of row, ch 3, dc2tog over next 2 sts, cont in MBSP patt as est to end, turn—5 (7, 9, 10, 11, 12) sts.

DEC ROW 2: Ch 2, sk first st, cont in MBSP patt as est to last 2 sts, hdc2tog over next 2 sts, turn—4 (6, 8, 9, 10, 11) sts.

DEC ROW 3: Ch 3, sk first st, dc2tog over next 2 sts, cont in MBSP patt as est to end, turn—3 (5, 7, 8, 9, 10) sts.

ROW 4: Ch 2, sk first st, hdc in each st across. Fasten off.

RIGHT FRONT
Shape Armholes and Front Neck

With front-neck shaping in progress, begin armhole shaping. Front-neck shaping and armhole shaping are worked simultaneously.

DEC ROW 1 (RS): Ch 3, sk first st, work next row of CABLE over next 18 sts, dc in next st, dc2tog over next 2 sts, work in MBSP to last 6 (6, 6, 7, 8, 9) sts before m (right side), dc2tog over next 2 sts, dc in next st, leave last 3 (2, 3, 3, 5, 5) sts before m unworked, turn—2 sts dec'd: 1 st dec'd for front neck, 1 st dec'd at armhole.

ROW 2: Work in MBSP patt as est to last 20 sts, hdc in next st, work next row of CABLE over next 18 sts, hdc in last st, turn.

DEC ROW 3: Ch 3, sk first st, work next row of CABLE over next 18 sts, dc in next st, work in MBSP patt as est to last 3 sts, dc2tog over next 2 sts, dc in last st, turn—1 st dec'd at armhole.

ROW 4: Rep Row 2.

S (M, L, XL, 2X) only

DEC ROW 5: Ch 3, sk first st, work next row of CABLE over next 18 sts, dc in next st, dc2tog over next 2 sts, work in MBSP to last 3 sts, dc2tog over next 2 sts, dc in last st, turn—2 sts dec'd: 1 st dec'd for front neck, 1 st dec'd at armhole.

ROW 6: Rep Row 2 of Armhole and Front-Neck shaping working next row of patts as est.

(M, L, XL, 2X)

ROWS 7– 8: Rep Rows 3–4 of Armhole and Front-Neck shaping, working next row of patts as est.

(L, XL, 2X)

ROWS 9–10: Rep Rows 5–6 of Armhole and Front-Neck shaping, working next row of patts as est.

(XL, 2X)

ROWS 11–12: Rep Rows 3–4 of Armhole and Front-Neck shaping, working next row of patts as est.

(2X)

ROWS 13–14: Rep Rows 5–6 of Armhole and Front-Neck shaping, working next row of patts as est.

(S, L, 2X)

ROW 7 (11, 15): Ch 3, sk first st, work next row of CABLE over next 18 sts, dc in next st, work in MBSP to last 3 sts, dc2tog over next 2 sts, dc in last st, turn—1 st dec'd.

ROW 8 (12, 16): Work in MBSP to last 20 sts, hdc in next st, work next row of CABLE over next 18 sts, hdc in last st, turn.

(ALL)

Cont in front-neck shaping as follows:

ROW 5 (9, 9, 13, 13, 17): Ch 3, sk first st, work next row of CABLE over next 18 sts, dc in next st, dc2tog over next 2 sts, work in MBSP to end, turn—1 st dec'd for front neck.

ROW 6 (10, 10, 14, 14, 18): Work next row of MBSP to last 20 sts, hdc in next st, work next row of CABLE over next 18 sts, hdc in last st, turn.

ROW 7 (11, 11, 15, 15, 19): Ch 3, sk first st, work next row of CABLE over next 18 sts, dc in next st, work next row of MBSP, turn.

ROW 8 (12, 12, 16, 16, 20): Work next row of MBSP to last 20 sts, hdc in next st, work next row of CABLE over next 18 sts, hdc in last st, turn.

ROWS 9 (13, 13, 17, 17, 21)–20 (20, 20, 24, 24, 28): Rep last 4 rows 3 (2, 2, 2, 2, 2) times as est—24 (25, 28, 28, 30, 30) sts.

(XS)

ROW 21: Ch 3, sk first st, work next row of CABLE over next 18 sts, dc in next st, dc2tog over next 2 sts, work in MBSP to end, turn—1 st dec'd for front neck, 23 sts rem.

(S)

ROW 21: Ch 3, sk first st, work next row of CABLE over next 18 sts, dc in next st, work in MBSP to end, turn.

ROWS 22–23: Work even in patt as est.

(S, M, XL)

ROW 21 (21, 25): Ch 3, sk first st, work next row of CABLE over next 18 sts, dc in next st, dc2tog over next 2 sts, work in MBSP to end, turn—1 st dec'd for front neck, 23 (27, 29) sts rem.

ROWS 22 (22, 26)–23 (23, 27): Work even in patt as est.

(L, 2X)

ROW 25 (29): Ch 3, sk first st, work next row of CABLE over next 18 sts, dc in next st, work next row of MBSP to end, turn.

Armhole measures about 7 (7¾, 7¾, 8¼, 9, 9¾)" (18 [18, 19.5, 21, 23, 25] cm).

COLLAR

ROW 1 (RS): Ch 3, sk first st, work next row of CABLE over next 18 sts, dc in next st, turn, leaving last 3 (5, 7, 8, 9, 10) sts unworked—20 sts.

ROW 2: Ch 2, sk first st, work next row of CABLE patt over next 18 sts, hdc in last st, turn.

ROW 3: Ch 3, sk first st, work next row of CABLE patt over next 18 sts, dc in last st, turn.

ROWS 4–7: Rep Rows 2–3 of Collar, 7 times.

Fasten off.

LEFT FRONT

With front-neck shaping in progress, begin armhole shaping. Front-neck shaping and armhole shaping are worked simultaneously.

DEC ROW 1 (RS): With new ball of yarn, sl st into 4th (3rd, 4th, 4th, 6th, 6th) st after m (left side), ch 3, dc2tog over next 2 sts, work in MBSP to last 22 sts, dc2tog over next 2 sts, dc in next st, work next row of CABLE over next 18 sts, dc in last st, turn—2 sts dec'd: 1 st dec'd for front neck, 1 st dec'd at armhole.

ROW 2: Ch 2, sk first st, work next row of CABLE over next 18 sts, hdc in next st, work in MBSP as est to end, turn.

DEC ROW 3: Ch 3, dc2tog over next 2 sts, work in MBSP as est to last 20 sts, dc in next st, work next row of CABLE over next 18 sts, dc in next st, turn—1 st dec'd at armhole.

ROW 4: Rep Row 2.

(S, M, L, XL, 2X)

DEC ROW 5: Ch 3, dc2tog over next 2 sts, work in MBSP to last 22 sts, dc2tog over next 2 sts, dc in next st, work next row of CABLE over next 18 sts, dc in last st, turn—2 sts dec'd: 1 st dec'd for front neck, 1 st dec'd at armhole.

ROW 6: Rep Row 2 of Armhole and Front-Neck shaping, working next row of patts as est.

(M, L, XL, 2X)

ROWS 7–8: Rep Rows 3–4 of Armhole and Front-Neck shaping, working next row of patts as est.

(L, XL, 2X)

ROWS 9–10: Rep Rows 5–6 of Armhole and Front-Neck shaping, working next row of patts as est.

(XL, 2X)

ROWS 11–12: Rep Rows 3–4 of Armhole and Front-Neck shaping, working next row of patts as est.

(2X)

ROWS 13–14: Rep Rows 5–6 of Armhole and Front-Neck shaping, working next row of patts as est.

(S, L, 2X)

ROW 7 (11, 15): Work in MBSP to last 22 sts, dc2tog over next 2 sts, dc in next st, work next row of CABLE over next 18 sts, dc in last st, turn—1 st dec'd.

ROW 8 (12, 16): Ch 2, sk first st, work next row of CABLE over next 18 sts, hdc in next st, work in MBSP patt as est to end, turn.

Cont in front-neck shaping as follows:

ROW 5 (9, 9, 13, 13, 17): Work in MBSP to last 22 sts, dc2tog over next 2 sts, dc in next st, work next row of CABLE over next 18 sts, dc in last st, turn—1 st dec'd for front neck.

ROW 6 (10, 10, 14, 14, 18): Ch 2, sk first st, work next row of CABLE over next 18 sts, hdc in next st, work in MBSP to end, turn.

ROW 7 (11, 11, 15, 15, 19): Work in MBSP to last 20 sts, dc in next st, work next row of CABLE over next 18 sts, dc in last st, turn.

ROW 8 (12, 12, 16, 16, 20): Ch 2, sk first st, work next row of CABLE over next 18 sts, hdc in next st, work in MBSP to end, turn.

ROWS 9 (13, 13, 17, 17, 21)–20 (20, 20, 24, 24, 28): Rep last 4 rows as est 3 (2, 2, 2, 2, 2) times—24 (25, 28, 28, 30, 30) sts.

(XS)

ROW 21: Work in MBSP to last 22 sts, dc2tog over next 2 sts, dc in next st, work next row of CABLE over next 18 sts, dc in last st, turn—1 st dec'd for front neck, 23 sts rem.

(S)

ROW 21: Ch 3, sk first st, work next row of CABLE over next 18 sts, dc in next st, work in MBSP to end, turn.

ROWS 22–23: Work even in patt as est.

(M, XL)

ROW 21 (21, 25): Work in MBSP to last 22 sts, dc2tog over next 2 sts, dc in next st, work next row of CABLE over next 18 sts, dc in last st, turn—1 st dec'd for front neck, 27, 29 sts rem.

ROWS 22 (22, 26)–23 (23, 27): Work even in patt as est.

(L, 2X)

ROW 25 (29): Work in MBSP to last 22 sts, dc2tog over next 2 sts, dc in next st, work next row of CABLE over next 18 sts, dc in last st, turn.

Armhole measures about 7 (7¾, 7¾, 8¼, 9, 9¾)" (18 [19.5, 19.5, 21, 23, 25] cm). Fasten off.

COLLAR

ROW 1 (RS): With new ball of yarn, sl st into 4th (6th, 8th, 9th, 10th, 11th) st, ch 3, sk first st, work next row in CABLE patt over next 18 sts, dc in last st, turn—20 sts.

ROW 2: Ch 2, sk first st, work next row in CABLE patt over next 18 sts, hdc in last st, turn.

ROW 3: Ch 3, sk first st, work next row in CABLE patt over next 18 sts, dc in last st, turn.

ROWS 4–17: Rep Rows 2–3 of Collar, 7 times. Fasten off.

SLEEVE

With smaller hook, fsc 33 (37, 37, 39, 39, 41).

RND 1 (WS): Ch 3 (counts as dc), sk first st, dc in each st across, sl st in first dc to join, turn.

RND 2: Ch 2 (counts as hdc), sk first st, * BPdc in next st, FPdc in next st, rep from * to last 2 sts, BPdc in next st, hdc in last st, sl st in first st, turn.

RND 3: Ch 2, sk first st, * FPdc in next st, BPdc in next st, rep from * to last 2 sts, FPdc in next st, hdc in last st, sl st in first st, turn.

RNDS 4–19: Rep Rnds 2–3, eight times. Change to larger hook.

(S, M)

DEC RND (RS): Ch 1, sc in next 2 sts, sc2tog, sc in next 4 sts, sc2tog, sc in next 17 sts, sc2tog, sc in next 4 sts, sc2tog, sc in last 2 sts, sl st in first sc to join, turn—33 (33) sts.

(XS, L, XL)

NEXT RND (RS): Ch 1, sc in each st across, turn—33 (39, 39) sc.

(2X)

DEC RND (RS): Ch 1, sc in next 2 sts, sc2tog, sc in each st across to last 4 sts, sc2tog, sc in last 2 sts, sl st in first sc to join, turn—39 sts.

(ALL)

RND 1 (WS): Ch 3 (counts as hdc and ch-1), sk first 2 sts, * hdc in next 5 sts, ch 1, sk next st, rep from * to last st, hdc in last st, sl st in first st to join, turn.

Cap It Off

Cap sleeve shaping can be the key to a great fitting sweater—or the sweater's downfall. Cap sleeve shaping adds a curved top to a straight sleeve (commonly called a drop sleeve). That curved area (or cap) basically just covers the shoulder to eliminate the extra bulk that a drop sleeve can cause under your arms.

In crochet, most of the time the cap usually resembles a trapezoid, generally 4"–6" (10–15 cm) tall, with a top edge shorter than the bottom edge, perhaps 3"–6" (7.5–15 cm) long. This standard fit makes a sleeve that works well in a fitted garment, one with up to 1" (2.5 cm) of ease in the bust.

There are some caveats, however, because not all caps are created equal. In general, the taller the cap height, the closer to the body the sleeve will fit. If you have broad shoulders, tall cap shaping might prevent you from raising your arms. But watch out: shallow (or short) cap shaping can position the sleeves far from the body. Imagine a nicely fitted sweater with bulky, puckering arms. Measure the cap height on a favorite sweater and record it. That way, when you choose a pattern, you can gauge how the sleeves will fit before you crochet the first stitch.

RND 2: Ch 3 (counts as dc), sk first hdc, 2dc-cl in st located 1 row below ch 1-sp, * dc in next 2 hdc, ch 1, sk next hdc, dc in next 2 hdc, 2 dc-cl in st located 1 row below ch-sp, rep from * to last st, dc in last hdc, sl st in first st to join, turn.

Shape Sleeves

Begin working MBSP as follows:

INC RND 1 (WS): Ch 2, sk first st, 2 hdc in next st, *ch 1, sk next st, hdc in next 5 sts, rep from * 4 (4, 4, 5, 5, 5) more times, ch 1, sk next st, 2 hdc in next st, hdc in last st, sl st in first st to join, turn—2 sts inc'd.

RND 2: Ch 3, sk first st, dc in next 2 sts, 2dc-cl in st one row below ch-1 sp, *dc in next 2 sts, ch 1, sk next st, dc in next 2 sts, 2dc-cl in st one row below ch-1 sp, rep from * to last 3 sts, dc in next 3 sts, sl st in first st to join, turn.

RND 3: Ch 2, sk first st, hdc in next 2 sts, ch 1, sk next st, *hdc in next 2 sts, 2dc-cl in st one row below ch-1 sp, hdc in next 2 sts, ch 1, sk next st: rep from * to last 3 sts, hdc in last 3 sts, sl st in first st to join, turn.

RND 4: Ch 3, sk first st, work MBSP as est, dc in last st, sl st in first st to join, turn.

RND 5: Ch 2, sk first st, 2 hdc in next st, work in MBSP as est to last 2 sts, 2 hdc in next st, hdc in last st, sl st in first st to join, turn—2 sts inc'd.

RNDS 6–33 (29, 21, 25, 13, 9): Rep Rnds 2–5 7 (6, 4, 5, 2, 1) times, working MBSP as est—51 (49, 45, 53, 47, 45) sts.

RND 34 (30, 22, 26, 14, 10): Rep Rnd 4.

INC RND 35 (31, 23, 27, 15, 11): Ch 2, sk first st, 2 hdc in next st, work in MBSP as est to last 2 sts, 2 hdc in next st, hdc in last st, sl st in first st to join, turn—2 sts inc'd.

RND 36 (32, 24, 28, 16, 12): Ch 3, sk first st, work in MBSP as est to last st, dc in last st, sl st in first st to join, turn.

RNDS 37 (33, 25, 29, 17, 13)-40 (40, 42, 42, 42, 44): Rep last 2 rounds 2 (4, 9, 7, 13, 16) times—57 (63, 69, 69, 75, 81) sts.

(S)

RNDS 41–42: Work in MBSP.

Sleeve measures about 17½ (18, 18, 18, 18, 19½)" (44.5 [45.5, 45.5, 45.5, 45.5, 49.5] cm) from beg. Fasten off.

Shape Sleeve Cap:

With RS facing and new ball of yarn, sl st into 4th (4th, 4th, 5th, 6th, 7th) st.

ROW 1 (RS): Ch 3 (counts as dc), sk first st, work in MBSP as est to last 3 (3, 3, 4, 5, 6) sts, leaving these last sts unworked, turn—51 (57, 63, 61, 65, 69) sts.

DEC ROW 2: Ch 2 (counts as hdc), sk first st, hdc2tog over next 2 sts, work in MBSP as est to last 3 sts, hdc2tog over next 2 sts, hdc in last st, turn—2 sts dec'd.

DEC ROW 3: Ch 3, sk first st, dc2tog over next 2 sts, work in MBSP to last 3 sts, dc2tog over next 2 sts, dc in last st, turn—2 sts dec'd.

DEC ROWS 4–15 (17, 19, 17, 19, 21): Rep last 2 rows 6 (7, 8, 7, 8, 9) times—23 (25, 27, 29, 29, 29) sts.

DEC ROW 16 (18, 20, 18, 20, 22): Rep Row 3 of Sleeve cap shaping—21 (23, 25, 27, 27, 27) sts.

DEC ROW 17 (19, 21, 19, 21, 23): Ch 3, sk first st, dc3tog over next 3 sts, work in MBSP to last 4 sts, dc3tog over next 3 sts, dc in last st, turn—4 sts dec'd.

DEC ROW 18 (20, 22, 20, 22, 24): Ch 2, sk first st, hdc3tog over next 3 sts, work in MBSP to last 4 sts, hdc3tog over next 3 sts, hdc in last st, turn—4 sts dec'd.

DEC ROW 19 (21, 23, 21, 23, 25): Ch 3, sk first st, dc3tog over next 3 sts, work in MBSP to last 4 sts, dc3tog over next 3 sts, dc in last st, turn—4 sts dec'd—9 (11, 13, 15, 15, 15) sts.

ROW 20 (22, 24, 22, 24, 26): Ch 2, sk first st, hdc in each st across. Fasten off.

Finishing
BLOCKING AND SEAMING

Block pieces to schematic size and spray with water. Allow to dry. Seam shoulder seams. Sew collar at center back neck and pin along back neck edge. Sew collar to back neck edge. Set in sleeves and sew sleeves to body. Attach 2 closures as pictured at right.

burnt plaid
DRESS

Colorwork in garments can make a huge impact. However, it can be quite challenging, even for an intermediate crocheter. This pattern uses color in the simplest way: stripes. The entire dress is crocheted with easy color changes—at the beginning and end of the rounds only. After the dress is blocked, the vertical lines of color are added to create the plaid look. The best part is that when you embroider the stripes on last, they also act as support threads to help keep the dress from "growing" from the weight of the yarn.

Materials

YARN

DK weight (#3 Light)

SHOWN: Filatura Di Crosa Zara (100% Lana extrafine merino superwash; 137 yd [125 m]/1.75 oz [50 g]): #805 Burnt Orange Chinè (MC), 11 (12, 14, 16, 18) balls; #1895 Cocoa (CC1), 2 (2, 2, 2, 2) balls; #1926 Periwinkle (CC2) 2 (2, 2, 2, 2) balls; #1798 Seafoam Green (CC3) 2 (2, 2, 2, 2) balls.

HOOK

Size H/8 (5.0 mm) or hook needed to obtain gauge.

NOTIONS

Stitch markers; tapestry needle for weaving in ends; spray bottle with water; straight pins for blocking.

Gauge

18 dc by 9 rows = 4" × 4" (10 × 10 cm).

7 V-sts by 9 rows = 4⅜" × 4" (11 × 10 cm).

Finished Size

Bust measurement is 31½ (36¾, 42, 47¼, 52½)" (80 [93.5, 106.5, 120, 133.5] cm). Waist measurement is 26.5 (31¾, 37, 42¼, 47½)" (67.5 [80.5, 94, 107.5, 120.5] cm). Hip measurement is 39 (45½, 52, 58½, 65)" (99 [115.5, 132, 148.5, 165] cm). Sized for Small (Medium, Large, X-large, and 2X) and a close fitting. Size shown is Medium.

Notes

Dress is worked from the bottom up to the shoulder. The bottom and collar edgings are added after the sleeves are attached. Throughout the pattern, you will be directed to change to a contrasting color (CC). Change color in the following sequence unless otherwise noted: CC3, CC1, CC1, CC2.

Special Stitches

FOUNDATION DOUBLE CROCHET (FDC)

Chain 4 (counts as fdc).

FIRST FDC: Yo, Insert hook into 4th ch from hook, yo and pull up lp, yo and draw through 1 lp (the "ch"), *yo and draw through 2 lps, rep from * once more (creates the "fdc").

SUBSEQUENT FDC: Yo, insert hook under 2 lps of the "ch" st of last fdc, yo and pull up lp, yo, and draw through 1 lp, *yo and draw through 2 lps, rep from * once more.

V-ST

(Dc, ch 1, dc) in st indicated.

DCTRTOG

Yo, insert hook into next indicated st, yo and draw up a lp, yo and draw through 2 lps, yo twice, insert hook into next indicated st, yo and draw up a lp, [yo and draw through 2 lps] twice, yo and draw through remaining 3 lps on hook—1 decrease made.

12 (14, 16, 18, 20) Stitch Repeats

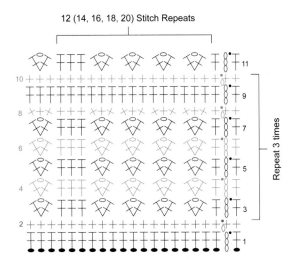

a. Skirt Stitch Diagram

Skirt

See Diagram A for assistance.

RND 1 (RS): Ch 4 (counts as fdc), 179 (209, 239, 269, 299) fdc with MC, sl st to top of tch, fasten off MC, turn—180 (210, 240, 270, 300) fdc.

RND 2: Join CC (following stripe sequence in notes), ch 1, sc in top of tch, sc in each dc around, sl st to first sc, fasten off CC, turn.

RND 3: Join MC, ch 3 (counts as dc), dc in next sc, *sk 1 sc, V-st in next sc, [sk 2 sc, V-st in next sc] 3 times, sk 1 sc, dc in next 3 sc, rep from * around to last 13 sc, sk 1 sc, V-st in next sc, [sk 2 sc, V-st in next sc] 3 times, sk 1 sc, dc in last sc, sl st to top of tch, turn—48 (56, 64, 72, 80) V-sts.

RND 4: Ch 3 (counts as dc), dc in each dc around, V-st in ch-1 sp of each V-st around, sl st to top of tch, turn.

RNDS 5–7: Rep Rnd 4 three times, fasten off MC, turn.

RND 8: Join CC, ch 1, sc in top of tch, sc in each dc around, 3 sc in each ch-1 sp around, sl st to first sc, fasten off CC, turn.

RND 9: Join MC, ch 3 (counts as dc), dc in each sc around, sl st to top of tch, fasten off MC, turn.

RND 10: Join CC, ch 1, sc in top of tch, sc in each dc around, sl st to first sc, fasten off CC, turn.

RNDS 11–26: Rep Rnds 3–10 twice more

Hip Shaping

See Diagram B for assistance.

RND 1 (RS): Join MC, ch 3 (counts as dc), dc in next sc, *sk 1 sc, V-st in next sc, sk 2 sc, 2 dc in next sc, place m, [sk 2 sc, V-st in next sc] twice, sk 1 sc, dc in each of next 3 sc*, **sk 1 sc, V-st in next sc, [sk 2 sc, V-st in next sc] 3 times, sk 1 sc, dc in next 3 sc**, rep from ** 3 (4, 5, 6, 7) times total, rep from * to ** once, rep from * to * once, rep from ** to ** 3 (4, 5, 6, 7) times total, rep from * to * once, sk 1 sc, V-st in next sc, [sk 2 sc, V-st in next sc] 3 times, sk 1 sc, dc in last sc, sl st to top of tch, turn—44 (52, 60, 68, 76) V-sts.

RND 2: Ch 3 (counts as dc), dc in each dc and V-st in ch-1 sp of each V-st around to m, dc bet dc of each marked group of 2 dc, move m to dc, sl st to top of tch, turn.

RND 3: Ch 3 (counts as dc), dc in each dc and V-st in ch-1 sp of each V-st around (sk marked dc), sl st to top of tch, turn.

RND 4: Ch 3 (counts as dc), dc in next dc, *V-st in next 2 V-sts, 2 dc in ch-1 sp of next V-st, place m, V-st in next V-st, dc in next 3 dc, V-st in next 3 V-sts, dc in next 3 dc*, [V-st in next 4 V-sts, dc in next 3 dc] 2 (3, 4, 5, 6) times, rep from * to * twice, [V-st in next 4 V-sts, dc in next 3 dc] 2 (3, 4, 5, 6) times, rep from * to last dc, sl st to top of tch, turn—40 (48, 56, 64, 72) V-sts.

RND 5: Rep Rnd 2 of hip shaping, fasten off MC, turn.

RND 6: Join CC, ch 1, sc in top of tch, sc in each dc and 3 sc in each ch-1 sps, move m to sc, sl st to first sc, fasten off CC, turn.

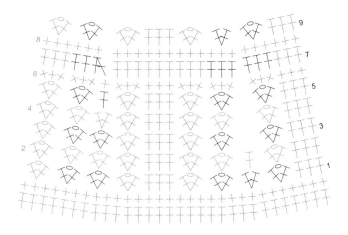

b. Skirt Hip Shaping Diagram

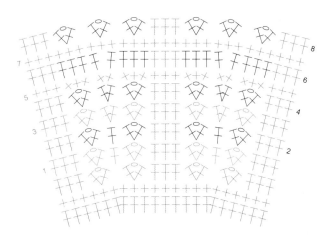

c. Bust Shaping Diagram

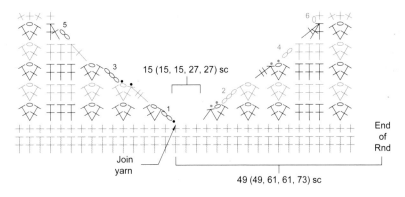

15 (15, 15, 27, 27) sc

End
of
Rnd

Join
yarn

49 (49, 61, 61, 73) sc

d. Neck Shaping Diagram

RND 7: Join MC, ch 3 (counts as dc), dc in each dc to m, dc2tog over next 2 sc, rep around, sl st to top of tch, fasten off MC, turn.

RND 8: Join CC, ch 1, sc in top of tch, sc in each dc around, sl st to first sc, fasten off CC, turn.

RND 9: Join MC, ch 3 (counts as dc), dc in next sc, *sk 1 sc, V-st in next sc, sk 2 sc, 2 dc in next sc, place m, sk 2 sc, V-st in next sc, sk 1 sc, dc in next 3 sc, sk 1 sc, V-st in next sc, [sk 2 sc, V-st in next sc] twice, sk 1 sc, dc in next 3 sc *, **sk 1 sc, V-st in next sc, [sk 2 sc, V-st in next sc] 3 times, sk 1 sc, dc in next 3 sc**, rep from ** to ** 2 (3, 4, 5, 6) times total, rep from * to * twice, rep from ** to ** 2 (3, 4, 5, 6) times total, rep from * to last sc, dc in last sc, sl st to top of tch, turn—36 (44, 52, 60, 68) V-sts.

RNDS 10–11: Rep Rnds 2–3 of hip shaping.

RND 12: Ch 3 (counts as dc), dc in next dc, *V-st in next V-st, 2 dc in ch-1 sp of next V-st, place m, V-st in next V-st, dc in next 3 dc, V-st in next 2 V-sts, dc in next 3 dc*, [V-st in next 4 V-sts, dc in next 3 dc] 2 (3, 4, 5, 6) times, rep from * to * twice, [V-st in next 4 V-sts, dc in next 3 dc] 2 (3, 4, 5, 6) times, rep from * to last dc, sl st to top of tch, turn—32 (40, 48, 56, 64) V-sts.

RNDS 13–16: Rep Rnds 5–8 of hip shaping.

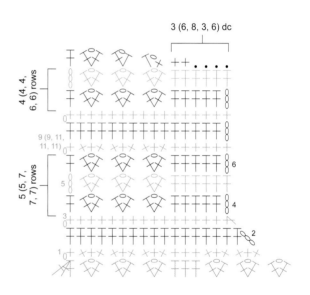

e. Front Right Panel Diagram

(S, L, 2X)

RND 17: Join MC, ch 3 (counts as dc), dc in next sc, *sk 1 sc, V-st in next sc, sk 2 sc, V-st in next sc, sk 1 sc, dc in next 3 sc*, rep from * once, **sk 1 sc, V-st in next sc, sk 2 sc, 2 dc in next sc, place m, [sk 2 sc, V-st in next sc] twice, sk 1 sc, dc in next 3 sc, sk 1 sc, V-st in next sc, [sk 2 sc, V-st in next sc] 3 times, sk 1 sc, dc in next 3 sc **, rep from ** to ** 0 (1, 2) more times, rep from * to * 4 times, rep from ** to ** 1 (2, 3) times, rep from * to* around to last sc, dc in last sc, sl st to top of tch, turn—30 (44, 58) V-sts.

(M, XL)

RND 17: Join MC, ch 3 (counts as dc), dc in next sc, *sk 1 sc, V-st in next sc, sk 2 sc, V-st in next sc, sk 1 sc, dc in next 3 sc*, rep from * once, **sk 1 sc, V-st in next sc, sk 2 sc, 2 dc in next sc, place m, [sk 2 sc, V-st in next sc] twice, sk 1 sc, dc in next 3 sc, sk 1 sc, V-st in next sc, [sk 2 sc, V-st in next sc] 3 times, sk 1 sc, dc in next 3 sc **, rep from ** to ** 0 (1) more times, sk 1 sc, V-st in next sc, sk 2 sc, 2 dc in next sc, place m, [sk 2 sc, V-st in next sc] twice, sk 1 sc, dc in next 3 sc, rep from * to * 4 times, rep from ** to ** 1 (2) times, sk 1 sc, V-st in next sc, sk 2

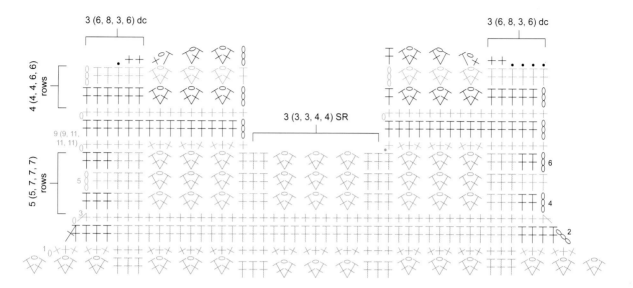

3 (6, 8, 3, 6) dc   3 (6, 8, 3, 6) dc

4 (4, 4, 6, 6) rows

9 (9, 11, 11, 11)

3 (3, 3, 4, 4) SR

5 (5, 7, 7, 7) rows

f. Back Panel Diagram

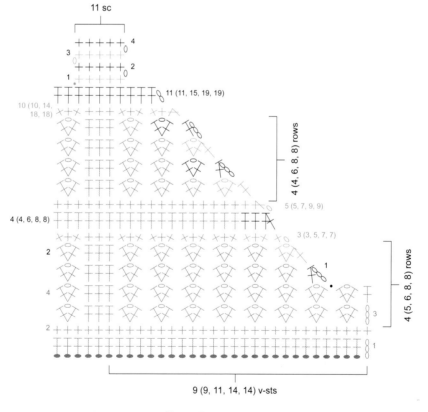

11 sc

4 (4, 6, 8, 8) rows

10 (10, 14, 18, 18)

11 (11, 15, 19, 19)

5 (5, 7, 9, 9)

4 (4, 6, 8, 8)

3 (3, 5, 7, 7)

4 (5, 6, 8, 8) rows

9 (9, 11, 14, 14) v-sts

g. Sleeve Diagram

sc, 2 dc in next sc, place m, [sk 2 sc, V-st in next sc] twice, sk 1 sc, dc in next 3 sc, rep from * to* around to last sc, dc in last sc, sl st to top of tch, turn—36 (50) V-sts.

(ALL)

RNDS 18–19: Rep Rnds 2–3 of hip shaping.

(S, L, 2X)

RND 20: Ch 3 (counts as dc), dc in next dc, [V-st in next 2 V-sts, dc in next 3 dc] twice, *V-st in next 2 V-sts, 2 dc in ch-1 sp of next V-st, place m, V-st in next V-st, dc in next 3 dc, V-st in next 3 V-sts, dc in next 3 dc*, rep from * to * 0 (1, 2) times, [V-st in next 2 V-sts, dc in next 3 dc] 4 times, rep from * to * 1 (2, 3) times, V-st in next 2 V-sts, dc in next 3 dc, V-st in next 2 V-sts, dc in last dc, sl st to top of tch, turn—28 (40, 52) V-sts.

(M, XL)

RND 20: Ch 3 (counts as dc), dc in next dc, [V-st in next 2 V-sts, dc in next 3 dc] twice, V-st in next 3 V-sts, dc in next 3 dc, *V-st in next 2 V-sts, 2 dc in ch-1 sp of next V-st, place m, V-st in next V-st, dc in next 3 dc, V-st in next 3 V-sts, dc in next 3 dc*, rep from * to * 0 (1) times, [V-st in next 2 V-sts, dc in next 3 dc] 4 times, V-st in next 3 V-sts, dc in next 3 dc, rep from * to * 1 (2) times, V-st in next 2 V-sts, dc in next 3 dc, V-st in next 2 V-sts, dc in last dc, sl st to top of tch, turn—34 (46) V-sts.

(ALL)

RNDS 21–24: Rep Rnds 5–8 of hip shaping once.

RND 25: Join MC, ch 3 (counts as dc), dc in next sc, *sk 1 sc, V-st in next sc, sk 2 sc, V-st in next sc, sk 1 sc, dc in next 3 sc*, rep from * once, **sk 1 sc, V-st in next sc, [sk 2 sc, V-st in next sc] twice, sk 1 sc, dc in next 3 sc**, rep from ** 1 (2, 3, 4, 5) more times, rep from * to* 4 times, rep from ** to ** 2 (3, 4, 5, 6) times, rep from * to * around to last sc, dc in last sc, sl st to top of tch, turn—28 (34, 40, 46, 52) V-sts.

Bust Shaping

See Diagram C (page 43) for assistance.

RND 1 (WS): Ch 3 (counts as dc), dc in next dc, *V-st in next V-st, dc bet V-sts, place m, V-st in next V-st, dc in next 3 dc*, rep from * once, [V-st in next 3 V-sts, dc in next 3 dc] 2 (3, 4, 5, 6) times, rep from * to * 4 times, [V-st in next 3 V-sts, dc in next 3 dc] 2 (3, 4, 5, 6) times, rep from * to * around to last dc, dc in last dc, sl st to top of tch, turn—8 additional dc.

RND 2: Ch 3 (counts as dc), V-st in each V-st and dc in each dc around, move m to st above, here and throughout, sl st to top of tch, turn.

RND 3: Ch 3 (counts as dc), dc in each dc and V-st in each V-st around to m, 2 dc in marked dc, move m, rep around, sl st to top of tch, turn—8 additional dc.

RND 4: Ch 3 (counts as dc), dc in each dc and V-st in each V-st around to m, 2 dc bet marked group of 2 dc, move m, rep

around, sl st to top of tch, turn, fasten off MC.

RND 5: Join CC, ch 1, sc in each dc and 3 dc in each ch-1 sp around to m, 2 sc bet marked group of 2 dc, move m, rep around, sl st to first sc, fasten off CC, turn.

RND 6: Join MC, ch 3 (counts as dc), dc in each sc around, move m, sl st to top of tch, fasten off MC, turn.

RND 7: Join CC, ch 1, sc in top of tch, sc in each dc around to m, sc bet marked dc and next dc, rep around, sl st to first sc, fasten off CC, turn—144 (168, 192, 216, 240) sc.

RND 8: Join MC, ch 3 (counts as dc), dc in next sc, *sk 1 sc, V-st in next sc, [sk 2 sc, V-st in next sc] twice, sk 1 sc, dc in next 3 sc, rep from * around to last 10 sc, sk 1 sc, V-st in next sc, [sk 2 sc, V-st in next sc] twice, sk 1 sc, dc in last sc, sl st to top of tch, turn—36 (42, 48, 54, 60) V-sts.

RND 9: Ch 3 (counts as dc), dc in each dc around, V-st in ch-1 sp of each V-st around, sl st to top of tch, turn.

RNDS 10–12 (12, 14, 14, 14): Rep Rnd 9 of bust shaping 3 (3, 5, 5, 5) times, fasten off MC, turn.

RND 13 (13, 15, 15, 15): Join CC, ch 1, sc in top of tch, sc in each dc around, 3 sc in each ch-1 sp around, sl st to first sc, fasten off CC, turn.

RND 14 (14, 16, 16, 16): Join MC, ch 3 (counts as dc), dc in each sc around, sl st to top of tch, fasten off MC, turn.

RND 15 (15, 17, 17, 17): Join CC, ch 1, sc in top of tch, sc in each dc around, sl st to first sc, turn, fasten off.

Neck Shaping

See Diagram D (page 43) for assistance.

Join MC with sl st 49 (49, 61, 61, 73) sts from end of previous round.

ROW 1: Ch 2, sk 1 sc, (hdc, ch 1, dc), [sk 2 sc, V-st in next sc] twice, sk 1 sc, *dc in next 3 sc, sk 1 sc, V-st in next sc, [sk 2 sc, V-st in next sc] twice, sk 1 ch, rep from * 8 (10, 12, 13, 15) more times, dc in next 3 sc, sk 1 sc, [V-st in next sc, sk 2 sc] twice, (dc, ch 1) in next sc, hdc2tog in previous and 2 sc away, turn—31 (37, 43, 46, 52) V-sts.

ROW 2: Sl st in hdc2tog, sl st in next ch-1 sp, ch 3, V-st in each V-st and dc in each dc across to last V-st, (dc, ch 1) in ch-1 sp of last V-st, dctrtog in last V-st and next ch-1 sp, turn—30 (36, 42, 45, 51) V-sts.

ROW 3: Rep Row 2—28 (34, 40, 43, 49) V-sts.

ROW 4: Sl st in first st, sl st in next ch-1 sp, ch 2, dc in each dc and V-st in each V-st across to last dc, dc2tog in last dc and ch-1 sp, turn—27 (33, 39, 42, 48) V-sts.

ROW 5: Ch 2, dc2tog over next 2 dc, V-st in each V-st and dc in each dc across to last 3 dc, dc3tog over last 3 dc, turn, fasten off MC.

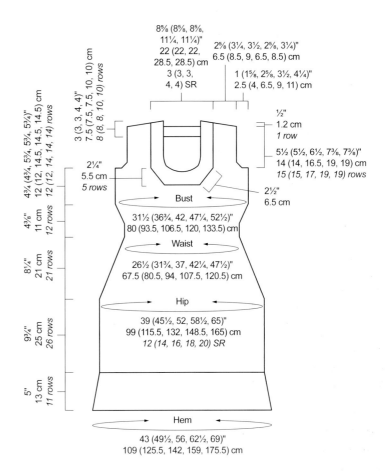

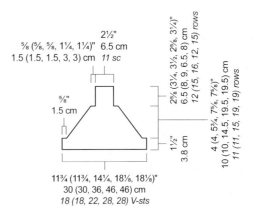

Right Front-Panel Shaping

See Diagram E (page 44) for assistance.

ROW 1: Join CC, sc in first st, 3 sc in each of next 3 ch-1 sps, sc in each of next 3 dc, 3 sc in each of next 1(2, 2, 1, 2) ch-1 sps, (L ONLY) 2 sc in next ch-1 sps, (ALL) fasten off CC, turn—16 (19, 21, 16, 19) sc.

ROW 2: Join MC, ch 3, sk 2 sc, dc in each sc across, fasten off MC, turn—14 (17, 19, 14, 17) dc.

ROW 3: Join CC, ch 1, sc in each dc across to last 2 dc, sc2tog over last 2 dc, turn—13 (16, 18, 13, 16) sc.

ROW 4: Join MC, ch 3 (counts as dc), dc in next 2 (5, 7, 2, 5) dc, sk 1 sc, V-st in next st, [sk 2 sc, V-st in next sc] twice, sk 1 sc, dc in last sc, turn.

ROW 5: Ch 3 (counts as dc), V-st in each V-st across, dc in each dc across, dc in top of tch, turn.

ROWS 6–8 (8, 10, 10, 10): Rep Row 5 of Right Front-Panel Shaping 3 (3, 5, 5, 5) times, fasten off MC.

ROW 9 (9, 11, 11, 11): Join CC, ch 1, sc in first dc, 3 sc in each ch-1 sp across, sc in each dc across, sc in top of tch, fasten off CC, turn.

ROW 10 (10, 12, 12, 12): Join MC, ch 3 (counts as dc), dc in each sc across, fasten off, turn.

ROW 11 (11, 13, 13, 13): Join CC, ch 1, sc in each dc across, sc in top of tch, fasten off, turn.

ROW 12 (12, 14, 14, 14): Rep Row 4.

ROWS 13 (13, 15, 15, 15)–15 (15, 17, 19, 19): Rep Row 5 of Right Front-Panel Shaping 3 (3, 3, 5, 5) times.

ROW 16 (16, 18, 20, 20): Sl st in next 1 (4, 6, 1, 4) dc, sc in next 2 dc, (sc, ch 1, hdc) in next ch-1 sp, (hdc, ch 1, dc) in next ch-1 sp, V-st in next V-st, dc in top of tch, fasten off.

Back-Panel Shaping

See Diagram F (page 45) for assistance.

(S) Sk 1 V-st, (M) sk [1 V-st, 3 dc, 1 V-st], (L) sk [3dc, 3 V-st, 3 dc], (XL) sk [2 V-st, 3 dc, 3 V-st, 3 dc, 2 V-st], (2X) sk [1 V-st, (3 dc, 3 V-st, 3 dc, 3 V-st, 3 dc, 1V-st] from end of first round of front panel. Join CC with sl st to next ch-1 sp.

ROW 1: (L) 2sc in first ch-1 sp, (ALL) 3 sc in next 1 (2, 2, 1, 2) ch-1 sps, *sc in next 3 dc, 3 sc in next 3 ch-1 sps, rep from * 4 (4, 4, 5, 5) more times, sc in next 3 dc, 3 sc in next 1(2, 2, 1, 2) ch-1 sps, (L ONLY) 2 sc in next ch-1 sps, (ALL) fasten off CC, turn—69 (75, 79, 69, 75) sc.

ROW 2: Join MC, ch 3, sk 2 sc, dc in each sc across to last 3 sc, dc2tog over next 2 sc, fasten off MC, turn—65 (71, 75, 65, 71) dc.

ROW 3: Join CC, ch 1, sc2tog in first 2 dc, sc in each dc across to last 2 dc, sc2tog over last 2 dc, fasten of CC, turn—63 (69, 73, 63, 69) sc.

ROW 4: Join MC, ch 3 (counts as dc), dc in next 2 (5, 7, 2, 5) dc, *sk 1 sc, V-st in next st, [sk 2 sc, V-st in next sc] twice, sk 1 sc, dc in next 3 dc, rep from * 4 (4, 4, 5, 5) more times, dc in each sc to end, turn.

ROW 5: Ch 3 (counts as dc), V-st in each V-st across, dc in each dc across, dc in top of tch, turn.

ROWS 6–8 (8, 10, 10, 10): Rep Row 5 of Back-Panel Shaping 3 (3, 5, 5, 5) times, fasten off MC.

Back Neck Shaping

ROW 1: Join CC, ch 1, sc in next 3 (6, 8, 3, 6) dc, 3 sc in each of next 3 ch-1 sps, sc in next dc, leave remaining sts unworked, fasten off CC, turn—13 (16, 18, 13, 16) sc.

ROW 2: Join MC, ch 3 (counts as dc), dc in each sc across, fasten off MC, turn.

ROW 3: Join CC, ch 1, sc in each dc across, fasten off CC, turn.

ROW 4: Join MC, ch 3 (counts as dc), sk 1 sc, V-st in next sc, [sk 2 sc, V-st in next sc] twice, sk 1 sc, dc in each sc across to end, turn.

ROW 5: Ch 3 (counts as dc), dc in each dc across, V-st in each V-st across, dc in top of tch, turn.

ROWS 6–7 (7, 7, 9, 9): Rep Row 5 of Back Neck Shaping 2 (2, 2, 4, 4) times.

ROW 8 (8, 8, 10, 10): Ch 3 (counts as dc), V-st in next V-st, (dc, ch 1, hdc) in next ch-1 sp, (hdc, ch 1, sc) in next ch-1 sp, sc in next 2 dc, sl st in next st, fasten off.

Opposite Back Neck Shaping

ROW 1: Sk (2 dc, [3 V-sts, 3 dc] 2 (2, 2, 3, 3) times, 3 V-sts, 2 dc) from end of first back neck shaping row. Join CC, sl st in next dc, sc in same dc, 3 sc in each of next 3 ch-1 sps, sc in each dc across, fasten off CC, turn—13 (16, 18, 13, 16) sc.

ROW 2: Join MC, ch 3 (counts as dc), dc in each sc across, fasten off MC, turn.

ROW 3: Join CC, ch 1, sc in each dc across, fasten off CC, turn.

ROW 4: Join MC, ch 3 (counts as dc), dc in next 2 (5, 7, 2, 5) sc, sk 1 sc, V-st in next sc, [sk 2 sc, V-st in next sc] twice, sk 1 sc, dc in last sc, turn.

ROW 5: Ch 3 (counts as dc), V-st in each V-st across, dc in each dc across, dc in top of tch, turn.

ROWS 6–7 (7, 7, 9, 9): Rep Row 5 of Opposite Back Neck Shaping 2 (2, 2, 4, 4) times.

ROW 8 (8, 8, 10, 10): Sl st in next 1 (4, 6, 1, 4) dc, sc in next 2 dc, (sc, ch 1, hdc) in next ch-1 sp, (hdc, ch 1, dc) in next ch-1 sp, V-st in next V-st, dc in top of tch, fasten off.

Left Front-Panel Shaping

(S) Sk 1 V-st, (M) sk [1 V-st, 3 dc, 1 V-st], (L) sk [3dc, 3 V-st, 3 dc], (XL) sk [2 V-st, 3 dc, 3 dc, 2 V-st], (2X) sk [1 V-st, 3 dc,

3 V-st, 3 dc, 3 V-st, 3 dc, 1 V-t] from end of first round of front panel. Join CC with sl st to next ch-1 sp.

ROW 1: (L) 2sc in first ch-1 sp, **(ALL)** 3 sc in next 1 (2, 2, 1, 2) ch-1 sps, sc in next 3 dc, 3 sc in each of next 3 ch-1 sps, sc in last st, fasten off CC, turn—16 (19, 21, 16, 19) sc.

ROW 2: Join MC, ch 3 (counts as dc), dc in each sc across to last 3 sc, dc2tog over next 2 sc, fasten off MC, turn—14 (17, 19, 14, 17) dc.

ROW 3: Join CC, ch 1, sc2tog in first 2 dc, sc in each dc across, turn—13 (16, 18, 13, 16) sc.

ROW 4: Join MC, ch 3 (counts as dc), sk 1 sc, V-st in next st, [sk 2 sc, V-st in next sc] twice, sk 1 sc, dc in each sc across, turn.

ROW 5: Ch 3 (counts as dc), dc in each dc across, V-st in each V-st across, dc in top of tch, turn.

ROWS 6–8 (8, 10, 10, 10): Rep Row 5 of Left Front-Panel Shaping 3 (3, 5, 5, 5) times, fasten off MC.

ROW 9 (9, 11, 11, 11): Join CC, ch 1, sc in next 3(6, 8, 3, 6) dc, 3 sc in each of next 3 ch-1 sps, sc in last dc, turn.

ROW 10 (10, 12, 12, 12): Join MC, ch 3 (counts as dc), dc in each sc across, fasten off MC, turn.

ROW 11 (11, 13, 13, 13): Join CC, ch 1, sc in each dc across, fasten off CC, turn.

ROW 12 (12, 14, 14, 14): Rep Row 4,

ROWS 13 (13, 15, 15, 15)–15 (15, 17, 19, 19): Rep Row 5 of Left Front-Panel Shaping 3 (3, 3, 5, 5) times.

ROW 16 (16, 18, 20, 20): Ch 3 (counts as dc), V-st in next V-st, (dc, ch 1, hdc) in next ch-1 sp, (hdc, ch 1, sc) in next ch-1 sp, sc in next 2 dc, sl st in next st, fasten off.

SLEEVES

Make 2. See Diagram G (page 45) for assistance.

ROW 1 (RS): Ch 4 (counts as fdc), 58 (58, 70, 88, 88) fdc with MC, fasten off MC, turn—59 (59, 71, 89, 89) fdc.

ROW 2: Join CC (following stripe sequence in notes), ch 1, sc in each dc across, sc in top of tch, fasten off CC, turn.

ROW 3: Join MC, ch 3 (counts as dc), *sk 1 sc, V-st in next sc, [sk 2 sc, V-st in next sc] 8 (8, 10, 13, 13) times, sk 1 sc, dc in next 3 sc, rep from * around to last sc, dc in last sc, turn—18 (18, 22, 28, 28) V-sts.

ROW 4: Ch 3 (counts as dc), dc in each dc and V-st in ch-1 sp of each V-st across, dc in top of tch, turn, fasten off.

Cap Shaping

ROW 1: Sk 1 V-st, join yarn with sl st bet next V-st, ch 3, dc in next V-st, V-st in each V-st and dc in each dc across to last 2 V-sts, dctrtog in next V-st and bet last 2 V-sts, turn—14 (14, 18, 24, 24) V-sts.

ROW 2: Ch 2, V-st in each V-st and dc in each dc across to last V-st, (dc, ch 1) in last ch-1 sp, dc2tog in last ch-1 sp and last dc, fasten off, turn.

(L, XL, 2X)

ROW 3: Ch 3, dc in next V-st, V-st in each V-st and dc in each dc across to last 2 V-sts, dctrtog in next V-st and bet last 2 V-sts, turn—16 (22, 22) V-sts.

(L)

ROW 4: Rep Row 2.

(XL, 2X)

ROWS 4–5: Rep Rows 2–3.

ROW 6: Rep Row 2—20 (20) V-sts.

(ALL)

ROW 3 (3, 5, 7, 7): Join CC, ch 1, sc in first ch-1 sp, 3sc in each ch-1 sp across and sc in each dc across to last V-st, sc in last V-st, fasten off, turn.

ROW 4 (4, 6, 8, 8): Join MC, ch 2, sk first sc, dc in each sc across to last 2 sc, dc2tog over last 2 sc, fasten off, turn.

ROW 5 (5, 7, 9, 9): Join CC, ch 1, sc2tog over first 2 dc, sc in each dc across to last 2 dc, sc2tog over last 2 dc, fasten off, turn.

ROW 6 (6, 8, 10, 10): Join MC, ch 3, sk 2 sc, V-st in next sc, [sk 2 sc, V-st in next sc] 4 (4, 6, 9, 9) times, sk 1 sc, dc in next 3 sc, sk

Side-Saddle in Stride

Side-saddle armholes seem so odd when you see them in schematic form, but in actuality, the side saddle is a typical cap sleeve with a strip on the top. Side saddles have a definite look that make a sweater more casual and sporty. They also help support heavy garments. In crochet, side-saddle sleeves work well when they're either all single crochet or a cable pattern worked tightly enough to support the weight of heavier garments.

1 sc, V-st in next sc, [sk 2 sc, V-st in next sc] 4 (4, 6, 9, 9) times, sk 2 sc, dc in last sc, turn—10 (10, 12, 16, 16) V-sts.

ROW 7 (7, 9, 11, 11): Ch 3, dc in first ch-1 sp, V-st in each V-st across, dc in each dc across to last V-st, dctrtog over last ch-1 sp and last dc, turn—8 (8, 10, 14, 14) V-sts.

ROW 8 (8, 10, 12, 12): Ch 2, V-st in each V-st across and dc in each dc across to last V-st, (dc, ch 1) in last ch-1 sp, dc2tog over last ch-1 sp and dc, turn.

ROW 9 (9, 11, 13, 13): Rep Row 7 (7, 9, 11, 11) once—6 (6, 8, 12, 12) V-sts.

(L, XL, 2X)

ROW 12 (14, 14): Rep previous 2 rows 1 (2, 2) times—6 (8, 8) V-sts.

(ALL)

Fasten off MC.

ROW 10 (10, 14, 18, 18): Join CC, ch 1, sc2tog in first 2 sts, 2 sc in first ch-1 sp, 3 sc in each ch-1 sp across, sc in each dc across, to last V-st, 2 sc in last ch-1 sp, sc2tog in last ch-1 sp and last dc, fasten off, turn.

ROW 11 (11, 15, 19, 19): Join MC, ch 3, sk 2 sc, dc in each sc across to last 3 sc, dc2tog over next and last sc, fasten off, turn.

Side-Saddle Strap

ROW 1: Sk 3 (3, 3, 6, 6) sts, join MC to next dc, sc in next 11 sc, turn.

ROW 2: Ch 1, sc in each sc across, turn.

ROWS 3–12 (15, 16, 12, 15): Rep Row 2 ten (13, 14, 10, 13) times, fasten off, weave in ends.

Finishing

BOTTOM EDGING

Join MC to bottom edge on RS at tch on foundation round.

RND 1: Ch 1, sc in each fdc around, sl st to first sc, turn.

RND 2: Ch 4 (counts as dc, ch-1 sp), dc in same sc, *sk 2 sc, V-st in next sc, rep from * around, sl st to 3rd ch of tch, turn.

RND 3: Sl st to ch-1 sp, ch 4 (counts as dc, ch-1 sp), dc in same ch-1 sp, V-st in each V-st around, sl st to 3rd ch of tch, turn.

RND 4: Sl st to ch-1 sp, ch 5 (counts as dc, ch-2 sp), dc in same ch-1 sp, (dc, ch 2, dc) in each V-st around, sl st to 3rd ch of tch, turn.

RND 5: Sl st to ch-2 sp, ch 5 (counts as dc, ch-2 sp), dc in same ch-2 sp, (dc, ch 2, dc) in each ch-2 sp around, sl st to 3rd ch of tch, turn.

RNDS 6–11: Rep Rnd 5 of Bottom Edging 6 times, fasten off.

BLOCKING, SEAMING, AND EMBROIDERY

Pin dress and sleeves to schematic size and spray with water. Allow to dry. Join CC to RS on foundation row with sl st. Using 3 dc groups as a guide, sl st up the dress by inserting the hook from the right side to the back side of the fabric. Follow the stripe note for changing colors. Pin RS of sleeve to RS of dress armhole edge. Whipstitch sleeve to armhole, sleeve seams and side saddle to shoulders. Join MC to RS edge of sleeve, sc around sleeve, sl st to first sc, fasten off.

COLLAR

Join MC to RS of back of neck.

RND 1: Sc evenly around neck, sl st to first sc, turn.

RND 2: Ch 1, sc in each sc across to 1 sc before back neck corner, sc3tog over corner sts, *sc in each sc to front neck inside edge, sc2tog over next 2 sts, rep from * 3 times, sc in each sc to 1 sc before back neck corner, sc3tog over corner sts, sc in each sc to end, sl st to first sc.

RND 3: Ch 1, sc in each sc to 1 sc before sc3tog, sc3tog over next 3 sc, *sc in each sc to sc2tog, sc2tog over next 2 sts, rep from * 3 times, sc in each sc to 1 sc before sc3tog, sc3tog over next 3 sc, sc in each sc to end, sl st to first sc, turn.

RNDS 4–8: Rep Rnd 3 five more times.

RND 9: Sl st in each sc around, fasten off.

Top-Down
and in-the-round
CONSTRUCTION

One thing I struggle with in making most garments is that you can't try them on as you work. Top-down construction changes all that. Also, they usually require very little seaming, which is definitely a bonus! You might encounter some challenges in shaping a yoke. For the most part, increases will either be spaced evenly on raglan lines as in the Rose Quartz Pullover (page 66), concentrated in corners as in the Magnolia Tank (page 54), or evenly spaced as in the Smoky Cropped Top (page 60). Increases are usually worked in every round, making it a bit hard to get into a crochet rhythm until you begin working the body.

Some stitch patterns are too large for increasing every round. For example, when you have a shell stitch pattern as in the Structured Cardigan (page 74), you might not increase on every round, but rather on every other (or more). And while top-down construction can involve quite lengthy directions, the garments are worth the effort.

magnolia
TANK

In this design, the yarn is the star. The natural drape of the cotton and bamboo yarn gives this stitch pattern movement. If you substitute a different yarn, put your swatch through its paces to make sure you still have natural drape. If you're concerned about having too much drape, always remember that you can strengthen the collar by adding some ribbon on the wrong side. The ribbon will help reinforce the garment without taking away the tank top's drape and flow.

Materials

YARN
DK weight (#3 Light)

SHOWN: Lion Brand LB Collection Cotton Bamboo (52% cotton, 48% rayon from bamboo; 245 yd [224 m]/3.5 oz [100 g]): #098 Magnolia (MC), 2 (3, 3, 4, 4, 5) skeins, #126 Chocolate Dahlia (CC), 1 (1, 1, 1, 1, 1) skein.

HOOK
Size I/9 (5.5 mm) or hook needed to obtain gauge.

NOTIONS
Tapestry needle for weaving in ends; spray bottle with water; straight pins for blocking.

Gauge
18 sts (3SR) by 8 rows (2 RR) = 4" × 4¼" (10 × 11 cm) in stitch pattern.

Finished Size
Bust measurement is 32 (34⅝, 37⅜, 42⅝, 45⅜, 50⅝)" (81.5 [88, 95, 108.5, 115, 128.5] cm). Sized for X-small (Small, Medium, Large, X-large, 2X). Size shown is Small.

Notes
Tank top is worked from the bottom up in turned rounds to the Front and Back Panels, which are then worked in rows. The collar is then worked from the top down and sewn to the tank at the end.

Special Stitches

SHELL (SH)

Work (2dc-cl, ch 2, 2dc-cl) in st indicated.

MAGNOLIA PETAL STITCH PATTERN (MPSP)

See Magnolia Petal Stitch Diagram Below for assistance.

Chain a multiple of 6 plus 3.

ROW 1 (RS): Sh in 6th ch from hook (sk ch counts as dc), *sk 2 ch, 2 dc in next ch, sk 2 ch, sh in next ch, rep from * across to last 3 ch, dc in last ch, turn.

ROW 2: Ch 3 (counts as dc here and throughout), *sh in next ch-2 sp of sh, FPdc in next 2 dc, rep from * across to last sh, sh in last ch-2 sp of sh, dc in top of tch, turn.

ROW 3: Ch 4 (counts as dc, ch-1 sp), 2dc-cl in first dc, *2 dc in ch-2 sp of sh, sh bet next 2 dc, rep from * across to last sh, 2 dc in last ch-2 sp of sh, (2 dc-cl, ch 1, dc) in top of tch, turn.

ROW 4: Ch 4 (counts as dc, ch-1 sp), 2 dc-cl in dc, *FPdc in next 2 dc, sh in next ch-2 sp of sh, rep from * across to last 2 dc, FPdc in next 2 dc, (2 dc-cl, ch 1, dc) in 3rd ch of tch, turn.

ROW 5: Ch 3, *sh bet next 2 dc, 2 dc in ch-2 sp of sh, rep from * to last 2 dc, sh bet next 2 dc, dc in 3rd ch of tch, turn.

Rep Rows 2–5 for pattern.

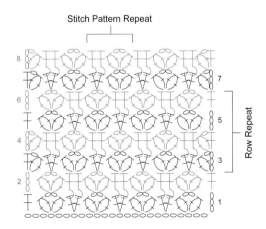

Magnolia Petal Stitch Diagram

Body

See Diagram A. Work 144 (156, 168, 192, 204, 228) fsc with MC, sl st to first sc, turn.

ROW 1 (WS): Ch 3, sk 2 sc, sh in next sc, *sk 2 sc, 2 dc in next sc, sk 2 sc, sh in next sc, rep from * across to last 2 sc, sk last 2 sc, dc in first sc, sl st to top of tch, turn—24 (26, 28, 32, 34, 38) sh.

ROW 2: Ch 3, cont in Row 2 of MPSP around to last stitch (tch), dc in top of last stitch, sl st to top of Row 2's tch, turn.

ROW 3: Ch 2, dc bet dc and tch, cont in Row 3 of MPSP around to beg, 2dc-cl bet dc and tch, hdc to first dc (counts as ch-2 sp), turn.

ROW 4: Ch 2, dc around post of hdc, cont in Row 4 of MPSP around to beg, 2dc-cl around post of hdc, hdc to first dc (counts as ch-2 sp), turn.

ROW 5: Ch 3, cont in Row 5 of MPSP around to beg, dc around post of hdc, sl st to top of tch, turn.

ROWS 6–21 (21, 21, 25, 25, 25): Rep Rows 2–5 of body four (4, 4, 5, 5, 5) times.

ROWS 22 (22, 22, 26, 26, 26)–24 (24, 24, 28, 28, 28): Rep Rows 2–4 of body once, turn, fasten off.

FRONT PANEL

See Diagram B. Join MC to ch-2 sp 1 (1, 1, 2, 2, 2) sh away from fastening off.

ROW 1 (WS): Ch 2, cont in Row 5 of MPSP for 10 (11, 12, 13, 14, 14) sh, hdc in next ch-2 sp, turn.

ROW 2: Ch 5 (counts as tr, ch-1 sp), 2 dc-cl in first ch-2 sp, FPdc in next 2 dc, cont in Row 2 of MPSP across to last sh, 2 dc-cl in ch-2 sp of last sh, ch 1, tr bet dc-cl and tch turn.

ROW 3: Ch 2, cont in Row 5 of MPSP across to last sh, sh bet next 2 dc, hdc in tch sp, turn—8 (9, 10, 11, 12, 12) sh.

(M, L, XL, 2X)

ROWS 4–5 (5, 7, 7, 9, 9): Rep Rows 2–3 of Front Panel 1 (1, 2, 2, 3, 3) times.

(ALL)

ROW 4 (6, 8, 8,10, 10): Rep Row 2 once, fasten off—8 (8, 8, 9, 9, 9) SR.

BACK PANEL

Join MC to ch-2 sp 2 (2, 2, 3, 3, 5) sh away from end of Row 1 of front panel.

ROW 1 (WS): Ch 2, cont in Row 5 of MPSP for 10 (11, 12, 13, 14, 14) sh, hdc in next ch-2 sp, turn.

ROW 2: Ch 5 (counts as tr, ch-1 sp), 2 dc-cl in first ch-2 sp, FPdc in next 2 dc, cont in Row 2 of MPSP across to last sh, 2 dc-cl in ch-2 sp of last sh, ch 1, tr bet dc-cl and tch turn.

ROW 3: Ch 2, cont in Row 2 of MPSP across to last sh, sh bet next 2 dc, hdc in tch sp, turn—8 (9, 10, 11, 12, 12) sh.

Rep Rows 2–3, two (3, 4, 4, 5, 5) times, Rep Row 2 once, do not turn—6 (6, 6, 7, 7, 7) SR.

EDGING RND: Ch 1, 2 sc in last sc, sc evenly down armhole edge, working in row ends, sc across armhole, sc evenly up opposite side, 2 sc in first st at top, sc evenly across top of panel, cont sc evenly around top of tank top, sl st to first sc, fasten off.

BOTTOM EDGING

Join CC to bottom edge of back panel on RS with sl st.

RND 1 (RS): Ch 2 (counts as hdc), hdc in each sc around, sl st to top of tch, turn—144 (156, 168, 192, 204, 228) hdc.

RND 2: Ch 1, sc in top of tch, sc in middle bar of each hdc around, sl st to first sc, turn.

RND 3: Ch 4 (counts as tr), tr in each sc around, sl st to top of tch, turn.

RND 4: Ch 1, sc in top of tch, sc in the middle bar of each tr around, sl st to first sc, turn.

RNDS 5–6: Rep Rnds 3–4 once.

RNDS 7–8: Rep Rnds 1–2 once.

RND 9: Sl st in each sc around, fasten off, weave in ends.

COLLAR

Ch 93 (93, 93, 105, 105, 105) with CC.

RND 1: Hdc in 3rd ch from hook (sk ch count as hdc), hdc in next 4 (4, 4, 7, 7, 7) ch, *[2 hdc in next ch, hdc in next 5 ch] twice, 2 hdc in next ch*, hdc in next 8 ch, rep from * to * once, hdc in next 12 (12, 12, 18, 18, 18) ch, rep from * to *, hdc in

next 8 ch, rep from * to *, hdc in each ch to end, sl st to top of tch, turn—104 (104, 104, 116, 116, 116) hdc.

RND 2: Ch 1, sc in top of tch, sc in middle bar (thoughout rnd) of next 5 (5, 5, 8, 8, 8) hdc, *[2 sc in next hdc, sc in next 3 hdc] 3 times, 2 sc in next hdc*, sc in next 8 hdc, rep from * to *, sc in next 12 (12, 12, 18, 18, 18) hdc, rep from * to *, sc in next 8 hdc, rep from * to *, sc in each hdc to end, sl st to first sc, turn—120 (120, 120, 132, 132, 132) sc.

RND 3: Ch 4 (counts as tr), tr in next 5 (5, 5, 8, 8, 8) hdc, *[2 tr in next sc, tr in next 3 sc] 4 times, 2 tr in next sc*, tr in next 8 sc, rep from * to *, tr in next 12 (12, 12, 18, 18, 18) sc, rep from * to *, tr in next 8 sc, rep from * to *, tr in each sc to end, sl st to top of tch, turn—140 (140, 140, 152, 152, 152) tr.

RND 4: Ch 1, sc in top of tch, sc in middle bar of tr around, sl st to first sc, turn.

RND 5: Ch 2 (counts as hdc), hdc in next 5 (5, 5, 8, 8, 8) sc, *2 hdc in next sc, hdc in next 9 sc, 2 hdc in next sc, hdc in next 10 sc, 2 hdc in next sc, hdc in next 8 sc, 2 hdc in next sc, hdc in next 10 sc, 2 hdc in next sc, hdc in next 9 sc, 2 hdc in next sc*, hdc in next 12 (12, 12, 18, 18, 18) sc, rep from * to *, hdc in each sc to end, sl st to top of tch, turn—152 (152, 152, 164, 164, 164) hdc.

RND 6: Rep Rnd 4.

RND 7: Ch 1, sc in next 6 (6, 6, 9, 9, 9) sc, *2 sc in next sc, sc in next 6 sc, 2 sc in next sc, sc in next 46 sc, 2 sc in next sc, sc in next 6 sc, 2 sc in next sc*, sc in next 12 (12, 12, 18, 18, 18) sc, rep from * to *, sc in each sc to end, sl st to first sc, do not turn—160 (160, 160, 172, 172, 172) sc.

RND 8: Sl st in each sc around, fasten off.

Join yarn to foundation ch, sl st in each ch around, fasten off.

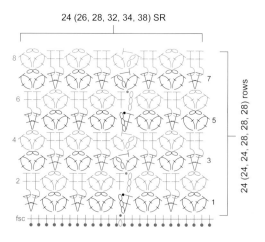

a. Body Stitch Diagram

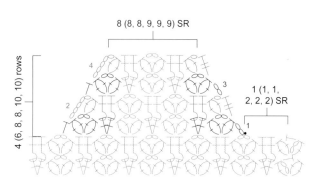

b. Front Panel Stitch Diagram

Shape Shifters

Increasing in the round can seem far-fetched, but it can be broken down to simple shapes. A round yoke is essentially an oval, but if you make it more like a rectangle by rounding the corners, you can work with easier shapes for math and still get a similar look.

In this case, the collar was designed with an inside collar circumference of 21" (53.5 cm) and a 2" (5 cm) width. The first round was imagined as a circle broken into equal arcs with long segments (the sides) separating them. The increasing rounds then followed a circular path and left the sides untouched.

The length of the sides can determine the style of the collar, as a scoop or boatneck, but the shaping doesn't have to change. For a complete top-down round yoke, you can continue increasing until the outside circumference matches the circumference around the front, back, and sleeves combined.

Finishing

BLOCKING AND SEAMING

Pin body and collar to schematic size and spray with water. Allow to dry. Pin the collar to the front panel by aligning the long side of the collar at the foundation chain with the top edge of the front panel. With the CC, backstitch the collar to the front panel. Pin the collar to the back panel by aligning the last round of the collar with the top corner of the armholes of the back panel. Backstitch the collar to the back panel.

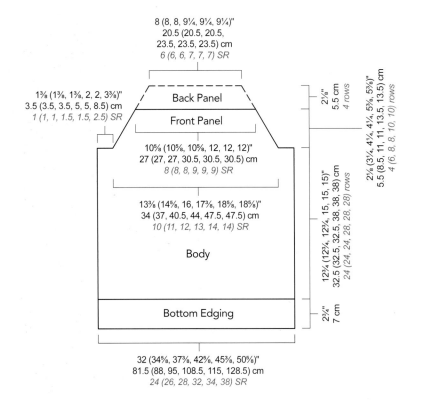

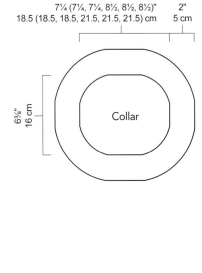

smoky CROPPED TOP

Worked from the top down, this flirty top involves a simple shell pattern delineated by the structure of front post stitches. All increases and decreases are hidden between columns of post stitches, creating clean lines and a tailored look. After bust shaping, you can crochet in stitch pattern to your perfect length to customize this top for your body before you add the bottom ruffle.

Designed by DREW EMBORSKY, AKA THE CROCHET DUDE

Materials

YARN

Sock Weight (#1 Superfine).

SHOWN: Cascade Yarns Heritage Silk (85% merino superwash wool, 15% mulberry milk; 437 yd (400 m)/3.5 oz (100 g): #5603 4 (4, 5, 5) hanks

HOOK

Size F/5 (3.75 mm) or hook needed to obtain gauge.

NOTIONS

Tapestry needle for weaving in ends.

Gauge

25 sts (6SR) by 12 rows = 4" × 4" (10 × 10 cm) in stitch pattern.

Finished Size

Bust measurement is 36 (40, 44, 48)" (91.5 [102, 112, 122] cm). Sized for Small (Medium, Large, X-large). Measurements includes 4" (10 cm) ease. Size shown is Small.

Notes

Do not join rnds unless indicated. It's helpful to use a stitch marker or a scrap piece of yarn to indicate the first st of the rnd so that you know when you've finished that rnd. When you start a new rnd, simply move the marker up to the first st.

Do not turn at the end of a rnd.

Special Stitches

See Columned V-stitch Pattern diagram for assistance.

COLUMNED V-ST STITCH PATTERN (FOR GAUGE SWATCH ONLY)

ROW 1 (RS): Ch 29, sk 3 ch, *dc in next ch, sk 1 st, (dc, ch 1, dc) in next ch (V-st made), sk 1 ch, rep from * across, dc in last 2 ch, turn—6 V-sts.

ROW 2: Ch 2 (counts as first st now and throughout), *BPdc around next st, (dc, ch 1, dc) in next ch-1 sp, rep from * across, BPdc around next st, hdc in last st, turn.

ROW 3: Ch 2, *FPdc around next st, (dc, ch 1, dc) in next ch-1 sp, rep from * across, FPdc around next st, hdc in last st, turn.

ROWS 4–13: Repeat Rows 2–3. Finish off.

Hint: Let the swatch rest overnight before measuring. Post stitches have a unique way of drawing up quite a bit as they rest.

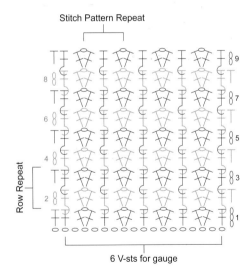

Columned V-st Stitch Pattern

Pattern

YOKE

See Diagram A (opposite) for assistance.

RND 1: Ch 176 (176, 180, 200), being careful not to twist ch, sl st in first ch to form ring, ch 3, *sk 1 ch, (dc, ch 1, dc) in next ch (V-st made), sk 1 ch, dc in next ch, rep from * around to within last st, sk last ch, do not join—176 (176, 180, 200) sts and 44 (44, 45, 50) V-sts.

RNDS 2–5: *FPdc around next dc, (dc, ch 1, dc) in next ch-1 sp, rep from * around.

(S)

RNDS 6–10: *FPdc around next dc, (2 dc, ch 1, dc) in next ch-1 sp, rep from * around—220 sts.

RNDS 11–15: *FPdc around next dc, (2 dc, ch 1, 2 dc) in next ch-1 sp, rep from * around—264 sts.

(M, L, XL)

RNDS 6–8: *FPdc around next dc, (2 dc, ch 1, dc) in next ch-1 sp, rep from * around—220 (225, 250) sts.

RNDS 9–11: *FPdc around next dc, (2 dc, ch 1, 2 dc) in next ch-1 sp, rep from * around—264 (270, 300) sts.

RNDS 12–15: *FPdc around next dc, (3 dc, ch 1, 2 dc) in next ch-1 sp, rep from * around—308 (315, 350) sts.

ARMHOLES

(S)

RND 16: [*FPdc around next dc, (2 dc, ch 1, 2 dc) in next ch-1 sp (sh made), rep from * 12 times total, ch 30, sk 10 FPdc] 2 times—24 sh.

RND 17: [*FPdc around next dc, (2 dc, ch 1, 2 dc) in next ch-1 sp, rep from * across to chains, ** dc in next ch, sk 2 ch, (2 dc, ch 1, 2 dc) in next ch, sk 2 ch, rep from ** 5 times total] 2 times—34 sh.

RNDS 18–28: *FPdc around next dc, (2 dc, ch 1, 2 dc) in next ch-1 sp, rep from * around.

RNDS 29–30: *FPdc around next dc, (3 dc, ch 1, 2 dc) in next ch-1 sp, rep from * around.

RNDS 31–38: *FPdc around next dc, (3 dc, ch 1, 3 dc) in next ch-1 sp, rep from * around.

(M, L, XL)

RND 16: *FPdc around next dc, (3 dc, ch 1, 2 dc) in next ch-1 sp (sh made), rep from * 12 (12, 15) times total, ch 30, sk 10 FPdc, ** FPdc around next dc, (3 dc, ch 1, 2 dc) in next ch-1 sp, rep from **12 (13,15) times total, ch 30, sk 10 FPdc—24 (25, 30) sh.

RND 17: [*FPdc around next dc, (3 dc, ch 1, 2 dc) in next ch-1 sp, rep from * across to chains, ** dc in next ch, sk 2 ch, (3 dc, ch 1, 2 dc) in next ch, sk 2 ch, rep from ** 5 times total] 2 times—34 (35, 40) sh.

RNDS 18–28: *FPdc around next dc, (3 dc, ch 1, 2 dc) in next ch-1 sp, rep from * around.

RNDS 29–38: *FPdc around next dc, (3 dc, ch 1, 3 dc) in next ch-1 sp, rep from * around.

BOTTOM RUFFLE

See Diagram B for assistance.

RND 39: *(FPdc, ch 1, FPdc) around next dc, (3 dc, ch 1, 3 dc) in next ch-1 sp, rep from * around.

RND 40: *FPdc around next dc, (dc, ch 1, dc) in next ch-1 sp, FPdc around next dc, (3 dc, ch 1, 3 dc) in next ch-1 sp, rep from * around.

RND 41: *FPdc around next dc, (2 dc, ch 1, dc) in next ch-1 sp, FPdc around next dc, (3 dc, ch 1, 3 dc) in next ch-1 sp, rep from * around.

RND 42: *FPdc around next dc, (2 dc, ch 1, 2 dc) in next ch-1 sp, FPdc around next dc, (3 dc, ch 1, 3 dc) in next ch-1 sp, rep from * around.

RND 43: *FPdc around next dc, (3 dc, ch 1, 2 dc) in next ch-1 sp, FPdc around next dc, (3 dc, ch 1, 3 dc) in next ch-1 sp, rep from * around.

RNDS 44–45: *FPdc around next dc, (3 dc, ch 1, 3 dc) in next ch-1 sp, rep from * around.

RND 46: Skipping all FPdc, (sc, ch 1) in blp of each st and each ch around, sl st to first sc, fasten off.

SLEEVES

(S, M)

RND 1: Hold project at armhole with body facing you. Attach yarn by working a FPdc around any FPdc from body towards center of armhole. Fpdc around each FPdc, (2 dc, ch 1, 2 dc) in same ch as sh on body at armhole, and in each ch-1 sp around—15 (15) sh.

RNDS 2–15: *FPdc around next dc, (2 dc, ch 1, 2 dc) in next ch-1 sp, rep from * around.

(L, XL)

RND 1: Hold project at armhole with body facing you. Attach yarn by working a FPdc around any FPdc from body toward center of armhole. Fpdc around each FPdc, (3 dc, ch 1, 2 dc) in same ch as sh on body at armhole, and in each ch-1 sp around—15 (15) sh.

RNDS 2–14: *FPdc around next dc, (3 dc, ch 1, 2 dc) in next ch-1 sp, rep from * around.

RND 15: *FPdc around next dc, (2 dc, ch 1, 2 dc) in next ch-1 sp, rep from * around.

(ALL)

RND 16: *FPdc around next dc, (2 dc, ch 1, dc) in next ch-1 sp, rep from * around.

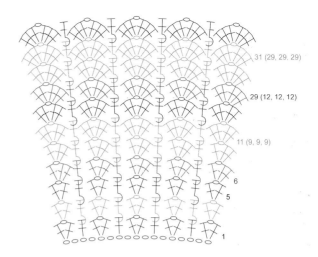

a. Increase Shaping Diagram

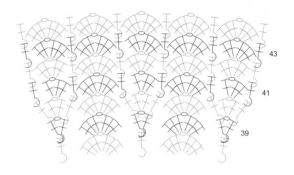

b. Bottom Ruffle Diagram

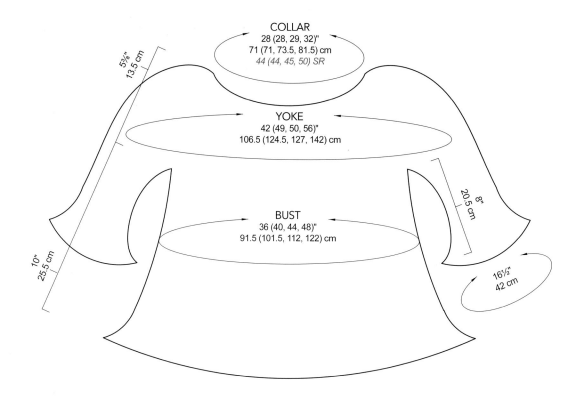

COLLAR
28 (28, 29, 32)"
71 (71, 73.5, 81.5) cm
44 (44, 45, 50) SR

YOKE
42 (49, 50, 56)"
106.5 (124.5, 127, 142) cm

BUST
36 (40, 44, 48)"
91.5 (101.5, 112, 122) cm

5⅜"
13.5 cm

8"
20.5 cm

10"
25.5 cm

16½"
42 cm

Shell Game

Increasing inside shell patterns can be a daunting task, especially for a first-time top-down crocheter. I like to look at the shells as just a bunch of stitches instead of the little motifs they actually are.

We all know that the easiest increase is just two of the same stitch in the same space or stitch. Using that simple knowledge, the easiest way to increase a shell is simply to add to it one extra stitch at a time. You can add an extra double crochet, as our pattern does, or add an extra chain in the center. The reverse will also work for decreasing. Take our pattern, for example. If after you crochet the collar you find it's too wide for your taste, you can always join the yarn to the collar and remove one stitch from each of the shells from Rnd 1 (you could simply remove the chain from the V-st around).

The beauty is clear in the finished top. The increasing may look like magic, but in reality it's as natural as making a stitch.

RNDS 17–18: *FPdc around next dc, (dc, ch 1, dc) in next ch-1 sp, rep from * around.

SLEEVE RUFFLE

RND 19: *2 FPdc around next dc, (dc, ch 1, dc) in next ch-1 sp, rep from * around.

RND 20: *FPdc around next dc, (dc, ch 1, dc) in next ch-1 sp, rep from * around.

RND 21: *FPdc around next dc, (2 dc, ch 1, dc) in next ch-1 sp, rep from * around.

RND 22: *FPdc around next dc, (2 dc, ch 1, 2 dc) in next ch-1 sp, rep from * around.

RND 23: *FPdc around next dc, (3 dc, ch 1, 2 dc) in next ch-1 sp, rep from * around.

RND 24: *FPdc around next dc, (3 dc, ch 1, 3 dc) in next ch-1 sp, rep from * around.

RND 25: Skipping all FPdc, (sc, ch 1) in blp of each st and each ch around, sl st to first sc, fasten off.

Finishing
BLOCKING

Pin tunic to schematic size and spray with water. Allow to dry.

rose quartz
PULLOVER

This classic pullover highlights my favorite elements of crochet: lace and ease. The lace inserts are stunning, and only you will know that it was actually a breeze to crochet them. Increasing for the yoke is done with simple stitches before and after the lace inserts, highlighting them beautifully. To get a perfect fit, try the pullover on as you go, and add or subtract any length from the body or the sleeves before crocheting the edging.

Materials

YARN

Sportweight (#2 Fine)

SHOWN: Blue Sky Alpacas Alpaca Silk (50% alpaca, 50% silk; 146 yd [133 m]/1.75 oz [50 g]): #101 Quartz, 8 (8, 9, 11, 12) hanks.

HOOK

Size G/6 (4.0 mm) or hook needed to obtain gauge.

NOTIONS

Stitch markers, tapestry needle for weaving in ends; spray bottle with water; straight pins for blocking, four ¼" (6 mm) diameter buttons.

Gauge

20 sts (2½ SR) by 12 rows (3 RR) = 4⅜" × 4⅜" (11 × 11 cm) in stitch pattern.

Finished Size

Bust measurement is 33 (36, 40½, 44, 47½)" (84 [91.5, 103, 112, 120.5] cm). Sized for X-Small (Small, Medium, Large, X-Large). Size shown is Small.

Special Stitches

CLUSTER DOTS STITCH PATTERN (CDSP)

See Cluster Dots Diagram (page 70) for assistance.

Chain a multiple of 8 plus 3.

ROW 1 (RS): Dc in 4th ch from hook (sk ch counts as dc), dc in next 5 dc, *ch 1, sk 1 ch, 3 dc-cl in next ch, ch 1, sk 1 ch, dc in next 5 ch, rep from * across to last 2 ch, dc in last 2 ch, turn.

ROW 2: Ch 2 (counts as hdc), *hdc in each dc across to ch-1 sp, hdc in ch-1 sp, hdc in 3 dc-cl, hdc in next ch-1 sp, rep from * across, hdc in each dc to tch, hdc in top of tch, turn.

ROW 3: Ch 3 (counts as dc here and throughout), dc in next 2 hdc, *ch 1, sk 1 hdc, 3 dc-cl in next hdc, ch 1, sk 1 hdc, dc in next 5 hdc, rep from * across to tch, dc in top of tch, turn.

ROW 4: Rep Row 2.

ROW 5: Ch 3, dc in next 6 hdc, *ch 1, sk 1 hdc, 3 dc-cl in next hdc, ch 1, sk 1 hdc, dc in next 5 hdc, rep from * across to last 2 sts, dc in next hdc, dc in top of tch, turn.

Rep Rows 2–5 for pattern.

YOKE

See Diagram A (page 70) for assistance.

Diagram shows increases surrounding lace panel. Cluster Dots stitch pattern is shown in size Small.

Work 122 (122, 122, 130, 130) fsc, turn.

ROW 1 (RS): Ch 3, dc in next sc, *ch 1, sk 1 sc, 3 dc-cl in next sc, ch 1, sk 1 sc, dc in next 5 sc*, rep from * twice omitting last 5 dc, dc in next 2 sc, **2 dc in next sc, place m, ch 1, sc in next sc, ch 3, sk 1 sc, sc in next sc, ch 1, 2 dc in next sc, place m**, dc in next 4 (4, 4, 6, 6) sc, rep from * to * 3 times omitting last 5 dc, dc in next 4 (4, 4, 6, 6) sc, rep from ** to **, dc in next 2 sc, rep from * to last sc, dc in last sc, turn—146 (146, 146, 154, 154) sts.

ROW 2: Ch 3, *sc bet marked dc group, move m, ch 1, 5 dc in ch-3 sp, ch 1, sc bet marked dc group, move m, ch 1, cont in Row 2 of CDSP across to m, ch 1, rep from * across to tch omitting last ch 1, hdc in top of tch, turn.

ROW 3: Ch 3, dc in first hdc, *dc in next 5 hdc, cont in Row 3 of CDSP across to last hdc, 2 dc in last hdc (incr made), **2 dc in marked sc, move m, [sc bet next 2 dc, ch 3] 3 times, sc bet next 2 dc, 2 dc in marked sc, move m, 2 dc in next hdc**, dc in next 7 (7, 7, 1, 1) hdc, cont in Row 3 of CDSP across to last 8 (8, 8, 2, 2) hdc, dc in next 7 (7, 7, 1, 1) hdc, 2 dc in next hdc, rep from ** to **, rep from * to tch omitting 2dc, dc in 2nd ch of tch, turn—8 add'l dc.

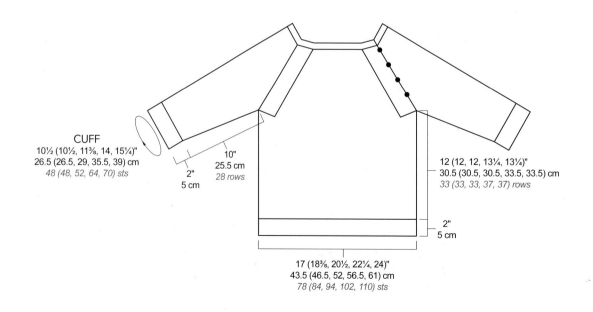

CUFF
10½ (10½, 11⅜, 14, 15¼)"
26.5 (26.5, 29, 35.5, 39) cm
48 (48, 52, 64, 70) sts

2"
5 cm

10"
25.5 cm
28 rows

12 (12, 12, 13¼, 13¼)"
30.5 (30.5, 30.5, 33.5, 33.5) cm
33 (33, 33, 37, 37) rows

2"
5 cm

17 (18⅜, 20½, 22¼, 24)"
43.5 (46.5, 52, 56.5, 61) cm
78 (84, 94, 102, 110) sts

ROW 4: Ch 2, *BPdc in next 2 dc, move m, ch 1, [sc in next ch-3 sp, ch 3] twice, sc in next ch-3 sp, ch 1, BPdc in next 2 dc, move m, 2 hdc in next dc (incr made), cont in Row 2 of CDSP to last dc before m, 2 hdc in last dc before m (incr made), rep from * across placing last increase in top of tch, turn—8 add'l hdc.

ROW 5: Ch 3, dc in first hdc, *dc in next 3 hdc, cont in Row 3 of CDSP across to last hdc before m, 2 dc in last hdc, **FPdc in next 2 dc, move m, ch 2, sc in next ch-3 sp, ch 3, sc in next ch-3 sp, ch 2, FPdc in next 2 dc, move m, 2 dc in next hdc**, dc in next 5 (5, 5, 7, 7) hdc, cont in Row 3 of CDSP across to m, 2 dc in next hdc, rep from ** to **, rep from * to tch omitting 2dc, dc in 2nd ch of tch, turn—8 add'l dc.

ROW 6: Ch 3, *sc bet marked dc group, move m, ch 2, 5 dc in ch-3 sp, ch 2, sc bet marked dc group, move m, ch 1, 2 hdc in next dc, cont in Row 2 of CDSP across to last dc before m, 2 hdc in last dc, ch 1, rep from * across to tch omitting last ch 1, 2 hdc in top of tch, turn—8 add'l hdc.

ROW 7: Rep Row 3 of yoke with 1 dc before SR on sleeves, and 3 (3, 3, 5, 5) dc before SR on front and back panel—8 add'l dc.

ROW 8: Rep Row 4 of yoke—8 add'l hdc.

ROW 9: Rep Row 5 of yoke with 7 dc before SR on sleeves, and 1 (1, 1, 3, 3) dc before SR on front and back panel—8 add'l dc.

ROW 10: Rep Row 6 of yoke—8 add'l hdc.

ROW 11: Rep Row 3 with 5 dc before SR on sleeves and 7 (7, 7, 1, 1) dc before SR on front and back—8 add'l dc.

ROW 12: Rep Row 4 of yoke—8 add'l hdc.

ROW 13: Rep Row 5 of yoke with 3 dc before SR on sleeves, and 5 (5, 5, 7, 7) dc before SR on front and back panel—8 add'l dc.

ROW 14: Rep Row 6 of yoke—8 add'l hdc.

ROW 15: Rep Row 3 with 1 dc before SR on sleeves and 3 (3, 3, 5, 5) dc before SR on front and back—8 add'l dc.

ROW 16: Rep Row 4, (S ONLY) do not increase on front and back panels (4 [8, 8, 8] add'l sts).

ROW 17: Rep Row 5 of yoke with 8 (8, 8, 7, 7) dc before SR on sleeves, and 1 (1, 1, 3, 3) dc before SR on front and back panel, (S, M, L) do not increase on sleeve panels, (S ONLY) do not increase on front and back panels—0 (4, 4, 8, 8) add'l sts.

ROW 18: Rep Row 6, (S, M, L) do not increase on sleeve panels, (S ONLY) do not increase on front and back panels—0 (4, 4, 8, 8) add'l sts.

ROW 19: Rep Row 3 with 4 (4, 4, 5, 5) dc before SR on sleeves and 5 (8, 7, 1, 1) dc before SR on front and back, (S, M) do not increase on front/ back panel and sleeves, (L) do not increase on sleeves—0 (0, 4, 8, 8) add'l sts.

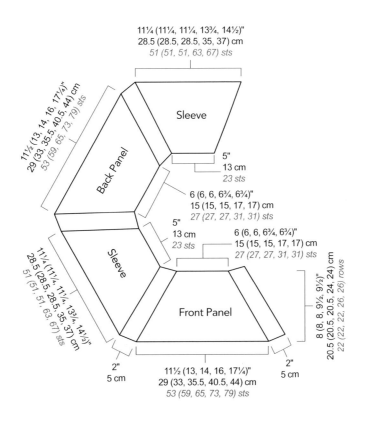

11¼ (11¼, 11¼, 13¾, 14½)"
28.5 (28.5, 28.5, 35, 37) cm
51 (51, 51, 63, 67) sts

11½ (13, 14, 16, 17¼)" cm
29 (33, 35.5, 40.5, 44) sts
53 (59, 65, 73, 79) sts

Back Panel

Sleeve

5"
13 cm
23 sts

6 (6, 6, 6¾, 6¾)"
15 (15, 15, 17, 17) cm
27 (27, 27, 31, 31) sts

5"
13 cm
23 sts

6 (6, 6, 6¾, 6¾)"
15 (15, 15, 17, 17) cm
27 (27, 27, 31, 31) sts

11¼ (11¼, 11¼, 13¾, 14½)"
28.5 (28.5, 28.5, 35, 37) cm
51 (51, 51, 63, 67) sts

Sleeve

Front Panel

8 (8, 8, 9½, 9½)"
20.5 (20.5, 20.5, 24, 24) cm
22 (22, 22, 26, 26) rows

2"
5 cm

11½ (13, 14, 16, 17¼)"
29 (33, 35.5, 40.5, 44) cm
53 (59, 65, 73, 79) sts

2"
5 cm

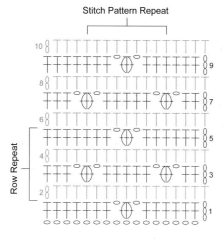

Stitch Pattern Repeat

Row Repeat

Cluster Dots Stitch Pattern

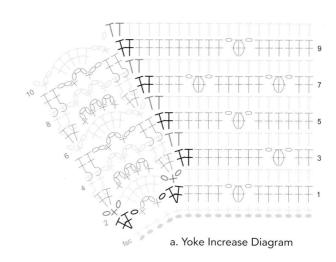

a. Yoke Increase Diagram

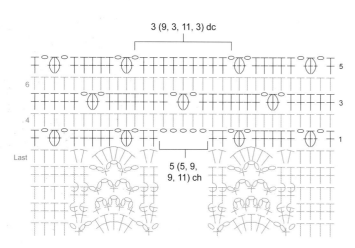

3 (9, 3, 11, 3) dc

5 (5, 9, 9, 11) ch

Last

b. Body Joining Diagram

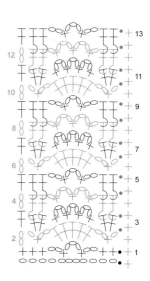

c. Bottom and Cuff Edging

ROW 20: Rep Row 4, (S, M) do not increase on front/ back panel and sleeves, (L) do not increase on sleeves—0 (0, 4, 8, 8) add'l sts.

ROW 21: Rep Row 5 of yoke with 8 (8, 8, 3, 3) dc before SR on sleeves, and 1 (4, 5, 7, 7) dc before SR on front and back panel, (S, M) do not increase in front/ back panel and sleeves, (L) do not increase in sleeves—0 (0, 4, 8, 8) add'l sts.

(S, M, L only)

ROW 22: Ch 2, *2 hdc bet marked dc group, 6 hdc in ch-3 sp, 2 hdc bet marked dc group, cont in Row 2 of CDSP across to m, rep from * across to tch, hdc in top of tch, turn—51 (51, 51) sts on the sleeves, 53 (59, 65) sts on the front and back.

(XL, 2X)

ROW 22: Rep Row 6—8 (8) add'l sts.

ROW 23: Rep Row 3 with 2 (1) dc before SR on sleeves and 5 (5) dc before SR on front and back, (XL) do not increase in sleeves—4 (8) add'l sts.

ROW 24: Rep Row 4, (XL) do not increase in front/ back panel and sleeves—0 (8) add'l sts.

ROW 25: Rep Row 5 of yoke with 6(8) dc before SR on sleeves, and 3 (3) dc before SR on front and back panel, (XL) do not increase in front/ back panel and sleeves, (2X) do not increase in sleeves—0 (4) add'l sts.

ROW 26: Ch 2, *2 hdc bet marked dc group, 6 hdc in ch-3 sp, 2 hdc bet marked dc group, 1 (2) hdc in next dc, cont in Row 2 of CDSP across to last dc before m, 1 (2) hdc in next dc, rep from * across to tch, hdc in top of tch, turn—63 (67) on the sleeves, 73 (79) on the front/back.

BODY

See Diagram B (opposite) for assistance.

Sl st to the top of the tch at the beg of the previous row on the front panel, turn. (Doing so closes the raglan seam.)

RND 1: Ch 8 (8, 12, 12, 14) (first 3 ch count as dc, remaining are underarm joining), dc in first marked hdc on back {sk all of sleeve panel 52 (52, 52, 64, 68) hdc}, dc in next 6 (1, 4, 0, 3) hdc, cont with CDSP across to last marked st on back panel for 73 (79, 85, 93, 99) sts total, ch 5 (5, 9, 9, 11), sk sleeve panel 51 (51, 51, 63, 67) sts, dc in first marked hdc on front, dc in next 6 (1, 4, 0, 3) hdc, cont with CDSP across to tch, sl st to 3rd ch of tch, turn.

RND 2: Ch 2 (counts as hdc), hdc in each ch, dc-cl, dc, and ch-1 sp around, sl st to top of tch, place m at first and last hdc of underarm, turn—156 (168, 188, 204, 220) hdc.

RND 3: Ch 3 (counts as dc), dc in next hdc, *ch 1, sk 1 hdc, 3 dc-cl in next hdc, ch 1, sk 1 hdc, dc in next 4 (7, 4, 8, 4) hdc, cont in CDSP across to 3 (6, 1, 5, 0) hdc before m, dc in next 4 (7, 4, 8, 4) hdc, rep from * around, sl st to top of tch, turn.

RND 4: Rep Rnd 2.

RND 5: (S) Ch 2, 2 dc-cl in same st, ch 1, sk 1 hdc, (M/XL) ch 3, (L) ch 4, sk 1 hdc, 3 dc-cl in next hdc, ch 1, sk 1 hdc, (2X) ch 3, dc in next hdc, ch 1, sk 1 hdc, 3 dc-cl in next hdc, ch 1, sk 1 hdc, (ALL) dc in next 3 (7, 3, 10, 3) hdc, ch 1, sk 1 hdc, 3 dc-cl in next hdc, ch 1, sk 1 hdc, cont in CDSP around to 2 (5, 0, 4, 7) hdc before m, ch 1, sk 1 hdc, 3 dc-cl in next hdc, ch 1, sk 1 hdc, dc in next 3 (9, 3, 11, 3) hdc, cont in CDSP across, sl st to 3rd ch of tch, turn.

RNDS 6–33 (33, 33, 37, 37): Rep Rnds 2–5 of Body 7 (7, 7, 8, 8) times.

RND 34 (34, 34, 38, 38): Rep Rnd 2 once more, fasten off.

BOTTOM EDGING

See Diagram C (opposite) for assistance.

Ch 11, sl st to any st on back edging. (Rows will be worked perpendicular to edge.)

ROW 1 (RS): Sl st to next st on edge, sc in next 2 ch, ch 2, sk 1 ch, sc in next ch, ch 3, sk 2 ch, sc in next ch, ch 2, sk 1 ch, sc in last 3 ch, turn.

ROW 2: Ch 3 (counts as hdc, ch 1-sp), sk 1 sc, sc bet next 2 sc, ch 2, 5 dc in ch-3 sp, ch 2, sc bet next 2 sc, ch 1, sl st to edge of bottom edge twice, turn. (Once will be to join, once for a turning ch, sk sts on edge as needed so edging does not ruffle.

ROW 3: Sk both sl st, 2 dc in next sc, [sc bet next 2 dc, ch 3] 3 times, sc bet next 2 dc, 2 dc in next sc, dc in 2nd ch of tch, turn.

ROW 4: Ch 2, BPdc around next 2 dc, ch 1, [sc in next ch-3 sp, ch 3] twice, sc in next ch-3 sp, ch 1, BPdc around next 2 dc, sl st twice to edge, turn.

ROW 5: Sk both sl st, FPdc around next 2 dc, ch 2, sc in next ch-3 sp, ch 3, sc in next ch-3 sp, ch 2, FPdc around next 2 dc, dc in top of tch, turn.

ROW 6: Ch 3, sk first dc, sc bet next 2 dc, ch 2, 5 dc in ch-3 sp, ch 2, sc bet next 2 dc, ch 1, sl st to edge twice, turn.

Rep Rows 3–6 around bottom edge ending with a Row 4, fasten off. Whipstitch last row to first row. Join yarn to bottom edge on RS, sc around ends of edging, sl st to first sc, fasten off, weave in ends.

The Case for Lace

Increasing in lace patterns can seem confusing when you're working in the round. As you may remember from my panel-construction projects, I like to sketch out all my shaping with symbols. All in-the-round projects simply involve four panels being crocheted at once.

Pretend that each panel (front/back/sleeves) is being crocheted separately, and figure out the symbols needed. Then, once you're ready to crochet, instead of turning, just keep crocheting one panel to the next. Now, if lace increasing still seems too confusing, skate around it.

In this pattern, the lace is in sections that do not increase; the more basic half double crochet and double crochet rounds are the ones that take the increasing. Thus, the lace inserts become the highlight of the sweater.

SLEEVES

See Diagram C (page 70) for assistance.

Join yarn to RS at middle ch of underarm joining with sl st.

RND 1: Ch 3 (counts as a dc), dc in next 6 (6, 8, 6, 9) sts, place m, cont in CDSP around to 4 (4, 4, 2, 4) sts before opposite underarm joining, place m, dc in next 13 (13, 9, 13, 11) sts, place m, cont with CDSP around, dc in each st to end, sl st to top of tch, turn—56 (56, 60, 72, 78) sts.

RND 2: Ch 2, hdc in each dc, dc-cl, and ch-1 sp around, sl st to top of tch, turn.

RND 3: Ch 3, dc in each hdc to 4 sts before m, place m, cont in CDSP across to 4 sts past m, place m, dc in each hdc till 4 sts before m, place m, cont in CDSP across to tch, sl st to top of tch, turn.

RND 4 AND EVERY EVEN RND: Rep Rnd 2.

RND 5: Ch 2 (does not count as dc), dc in each hdc to 4 sts after m, place m, cont in CDSP across to 4 sts before m, place m, dc in each hdc till 4 sts past m, place m, cont in CDSP across to tch, sl st to top of tch, turn—55 (55, 59, 71, 77) sts.

RND 7: Ch 2 (does not count as dc), dc in each hdc to 4 sts before m, place m, cont in CDSP across to 4 sts past m, place m, dc in each hdc till 4 sts before m, place m, cont in CDSP across to tch, sl st to top of tch, turn—54 (54, 58, 70, 76) sts.

RND 9: Ch 3, dc in each hdc to 4 sts after m, place m, cont in CDSP across to 4 sts before m, place m, dc in each hdc till 4 sts past m, place m, cont in CDSP across to tch, sl st to top of tch, turn.

RND 11: Rep Rnd 7—53 (53, 57, 69, 75) sts.

RND 13: Rep Rnd 5—52 (52, 56, 68, 74) sts.

RND 15: Rep Rnd 3.

RNDS 16–27: Rep Rnds 4–15 once.

RND 28: Rep Rnd 2 once, fasten off—48 (48, 52, 64, 70) sts.

Rep bottom edging around cuffs, fasten off.

Finishing

BLOCKING

Pin pullover to schematic size and spray with water. Allow to dry.

COLLAR EDGING

Join yarn to edge of collar with sl st, ch 5 (counts as dc), ch 2.

ROW 1: Dc in 4th ch from hook, dc in next dc, sl st to edge of collar twice (once to join, once for turning ch), turn.

ROW 2: Sk both sl sts, BPdc around next 2 dc, hdc in top of tch, turn.

ROW 3: Ch 3, FPdc around next 2 dc, sl st to edge of collar twice, turn.

ROWS 4–5: Rep Rows 2–3 around collar, fasten off.

Join yarn to raglan seam, sc up raglan seam to collar, 3 sc at edge, sc around collar to opposite raglan seam, 3 sc at edge, sc down raglan seam, fasten off.

BUTTONBAND: Join yarn to bottom of raglan seam, *sl st in next 5 sts, ch 3 (buttonhole made), rep from * 3 times, sl st to top of raglan seam. Sew buttons to opposite raglan seam.

structured
CARDIGAN

Hone your "top-down shaping" skills with this classic cardigan! The simple stitch pattern aligns to help you keep track as you work your way down the sweater, while the low V-neck shaping keeps you on your toes.

Materials

YARN
DK weight (#3 Light)

SHOWN: Filatura Di Crosa Zara (100% Lana extrafine merino superwash; 136.5 yd [125 m]/1.75 oz [50 g]): #1494 Light Gray, 7 (8, 10, 11, 13) balls.

HOOK
Size H/8 (5.0 mm) or hook needed to obtain gauge.

NOTIONS
Stitch markers, tapestry needle for weaving in ends; spray bottle with water; straight pins for blocking; hook-and-eye fastener; matching sewing thread.

Gauge
3 sh (3SR) by 12 rows (6 RR) = 4⅛" × 4½" (10.5 × 11.5 cm) in stitch pattern.

Finished Size
Bust measurement is 33 (35¾, 41¼, 44, 49½)" (84 [91, 105, 112, 125.5] cm). Sized for Small (Medium, Large, X-Large, 2X). Size shown is Medium.

Notes
As with many top-down sweaters, over time the weight of the sweater can make the necklines grow. Sewing grosgrain ribbon around the inside of the sweater neck collar will ensure that you'll enjoy years of crisp wear.

Special Stitches

SHELL (SH)
Work (2dc, ch 2, 2dc) in st indicated.

INCREASE
Work (2 dc, ch 1, sc, ch 1, 2 dc) in st indicated.

LOVELY LACE STITCH PATTERN (LLSP)
See Lovely Lace Diagram (page 77) for assistance.

Chain a multiple of 6 plus 2.

ROW 1 (RS): Sc in 2nd ch from hook, *sk 2 ch, sh in next ch, sk 2 ch, sc in next ch; rep from * across, turn.

ROW 2: Ch 3 (counts as dc here and throughout), dc in first sc, *ch 2, sc in next ch-2 sp, ch 2, 2 dc in next sc; rep from * across, turn.

ROW 3: Ch 1, sc in first dc, *sh in next sc, sc bet next 2 dc; rep from * across to last sc, sh in last sc, sc bet last dc and tch, turn.

Rep Rows 2–3 for pattern.

Yoke
See Diagrams A and B (page 77) for assistance for increasing yoke.

Work 41 (41, 45, 45, 45) fsc.

ROW 1 (RS): Ch 1, sc in first sc, *sk 1 sc, sh in next sc, sk 1 sc, sc in next sc; rep from * across, turn—10 (10, 11, 11, 11) sh.

ROW 2: Ch 1, (sc, ch 1, 2 dc) in first sc, [ch 2, sc in ch-2 sp, ch 2, 2 dc in next sc] twice, *ch 2, sc in ch-2 sp, ch 2, increase in next sc (place m in sc of increase)*, [ch 2, sc in ch-2 sp, ch 2, 2 dc in next sc] 3 (3, 4, 4, 4) times, rep from * to * once, [ch 2, sc in ch-2 sp, ch 2, 2 dc in next sc] twice, ch 2, sc in ch-2 sp, ch 2, (2 dc, ch 1, sc) in last sc, turn.

ROW 3: Ch 5, 2 dc in first sc, sc bet next 2 dc, rep Row 3 of LLSP across to last sc, (2 dc, ch 1, tr) in last sc, turn—12 (12, 13, 13, 13) sh + 2 half sh.

ROW 4: Ch 2, sc in ch-1 sp, ch 2, 2 dc in next sc, cont in Row 2 of LLSP across to last sc, 2 dc in last sc, ch 2, (sc, hdc) in tch-sp, turn.

ROW 5: Ch 4, (tr, ch 1, 2 dc) in sc, cont in Row 3 of LLSP across to last sc, (2 dc, ch 1, tr) in last sc, tr in top of tch, turn—12 (12, 13, 13, 13) sh + 2 half sh.

ROW 6: Ch 1, sc in first tr, ch 1, sc in ch-1 sp, ch 2, *increase in next sc, place m in sc of increase, cont in Row 2 of LLSP to sc after m; rep from * across to last sc, increase in last sc (place m in sc), ch 2, sc in ch-1 sp, ch 1, sc in top of tch, turn.

ROW 7: Ch 2, sk first sc, sh in next sc, sc bet next 2 dc, cont in Row 3 of LLSP across to last 2 sc, sh in next sc, hdc in last sc, turn—18 (18, 19, 19, 19) sh.

ROW 8: Ch 5, sc in ch-2 sp, ch 2, 2 dc in next sc, cont in Row 2 of LLSP across to last sc, 2 dc in last sc, ch 2, sc in ch-2 sp, ch 2, dc in top of tch, turn.

ROW 9: Ch 1, sc in first dc, cont in Row 3 of LLSP across to last sc, sh in last sc, sc in 3rd ch of tch, turn.

ROW 10: Ch 3, dc in first sc, cont in Row 2 of LLSP across to sc before m, *increase in next sc, cont in Row 2 of LLSP across to sc before m; rep from * across to last sc, 2 dc in last sc, turn.

ROW 11: Ch 2, sc bet first 2 dc, sh in next sc, cont in Row 3 of LLSP across to tch, sc bet last dc and tch, hdc in top of tch, turn—22 (22, 23, 23, 23) sh.

ROW 12: Ch 3, 2 dc in first sc, cont in Row 2 of LLSP across to last sc, 2 dc in last sc, dc in top of tch, turn.

ROW 13: Ch 4, (dc, hdc) in first dc, sc bet next 2 dc, sh in next sc, cont in Row 3 of LLSP across to tch, (hdc, dc, tr) in top of tch, turn.

ROW 14: Ch 1, sc in first tr, ch 2, 2 dc in next sc, cont in Row 2 to sc after m, *increase in next sc (place m), cont in Row 2 of LLSP across to sc after m; rep from * across to last sc, 2 dc in last sc, ch 2, sc in top of tch, turn.

ROW 15: Ch 5, 2 dc in first sc, sc bet next 2 dc, cont in Row 3 of LLSP across to last sc, (2 dc, ch 1, tr) in last sc, turn—26 (26, 27, 27, 27) sh + 2 half sh.

ROW 16: Ch 2, sc in ch-1 sp, ch 2, 2 dc in next sc, cont in Row 2 of LLSP across to tch, ch 2, (sc, hdc) in tch-sp, turn.

ROW 17: Ch 4, (tr, ch 1, 2 dc) in next sc, sc bet next 2 dc, cont in Row 3 of LLSP across to last sc, (2 dc, ch 1, tr) in last sc, tr in top of tch, turn.

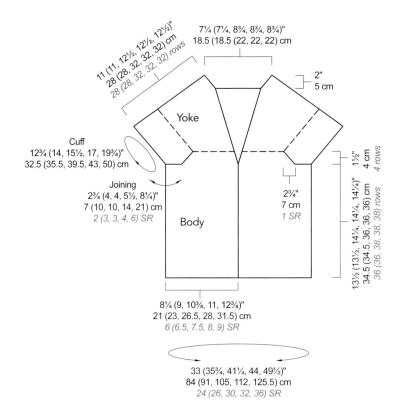

7¼ (7¼, 8¾, 8¾, 8¾)"
18.5 (18.5, 22, 22, 22) cm

11 (11, 12½, 12½, 12½)"
28 (28, 32, 32, 32) cm
28 (28, 32, 32, 32) rows

2"
5 cm

Yoke

Cuff
12¾ (14, 15½, 17, 19¾)"
32.5 (35.5, 39.5, 43, 50) cm

1½"
4 cm
4 rows

Joining
2¾ (4, 4, 5½, 8¼)"
7 (10, 10, 14, 21) cm
2 (3, 3, 4, 6) SR

Body

2¾"
7 cm
1 SR

13½ (13½, 14¼, 14¼, 14¼)"
34.5 (34.5, 36, 36, 36) cm
36 (36, 36, 38, 38) rows

8¼ (9, 10⅜, 11, 12⅜)"
21 (23, 26.5, 28, 31.5) cm
6 (6.5, 7.5, 8, 9) SR

33 (35¾, 41¼, 44, 49½)"
84 (91, 105, 112, 125.5) cm
24 (26, 30, 32, 36) SR

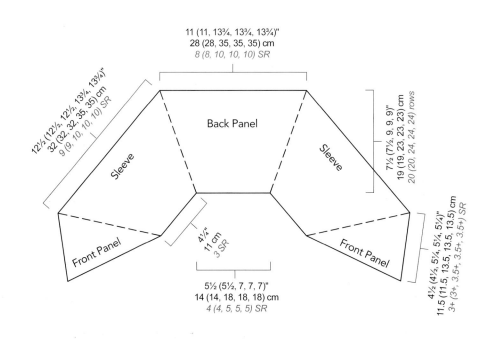

11 (11, 13¾, 13¾, 13¾)"
28 (28, 35, 35, 35) cm
8 (8, 10, 10, 10) SR

Back Panel

Sleeve

Sleeve

12½ (12½, 12½, 13¾, 13¾)"
32 (32, 32, 35, 35) cm
9 (9, 10, 10, 10) SR

7½ (7½, 9, 9, 9)"
19 (19, 23, 23, 23) cm
20 (20, 24, 24, 24) rows

Front Panel

Front Panel

4¼"
11 cm
3 SR

4½ (4½, 5¼, 5¼, 5¼)"
11.5 (11.5, 13.5, 13.5, 13.5) cm
3+ (3+, 3.5+, 3.5+, 3.5+) SR

5½ (5½, 7, 7, 7)"
14 (14, 18, 18, 18) cm
4 (4, 5, 5, 5) SR

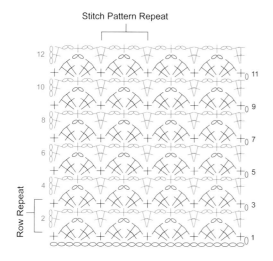

Stitch Pattern Repeat

Lovely Lace Stitch Pattern

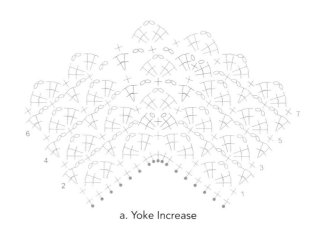

a. Yoke Increase

b. Neck Line Increase Shaping

ROW 18: Ch 1, sc in first tr, ch 1, sc in ch-1 sp, ch 2, 2 dc in next sc, cont in Row 2 to sc before m, *increase in next sc (place m), cont in Row 2 of LLSP across to sc before m; rep from * across to last ch-1 sp, ch 2, sc in ch-1 sp, ch 1, sc in top of tch, turn.

ROW 19: Ch 2, sk first sc, sh in next sc, sc bet next 2 dc, cont in Row 3 of LLSP across to last 2 sc, sh in next sc, hdc in last sc, turn—32 (32, 33, 33, 33) sh.

ROW 20: Ch 5, sc in ch-2 sp, ch 2, 2 dc in next sc, cont in Row 2 of LLSP across to last sc, 2 dc in next sc, ch 2, sc in next ch-2 sp, ch 2, dc in top of tch, turn.

(L, XL, 2X)

ROWS 21–24: Rep Rows 9–12—37 (37, 37) sh.

Joining for Body

See Diagram C (page 78) for assistance.

FRONT PANEL

(S, M)

ROW 1: Cont in Row 3 of LLSP for 3 sh, turn.

ROW 2: Ch 6, 2dc in first sc, cont in Row 2 of LLSP across to end, turn.

ROW 3: Ch 2, sc bet next 2 dc, cont in Row 3 of LLSP across to tch, (2 dc, ch 2, dc) in 4th ch of tch, turn—3 sh + 1 half sh.

ROW 4: Ch 4, sc in next ch-2 sp, ch 2, 2 dc in next sc, cont in Row 2 of LLSP across to tch, dc in top of tch, fasten off, turn.

(L, XL, 2X)

ROW 1: Ch 4, (dc, hdc) in first dc, sc bet next 2 dc, cont in Row 3 of LLSP for 3 sh, sc bet next 2 dc, (2 dc, ch 2, dc) in next sc, turn.

ROW 2: Ch 4, sc in next ch-2 sp, ch 2, 2 dc in next sc, cont in Row 2 of LLSP across to tch, sc in top of tch, turn.

ROW 3: Ch 5, 2 dc in first sc, sc bet next 2 dc, cont in Row 3 of LLSP across to tch, sc in 2nd ch of tch, turn—4 sh + 1 half sh.

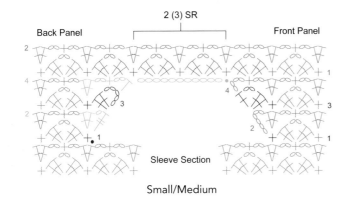

Back Panel   2 (3) SR   Front Panel

Sleeve Section

Small/Medium

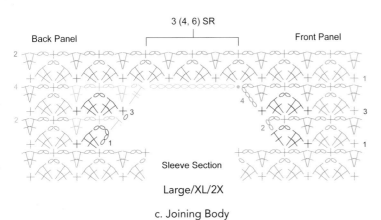

Back Panel   3 (4, 6) SR   Front Panel

Sleeve Section

Large/XL/2X

c. Joining Body

ROW 4: Ch 6, 2 dc in first sc, cont in Row 2 of LLSP across to tch, sc in tch-sp, hdc in 4th ch of tch, fasten off, turn.

BACK PANEL

(S, M)

Sk 9 sc on last row of yoke, join yarn with sl st bet next 2 dc. (Sk sts will become sleeve section.)

ROW 1: Sc in same sp as sl st, cont in Row 3 of LLSP across for 8 sh, turn.

ROW 2: Ch 6, 2 dc in first sc, cont in Row 2 of LLSP across to last sc, (2 dc, ch 1, tr) in last sc, turn.

ROW 3: Ch 5, 2 dc in tr, cont in Row 3 of LLSP across to tch, (2 dc, ch 2, dc) in 4th ch of tch, turn—8 sh + 2 half sh.

ROW 4: Ch 4, sc in next ch-2 sp, ch 2, 2 dc in next sc, cont in Row 2 of LLSP across to last sc, 2 dc in last sc, ch 2, sc in tch-sp, ch 2, hdc in 3rd ch of tch, ch 11 (17), sl st to 2nd ch of tch in Row 4 of front panel (back and front now joined), fasten off, turn.

(L, XL, 2X)

Sk 20 dc on last row of yoke, join yarn with sl st in next sc. (Sk sts will become sleeve section.)

ROW 1: Ch 5, 2 dc in same sc, sc bet next 2 dc, cont in Row 3 of LLSP across for 9 sh, sc bet next 2 dc, (2 dc, ch 2, dc) in next sc, turn—9 sh + 2 half sh.

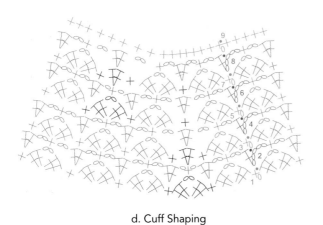

d. Cuff Shaping

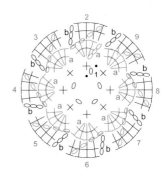

e. Flower Motif

ROW 2: Ch 4, sc in next ch-2 sp, ch 2, 2 dc in next sc, cont in Row 2 of LLSP across to last sc, 2 dc in last sc, ch 2, sc in tch-sp, ch 2, hdc in 3rd ch of tch, turn.

ROW 3: Ch 1, sc in hdc, cont in Row 3 of LLSP across to tch, sc in 2nd ch of tch, turn—11 sh.

ROW 4: Ch 6, 2dc in first sc, cont in Row 2 of LLSP across to last sc, (2 dc, ch 1, tr) in last sc, ch 17 (23, 35), sl st to 2nd ch of tch in Row 4 of front panel (back and front now joined), fasten off, turn.

OPPOSITE FRONT PANEL

(S, M)

Sk 9 sc on last row of yoke, join yarn with sl st bet next 2 dc. (Sk sts will become sleeve section.)

ROW 1: Sc in same sp as sl st, cont in Row 3 of LLSP across for 3 sh, turn.

ROW 2: Ch 3, dc in first sc, cont in Row 2 of LLSP across to last sc, (2 dc, ch 1, tr) in last sc, turn.

ROW 3: Ch 5, 2 dc in tr, cont in Row 3 of LLSP across to tch, sc bet last dc and tch, hdc in top of tch, turn—3 sh + 1 half sh.

ROW 4: Ch 3, 2 dc in first sc, cont in Row 2 of LLSP across to last sc, 2 dc in last sc, ch 2, sc in tch-sp, ch 2, hdc in 3rd ch of tch, ch 11 (17), sl st to 2nd ch of tch in Row 4 of back panel, fasten off, turn.

(L, XL, 2X)

Sk 20 dc on last row of yoke, join yarn with sl st in next sc (sk sts will become sleeve section).

ROW 1: Ch 5, 2 dc in same sc, sc bet next 2 dc, cont in Row 3 of LLSP to tch, (hdc, dc, tr) in top of tch, turn—3 sh + 1 half sh.

ROW 2: Ch 1, sc in tr, ch 2, 2 dc in first sc, cont in Row 2 of LLSP across to last sc, 2 dc in last sc, ch 2, sc in tch-sp, ch 2, hdc in 3rd ch of tch, turn.

ROW 3: Ch 1, sc in hdc, cont in Row 3 of LLSP across to last sc, (2 dc, ch 1, tr) in last sc, turn—4 sh + 1 half sh.

ROW 4: Ch 2, sc in ch-1 sp, ch 2, 2 dc in first sc, cont in Row 2 of LLSP across to last sc, (2 dc, ch 1, tr) in last sc, ch 17 (23, 35), sl st to 2nd ch of tch in Row 4 of front panel, fasten off, turn.

BODY

(S, M)

Join yarn to RS of front panel with sl st in dc.

ROW 1: Ch 4, (dc, hdc) in first dc, sc bet next 2 dc, sh in next sc, *cont in Row 3 of LLSP across to tch of front panel, sc in 2nd ch of tch, [sk 2 ch, sh in next ch, sk 2 ch, sc in next ch] 1 (2) times, sk 2 ch, sh in next ch, sk 2 ch, sc in hdc; rep from * once, cont in Row 3 of LLSP across to tch, (hdc, dc, tr) in top of tch, turn—22 (24) sh.

ROW 2: Ch 1, sc in first tr, ch 2, 2 dc in next sc, cont in Row 2 of LLSP to last sc, 2 dc in last sc, ch 2, sc in top of tch, turn.

ROW 3: Ch 5, 2 dc in first sc, sc bet next 2 dc, cont in Row 3 of LLSP across to last sc, (2 dc, ch 1, tr) in last sc, turn—22 (24) sh + 2 half sh.

ROW 4: Ch 2, sc in ch-1 sp, ch 2, 2 dc in next sc, cont in Row 2 of LLSP to last sc, 2 dc in last sc, ch 2, sc in tch-sp, hdc in 4th ch of tch, turn.

ROW 5: Ch 4, (tr, ch 1, 2 dc) in first sc, sc bet next 2 sc, cont in Row 3 of LLSP across to last sc, (2 dc, ch 1, tr) in last sc, tr in top of tch, turn.

ROW 6: Ch 1, sc in first tr, ch 1, sc in ch-1 sp, ch 2, cont in Row 2 of LLSP to last sc, 2 dc in last sc, ch 2, sc in ch-1 sp, ch 1, sc in top of tch, turn.

ROW 7: Ch 2, sk first sc, sh in next sc, sc bet next 2 sc, cont in Row 3 of LLSP across to last 2 sc, sh in next sc, hdc in last sc, turn—24 (26) sh.

ROW 8: Ch 5, sc in ch-2 sp, ch 2, 2 dc in next sc, cont in Row 2 of LLSP across to last sc, 2 dc in last sc, ch 2, sc in ch-2 sp, ch 2, dc in top of tch, turn.

Increase Your Comfort Level

In top-down sweaters, increasing is a challenge, especially coming up with a unique way to increase for each stitch pattern you crochet. I love to increase within shells, and I'll share why. You can use increasingly larger shells for a uniform increase. The Structured Cardigan increases along raglan seams (that are pretty hidden in the fabric) by adding an entire shell every other odd row at each raglan line. While this shaping is occurring, you're also creating the front neckline edge. In shaping, the neckline is the easiest part to figure out. You know where the neckline starts (at the corners of the back panel and sleeve) and ends (at the middle of the width of the cardigan). The depth is up to you to determine. The rest involves using your handy symbols to increase slowly to the full width of the sweater. The biggest challenge is figuring out when to put in that first increase for the yoke shaping at the neckline. In very deep necklines, I do half an increase in the first few rows to get the ball rolling. In shallower necklines, I may do a full increase instead. Everything is trial and error, which is why top-down construction is great.

ROW 9: Ch 1, sc in first dc, cont in Row 3 of LLSP across to last sc, sh in last sc, sc in 3rd ch of tch, turn.

ROW 10: Rep Row 2 of LLSP.

ROW 11: Rep Row 3 of LLSP.

ROWS 12–35: Rep Rows 10–11 twelve times.

ROW 36: Rep Row 2 of LLSP.

ROW 37: Ch 1, sc bet next 2 dc, 2 sc in each ch-2 sp across, sc bet each 2dc group across, fasten off.

(L, XL, 2X)

Join yarn to RS of front panel with sl st in hdc.

ROW 1: Ch 4, (tr, ch 1, 2 dc) in first sc, sc bet next 2 sc, cont in Row 3 of LLSP across to tch of front panel, **sh in 4th ch of tch, sk 2 ch, *sc in next ch, sk 2 ch, sh in next ch, sk 2 ch; rep from * across to last 3 ch, sc in next ch, sh in tr, sc bet next 2 sc, cont in Row 3 of LLSP across to tch of back panel, rep from ** across to last sc, (2 dc, ch 1, tr) in last sc, tr in top of tch, turn—27 (29, 33) sh + 2 half sh.

ROW 2: Ch 1, sc in first tr, ch 1, sc in ch-1 sp, ch 2, cont in Row 2 of LLSP to last sc, 2 dc in last sc, ch 2, sc in ch-1 sp, ch 1, sc in top of tch, turn.

ROW 3: Ch 2, sk first sc, sh in next sc, sc bet next 2 dc, cont in Row 3 of LLSP across to last 2 sc, sh in next sc, hdc in last sc, turn—29 (31, 35) sh.

ROW 4: Ch 5, sc in ch-2 sp, ch 2, 2 dc in next sc, cont in Row 2 of LLSP across to last sc, 2 dc in last sc, ch 2, sc in ch-2 sp, ch 2, dc in top of tch, turn.

ROW 5: Ch 1, sc in first dc, cont in Row 3 of LLSP across to last sc, sh in last sc, sc in 3rd ch of tch, turn.

ROW 6: Ch 3, dc in first sc, cont in Row 2 of LLSP across to last sc, 2 dc in last sc, turn.

ROW 7: Ch 2, sc bet first 2 dc, sh in next sc, cont in Row 3 of LLSP across to tch, sc bet last dc and tch, hdc in top of tch, turn.

ROW 8: Ch 3, 2 dc in first sc, cont in Row 2 of LLSP across to last sc, 2 dc in last sc, dc in top of tch, turn.

ROW 9: Ch 4, (dc, hdc) in first dc, sc bet next 2 dc, sh in next sc, cont in Row 3 of LLSP across to tch, (hdc, dc, tr) in top of tch, turn.

ROW 10: Ch 1, sc in first tr, ch 2, 2 dc in next sc, cont in Row 2 of LLSP to last sc, 2 dc in last sc, ch 2, sc in top of tch, turn.

ROW 11: Ch 5, 2 dc in first sc, sc bet next 2 dc, cont in Row 3 of LLSP across to last sc, (2 dc, ch 1, tr) in last sc, turn (29, 31, 35) sh + 2 half sh.

ROW 12: Ch 1, sc in first tr, ch 2, 2 dc in next sc, cont in Row 2 of LLSP to last sc, 2 dc in last sc, ch 2, sc in 4th ch of tch, turn.

ROWS 13–38: Rep Rows 11–12 thirteen times.

ROW 39: Ch 1, sc in first sc, 2 sc in each ch-2 sp across, sc bet each group of 2 dc, sc in last sc, fasten off.

ARM CUFFS

See Diagram D (page 78) for assistance.

Join yarn to RS of underarm with sl st to first ch.

ROW 1: Ch 1, sc in same ch, *sh in same ch as sh, sc in same ch as sc; rep from * across underarm ch, sc in side of front panel (around row ends), sh in side of front panel (around row ends), cont in Row 3 of LLSP across sleeve, sc in side of panel, sh in side of panel, sl st to first sc, turn—13 (14, 15, 16, 18) sh.

ROW 2: Ch 5, sc in ch-2 sp, cont in Row 2 of LLSP across to last 2 sc, 2 dc in next sc, ch 1, sc in ch-2 sp, ch 1, 2 dc in last sc, ch 2, sc in ch-2 sp, ch 2, dc in first sc, sl st to 3rd ch of tch, turn.

ROW 3: Ch 1, sc bet dc and tch, sh in sc, sc bet 2 dc, 2 dc in sc, sc bet 2 dc, cont in Row 3 of LLSP around, sl st to first sc, turn—12 (13, 14, 15, 17) sh.

ROW 4: Ch 5, sc in ch-2 sp, cont in Row 2 of LLSP across to last 2 sc, 2 dc bet next 2 dc, ch 2, sc in ch-2 sp, ch 2, dc in first sc, sl st to 3rd ch of tch, turn.

Finishing

BLOCKING AND EDGING

Pin body to schematic size and spray with water. Allow to dry.

Join yarn to back bottom edge, sc evenly around bottom, collar, and neck edge (around ends of rows and 1 in each sc), sl st to first sc, do not turn. Reverse sc in each sc around, sl st to first st, fasten off.

FLOWERS AND CLOSURE

See Diagram E (page 78) for assistance.

Make 7 (7, 9, 9, 9) flowers.

Ch 4, sl st to first ch to form ring.

RND 1: Ch 1, 8 sc in ring, sl st to first sc to join, turn.

PETAL 2A: Ch 3, 4 dc in first sc, turn. **B:** Ch 3, sk first dc, dc in each dc across, ch 4, turn.

PETAL 3A: 5 dc in next sc, turn. **B:** Ch 3, sk first dc, dc in each dc across, ch 4, turn.

Rep Petal 3 to last sc.

PETAL 9A: 5 dc in last sc, turn. **B:** Ch 3, sk first dc, dc in each dc across, ch 2, hdc in top of tch of row A of Petal 1, fasten off.

Using leftover yarn, sew flowers to side of neckline.

Sew eye closure to wrong side of cardigan under flowers. Sew hook to right side of fabric on opposite cardigan side.

ROW 5: Ch 1, sc bet dc and tch, cont in Row 3 of LLSP around, sl st to first sc, turn.

ROW 6: Ch 5, sc in ch-2 sp, cont in Row 2 of LLSP across to last 3 sc, 2 dc in next sc, ch 1, sc in ch-2 sp, ch 1, 2 dc in next sc, cont in Row 2 of LLSP around to first sc, dc in first sc, sl st to 3rd ch of tch, turn.

ROW 7: Ch 1, sc bet dc and tch, [sh in next sc, sc bet next 2 dc] twice, 2 dc in sc, sc bet 2 dc, cont in Row 3 of LLSP around, sl st to first sc, turn—11 (12, 13, 14, 16) sh.

ROW 8: Ch 5, sc in ch-2 sp, cont in Row 2 of LLSP across to last 3 sc, 2 dc bet next 2 dc, cont in Row 2 of LLSP around to first sc, dc in first sc, sl st to 3rd ch of tch, turn.

ROW 9: Ch 1, sc bet dc and tch, 2 sc in each ch-2 sp around, sc bet each 2 dc group around, sl st to first sc, turn.

ROW 10: Ch 1, sc in each sc around, sl st to first sc, turn.

ROW 11: Sl st to each sc around, fasten off.

Rep on other arm cuff.

Granny Motif
CONSTRUCTION

I love motifs, especially squares. I think it's because the little squares remind me of building blocks, and my engineer's mind just clicks into action. I also love the seamless look of granny motifs, such as in the Shiitake Tunic (page 90). However, the drawback of motifs is in sizing. With classic construction you can add or subtract a stitch to get the size you need, but with motifs you have to work in whole blocks—or do you? The solution lies in those handy symbols, which you can use to transform blocks into triangles, rectangles, and more. Use partial blocks to get your necklines and armholes to fit perfectly, such as in the Ruby Cropped Cardi (page 100). Another great tool is your hook. If you want waist shaping in a motif sweater, just drop a hook size, such as in the Harvest Cowl Shift (page 84). Finally, when changing hooks and making smaller motifs isn't enough, use edgings such as as in the Calypso Kimono (page 107). By the end of this chapter, I hope you'll see that motifs can be as amazing in garments as their stitch-pattern counterparts.

harvest
COWL SHIFT

Shaping doesn't have to be scary, especially when you're crocheting motif garments. For this top, shaping is as simple as changing a hook size. When you increase the hook size, the sweater widens gently. With motif patterns, if your size falls between two sizes, changing hook size to modify a garment works well.

Materials

YARN

DK Weight (#3 Light).

SHOWN: Blue Sky Alpacas Suri Merino (60% baby suri alpaca, 40% merino; 164 yd [150 m]/3.5 oz [100 g]): #415 Harvest 6 (6, 7, 8, 9) hanks.

HOOK

Size G/6 (4.0 mm), size G/7 (4.5 mm), size H/8 (5.0 mm), size I/9 (5.5 mm) or hook needed to obtain gauge.

NOTIONS

Tapestry needle for weaving in ends; spray bottle with water; straight pins for blocking; stitch markers

Gauge

Diagonally across motif trefoil to trefoil = 4" (10 cm) with size G/6 hook, 4½" (11.5 cm) with size G/7 hook, 5" (12.5 cm) with size H/8 hook, 5½" (14 cm) with size I/9 hook.

16 sc by 20 rows = 4" × 4" (10 × 10 cm) with size G/7 hook.

Finished Size

Bust measurement is 32 (36, 40, 45, 50)" (81.5 [91.5, 101.5, 114.5, 127] cm). Sized for Small (Medium, Large, X-Large, and 2X). Sweater is close-fitting. Size shown is Small.

Notes

For S size, small hook is size G/6 (4.0 mm) and large hook is size G/7 (4.5 mm). For M and XL sizes, small hook is size G/7 (4.5 mm) and large hook is size H/8 (5.0 mm). For L and 2X sizes, small hook is size H/8 (5.0 mm) and large hook is size I/9 (5.5 mm). For edging on all sizes, you'll use size G/7 (4.5 mm) and size H/8 (5.0 mm).

This jumper is designed to stretch. After you block it to the schematic's measurements, it will lengthen as you wear it.

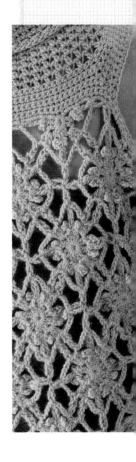

Special Stitches

TREFOIL

Ch 5, sl st in flp of first previous st, ch 7, sl st in flp of previous sl st, ch 5, sl st in flp of previous sl st, sl st in first st.

Note: To get picot to stay on top of st, sl st in flp and vertical strand of previous st at the same time.

LARGE PICOT

Ch 6, sl st in flp of previous st.

LARGE PICOT JOIN

Ch 2, sl st to adjoining motif's large picot, ch 3, sl st in flp of previous st.

SMALL PICOT

Ch 4, sl st in flp of previous st.

SMALL PICOT JOIN

Ch 1, sl st to adjoining motif's small picot, ch 2, sl st in flp of previous st.

FOUNDATION SINGLE CROCHET (FSC)

Ch 2 (does not count as fsc), insert hook in 2nd ch from hook, yo and pull up lp, yo and draw through 1 lp (the "ch"), yo and draw through 2 lps (the "fsc"), * insert hook under 2 lps of the "ch" st of last fsc , yo and pull up lp, yo and draw through 1 lp, yo and draw through 2 lps, rep from * for length of foundation.

EXTENDED SINGLE CROCHET (ESC)

Insert hook in next stitch, yo and draw up lp, yo, draw through 1 lp on hook, yo, draw through remaining 2 lps on hook.

Motifs

Flor de Elia Motif

See Flor de Elia Motif diagram. Make 1 with small hook. Join 37 (37, 37, 43, 43) with small hook. Join 24 (24, 24, 40, 40) with large hook.

Make an adjustable ring.

RND 1 (RS): Ch 4 (counts as dc, ch-1 sp), [2 dc, trefoil, 2 dc, ch 1] 3 times in ring, (2 dc, trefoil, dc), sl st to 3rd ch of tch, pull ring closed, do not turn—4 trefoils.

RND 2: Ch 3 (counts as dc), dc in 4th ch of tch, *small picot, ch 5, sc in ch-7 sp of trefoil, large picot, ch 5, small picot, 3 dc in ch-1 sp, rep from * around to last ch-1 sp, small picot, ch 5, sc in ch-7 sp of trefoil, large picot, ch 5, small picot, dc in ch-sp formed by tch, sl st to top of tch, fasten off—12 picots.

Joining

Connecting Flor de Elia Motifs

Join 37 (37, 37, 43, 43) motifs with small hook and join 24 (24, 24, 40, 40) motifs with large hook by following the directions for a flor de elia motif through Rnd 1. In Rnd 2, when next to an adjoining motif, substitute a picot join for a picot (see Diagram A), thus seamlessly connecting the two. Follow the sweater's layout diagram (page 88) for location of adjoining motifs. Note that motifs labeled A connect to adjoining A motifs at the arm opening. Note that B motifs do not connect to opposite B motifs, which means that you do not seam the front and back together at the top of the sweater. The cowl will connect the front and back panels later.

Connecting Half Motifs

Join 4 (4, 4, 4, 4) with small hook. Join 8 (8, 8, 10, 10) with large hook. Follow Diagram B and the sweater layout diagrams (page 88) for location of adjoining motifs.

Make an adjustable ring.

ROW 1 (WS): Ch 10 (counts as dc, ch-7 sp), sl st to 7th ch from hook, ch 5, sl st to flp of previous sl st, (2 dc, ch 1, 2 dc, trefoil) in ring, (2 dc, ch 1, 3 dc) in ring, ch 5, sl st to flp of previous st, ch 3, tr in top of previous dc, pull ring closed, turn—10 dc.

ROW 2: Ch 1, sc in tr, large picot join, *ch 5, small picot join, 3 dc in ch-1 sp, small picot join, ch 5, sc in ch-7 sp of trefoil, large picot join, rep from * once more, fasten off—7 picots.

Joining Quarter Motifs

See Diagram C. Join 0 (0, 0, 4, 4) with small hook.

Make an adjustable ring.

ROW 1 (WS): Ch 10 (counts as dc, ch-7 sp), sl st to 7th ch from hook, ch 5, sl st to flp of previous sl st, (2 dc, ch 1, 3 dc) in ring, ch 5, sl st to flp of previous st, ch 3, tr in top of previous dc, pull ring closed, turn—6 dc.

ROW 2: Ch 1, sc in tr, large picot join, ch 5, small picot join, 3 dc in ch-1 sp, small picot join, ch 5, sc in ch-7 sp of trefoil, large picot join, fasten off—4 picots.

Finishing

BLOCKING

Pin to schematic measurements and spray with water. Allow to dry.

COLLAR EDGING

Join yarn with size G/7 hook to back panel upper edge with sl st on RS. See Diagram D.

RND 1 (RS): Ch 1, sc across top edge (around row ends of half motifs) to opposite side (end with an even number of sts), 36 (36, 36, 28, 28) fsc (forms arm strap), sc across top edge of front panel (end with an even number of sts), 36 (36, 36, 28, 28) fsc, sl st to first sc, turn. Place stitch marker at the first and last sc of each arm strap.

RND 2: Ch 1, *sc in each sc to m, sc2tog over next 2 sc, move marker to sc2tog, rep from * around, sl st to first sc, turn.

RNDS 3–8: Rep Rnd 2 of Collar Edging 6 more times. Change to size H/8 hook.

RND 9: Ch 3 (counts as esc, ch-1 sp), *sk 1 sc, esc in next sc, ch 1, rep from * around, sl st to 2nd ch of tch, do not turn.

RND 10: Ch 3 (counts as esc, ch-1 sp), *esc in next esc, sk ch-1 sp, ch 1, rep from * around, sl st to 2nd ch of tch, do not turn.

Rep Rnd 10 until collar measures 8" (20.5 cm), fasten off.

To block cowl neck, submerge in cool water. Towel dry and pin to size. Allow to dry. The cowl will be very soft with lots of drape.

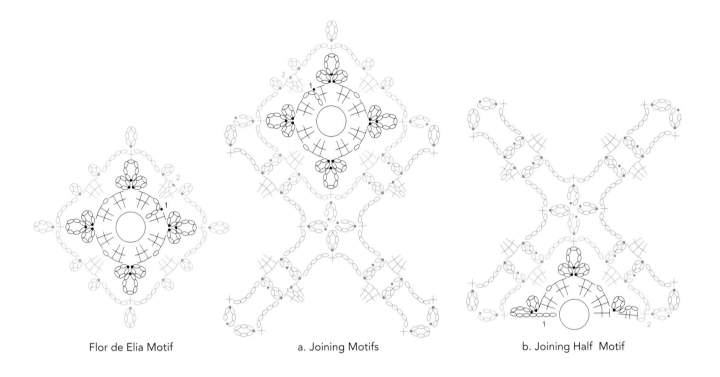

Flor de Elia Motif

a. Joining Motifs

b. Joining Half Motif

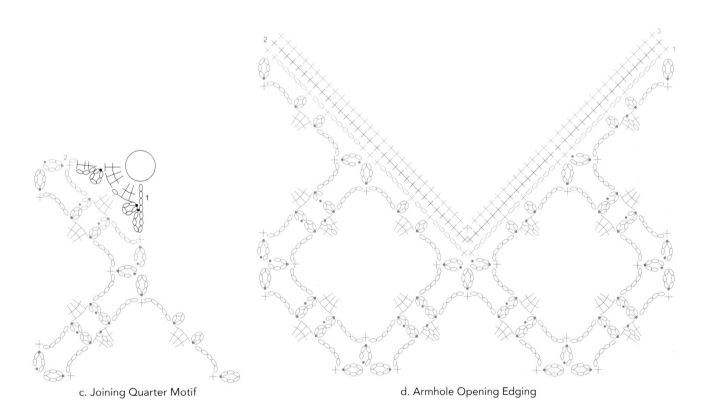

c. Joining Quarter Motif

d. Armhole Opening Edging

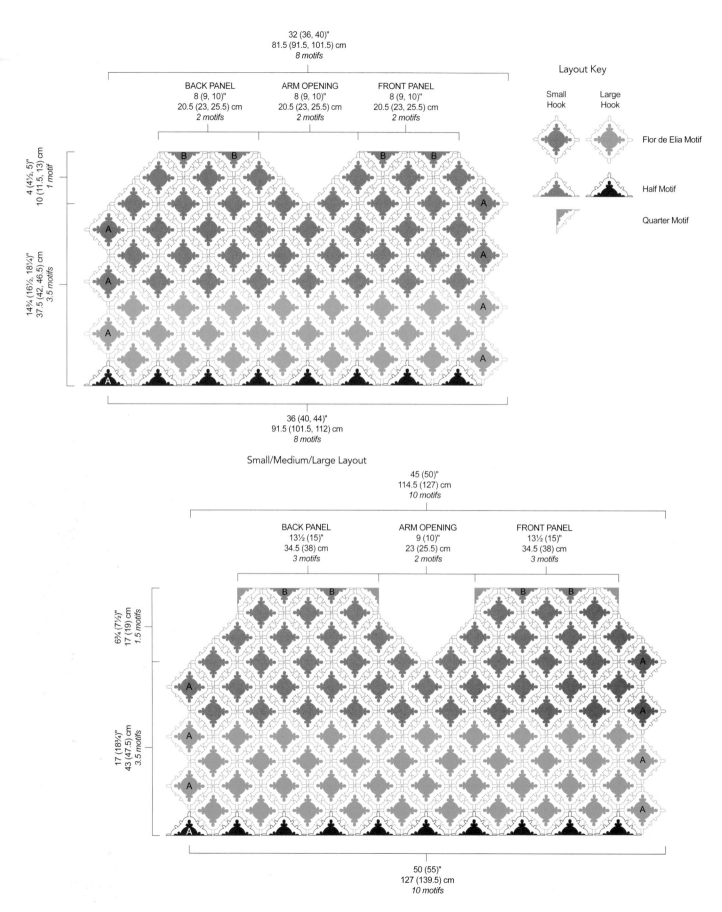

32 (36, 40)"
81.5 (91.5, 101.5) cm
8 motifs

BACK PANEL
8 (9, 10)"
20.5 (23, 25.5) cm
2 motifs

ARM OPENING
8 (9, 10)"
20.5 (23, 25.5) cm
2 motifs

FRONT PANEL
8 (9, 10)"
20.5 (23, 25.5) cm
2 motifs

Layout Key

Small Hook

Large Hook

Flor de Elia Motif

Half Motif

Quarter Motif

4 (4½, 5)"
10 (11.5, 13) cm
1 motif

14¾ (16½, 18¼)"
37.5 (42, 46.5) cm
3.5 motifs

36 (40, 44)"
91.5 (101.5, 112) cm
8 motifs

Small/Medium/Large Layout

45 (50)"
114.5 (127) cm
10 motifs

BACK PANEL
13½ (15)"
34.5 (38) cm
3 motifs

ARM OPENING
9 (10)"
23 (25.5) cm
2 motifs

FRONT PANEL
13½ (15)"
34.5 (38) cm
3 motifs

6¾ (7½)"
17 (19) cm
1.5 motifs

17 (18¾)"
43 (47.5) cm
3.5 motifs

50 (55)"
127 (139.5) cm
10 motifs

X-Large/2X Layout

SLEEVE EDGING

Join yarn with size G/7 hook to armhole edge with sl st on RS.

RND 1 (RS): Ch 1, **(XL, 2X)** sc evenly down quarter motif edge, **(ALL)** *2 sc in large picot, ch 5, sc in small picot, ch 2, sc in small picot, ch 5, sc in large picot, rep from * to bottom of valley of armhole opening, **sc in next large picot, ch 5, sc in small picot, ch 2, sc in small picot, ch 5, 2 sc in next large picot, rep from ** once, **(XL, 2X)** sc evenly up quarter motif, turn.

RND 2: Sl st in first st, sc in each sc, 5 sc in each ch-5 sp, 2 sc in each ch-2 sp, sk 2 sc at valley of armhole opening, sl st in last st, turn.

RND 3: Sl st in first st, sc in each sc to valley, sc4tog over middle 4 sc, sc in each sc to last, sl st to last sc, fasten off.

BOTTOM EDGING

Join yarn with size G/7 hook to back panel bottom edge with sl st on RS.

RND 1 (RS): Ch 1, sc evenly across bottom edge (around row ends of half motifs), sl st to first sc, turn.

RNDS 2–3: Ch 1, sc in each sc around, fasten off.

Stretch Happens

No one wants to admit to unwanted stretch in garments, but it's a common occurrence—especially in lacy crochet projects. Lace is delicate and crochet is heavy; the resulting stretch is predictable. What can you do? In the case of this cowled shift, you can go with it. It was designed to stretch. The degree of stretch varies with the yarn blend and natural weight of the fiber. Therefore, if you crochet this tunic with a lighter-weight yarn (for example, with acrylic, which weighs less than alpaca), the yarn, and therefore your sweater, won't stretch as much. Although this sweater will look cute either way, you'll need to swatch with your yarn to know in advance how much it will stretch. Try swatching four of the motifs, then join them together and block them. Hang the swatch from a clothes hanger with clothespins, add clothespins to the bottom, and let it hang overnight. If it stretches significantly, then the yarn will give you a long slinky tunic; if it doesn't stretch, the yarn will give you a shorter, more flowing tunic. Either way, you'll know what to expect.

shiitake
TUNIC

If you're new to crocheting garments but you're a fan of doilies, the Shiitake Tunic is a great first project. The main motif may look complex but it's made up of basic stitches, and there's no shaping. The project lets beginner garment makers test their crochet skills—and it's still challenging enough to grow them.

Materials

YARN

Sportweight (#2 Fine).

SHOWN: Blue Sky Alpacas Spud and Chloe Fine (80% superwash wool 20% silk; 248 yd [227 m]/2.29 oz [65 g]): #7814 Shiitake, 5 (5, 6, 6, 8, 8) hanks.

HOOK

Size E/4 (3.5 mm) for X-Small, Medium, and X-Large sizes, size G/6 (4.0 mm) for Small, Large, and 2X sizes, or hook needed to obtain gauge.

NOTIONS

Tapestry needle for weaving in ends; spray bottle with water; straight pins for blocking; stitch markers.

Gauge

Dimension across snowflake trefoil to trefoil = 4" (10 cm) with smaller hook, 4½" (11.5 cm) with larger hook.

Finished Size

Bust measurement is 32 (36, 40, 45, 48, 54)" (81.5 [91.5, 101.5, 114.5, 122, 137] cm). Sized as X-Small (Small, Medium, Large, X-Large, 2X). Sweater fit is relaxed. Size shown is Small.

Notes

Use small hook for XS, M, and XL sizes; use large hook for S, L, and 2X sizes. Construct tunic by connecting all the snowflakes first, then fill in each void with a joining motif. After all the motifs are connected, block before finishing. Tunic opens in front. One size can accommodate many, depending on how far you overlap the tunic fronts.

Special Stitches

TREFOIL

Ch 3, sl st in flp of previous st, [ch 3, sl st in flp of previous sl st] 2 times, sl st in first st.

Note: To get picot to stay on top of stitch, sl st in flp and vertical strand of previous st at the same time.

TREFOIL JOIN

Ch 3, sl st in flp of previous st, ch 1, sl st to adjoining motif's trefoil, ch 1, sl st in flp of previous sl st, ch 3, sl st in flp of previous sl st, sl st in first st.

DOUBLE PICOT

Ch 4, sl st in flp of previous st, ch 4, sl st in flp of prev sl st.

Motifs

MAGAIRLIN SNOWFLAKE

See Magairlin Snowflake diagram (page 92).

Make 1. Join 47 (43, 52, 47, 77, 71).

Make an adjustable ring with MC.

RND 1 (RS): Ch 2 (counts as hdc), 23 hdc in ring, pull ring closed, sl st to top of tch, do not turn—24 hdc.

RND 2: Ch 1, sc in top of tch, *ch 3, sk 2 hdc, sc in next hdc, rep from * around to last 2 hdc, ch 3, sl st to first sc, do not turn—8 ch-3 sps.

RND 3: Ch 1, (sc, hdc, dc, trefoil, dc, hdc, sc) in each ch-3 sp around, sl st to first sc, do not turn—8 trefoil.

RND 4: Ch 1, sc in sl st, *ch 5, sk 1st ch-3 sp of trefoil, sc in 2nd ch-3 sp of trefoil, ch 5, sc bet next 2 sc, rep from * around, sl st to first sc, do not turn—16 ch-5 sps.

RND 5: Ch 1, *6 sc in next ch-5 sp, trefoil, 6 sc in next ch-5 sp, rep from * around, sl st to first sc, fasten off—8 trefoil.

Magairlin Snowflake

HALF SNOWFLAKE

See Diagram B (page 94). Join 0 (0, 14, 14, 0, 0).

Make an adjustable ring with MC.

RND 1 (RS): Ch 2 (counts as hdc), 12 hdc in ring, pull ring closed, turn—13 hdc.

RND 2: Ch 1, sc in first hdc, *ch 3, sk 2 hdc, sc in next hdc, rep from * around, turn—4 ch-3 sps.

RND 3: Ch 1, (sc, hdc, dc, trefoil, dc, hdc, sc) in each ch-3 sp around, turn—4 trefoil.

RND 4: Ch 1, sc in first sc, *ch 5, sk 1st ch-3 sp of trefoil, sc in 2nd ch-3 sp of trefoil, ch 5, sc bet next 2 sc, rep from * around, sc in last sc, turn—8 ch-5 sps.

RND 5: Ch 1, *6 sc in next ch-5 sp, trefoil, 6 sc in next ch-5 sp, rep from * around, fasten off—4 trefoil.

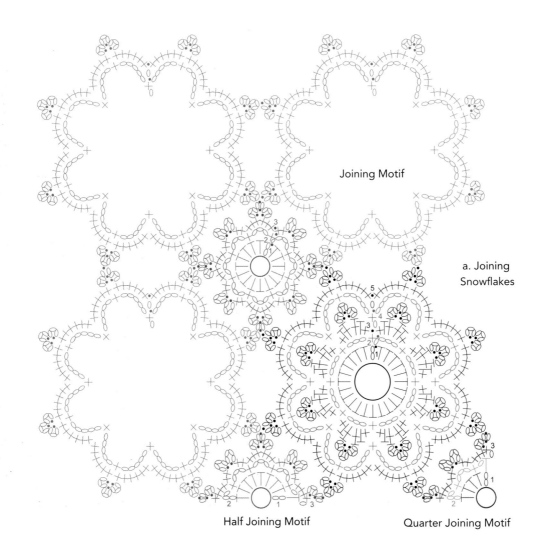

Joining Motif

a. Joining Snowflakes

Half Joining Motif

Quarter Joining Motif

Joining

Connecting Snowflakes

Join 47 (43, 52, 47, 77, 71) snowflakes by following the directions for a Magairlin Snowflake through Rnd 4. In Rnd 5, substitute a trefoil join for a trefoil (see Diagram A) when next to an adjoining snowflake, thus seamlessly connecting the two. Follow the tunic layout diagrams (pages 96–98) for the location of adjoining snowflakes. Note that front-panel A snowflakes connect to adjoining back-panel A snowflakes, and front-panel B snowflakes connect to adjoining back-panel B snowflakes. However, also note that C snowflakes do not connect to the opposite C snowflakes across the front-panel opening. (Do not seam up the tunic's front opening.)

Connecting Half Snowflakes

Join 0 (0, 14, 14, 0, 0) half snowflakes by following the directions for a half snowflake through Rnd 4. In Rnd 5, substitute a trefoil join for a trefoil (see Diagram A) when next to an adjoining snowflake, thus seamlessly connecting the two. Follow the tunic layout diagrams for the location of adjoining snowflakes.

JOINING MOTIFS

After connecting all the snowflakes, fill in each void with a joining motif. See the Tunic Layout diagram (pages 96–98) for the location of each motif. See Diagram A.

Join 30 (26, 48, 42, 57, 50).

Make an adjustable ring with CC.

RND 1 (RS): Ch 2 (counts as hdc), 15 hdc in ring, pull ring closed, do not turn—16 hdc.

RND 2: Ch 1, sc in top of tch, *ch 3, sk 1 hdc, sc in next hdc, rep from * around to last hdc, ch 3, sl st to first sc, do not turn—8 ch-3 sps.

RND 3: Ch 1, *(3 sc, trefoil join, 3 sc) in next ch-3 sp, (2 sc, double picot, 2 sc) in next ch-3 sp, rep from * around, fasten off—4 trefoil.

HALF JOINING MOTIFS

See Diagram A. Join 29 (25, 18, 16, 35, 33).

Make an adjustable ring with CC.

RND 1 (RS): Ch 2 (counts as hdc), 8 hdc in ring, pull ring closed, turn—9 hdc.

RND 2: Ch 3 (counts as hdc, ch-1 sp), sk first hdc, sc in next hdc, *ch 3, sk 1 hdc, sc in next hdc, rep from * around to tch, ch 1, hdc in top of tch, turn—5 ch-sps.

RND 3: Ch 1, sc in hdc, ch 1, sl st to adjoining motif's trefoil, ch 1, sl st to flp of previous sc, ch 3, sl st in flp of previous sl st, 3 sc in ch-1 sp, (2 sc, double picot, 2 sc) in next ch-3 sp, (3 sc, trefoil join, 3 sc) in next ch-3 sp, (2 sc, double picot, 2 sc) in next ch-3 sp, 3 sc in last ch-sp, ch 3, sl st in flp of previous sc,

ch 1, sl st to adjoining motif's trefoil, ch 1, sl st to flp of previous sl st, sc in 2nd ch of tch, fasten off—3 trefoil.

QUARTER JOINING MOTIFS

See Diagram A. Join 6 (6, 4, 4, 6, 6).

Make an adjustable ring with CC.

RND 1 (RS): Ch 2 (counts as hdc), 4 hdc in ring, pull ring closed, turn—5 hdc.

RND 2: Ch 3 (counts as hdc, ch-1 sp), sk first hdc, sc in next hdc, ch 3, sk 1 hdc, sc in next hdc, ch 1, hdc in top of tch, turn—3 ch-sps.

RND 3: Ch 1, sc in hdc, ch 1, sl st to adjoining motif's trefoil, ch 1, sl st to flp of previous sc, ch 3, sl st in flp of previous sl st, 3 sc in ch-1 sp, (2 sc, double picot, 2 sc) in next ch-3 sp, 3 sc in last ch-sp, ch 3, sl st in flp of previous sc, ch 1, sl st to adjoining motif's trefoil, ch 1, sl st to flp of previous sl st, sc in 2nd ch of tch, fasten off—2 trefoil.

b. Half Snowflake

c. Open Joining Motif

Back Panel

Front Panel

OPEN-JOINING MOTIFS

Note: Open-joining motifs are used at the side opening on the bottom seam (for all sizes) and arm openings (for S, L, 2X) for more room to move. Make sure you connect motifs to both front and back panel snowflakes. See Diagram C.

Join 2 (4, 2, 4, 2, 4).

Make an adjustable ring with CC.

RND 1 (RS): Ch 2 (counts as hdc), 16 hdc in ring, pull ring closed, turn—17 hdc.

RND 2: Ch 3 (counts as hdc, ch-1 sp), sk first hdc, sc in next hdc, *ch 3, sk 1 hdc, sc in next hdc, rep from * around to tch, ch 1, hdc in top of tch, turn—9 ch-sps.

RND 3: Ch 1, sc in hdc, ch 1, sl st to adjoining motif's trefoil, ch 1, sl st to flp of previous sc, ch 3, sl st in flp of previous sl st, 3 sc in ch-1 sp, *(2 sc, double picot, 2 sc) in next ch-3 sp, (3 sc, trefoil join, 3 sc) in next ch-3 sp, rep from * to last ch-3 sp, (2 sc, double picot, 2 sc) in last ch-3 sp, 3 sc in last ch-sp, ch 3, sl st in flp of previous sc, ch 1, sl st to adjoining motif's trefoil, ch 1, sl st to flp of previous sl st, sc in 2nd ch of tch, fasten off—5 trefoil.

Finishing

BLOCKING

Pin to schematic measurements and spray with water. Allow to dry.

SLEEVE EDGING

Join MC with sl st to RS of back panel at any trefoil after joining motif.

RND 1 (RS): Ch 1, sc in same trefoil, *ch 8, sc in next trefoil, sc evenly across edge of joining motif, sc in next trefoil, rep from * around, sl st to first sc, do not turn.

RND 2: Ch 1, 8 sc in each ch-8 sp, sc in each sc around, sl st to first sc, do not turn.

RND 3: Sl st in each sc around, fasten off.

XS (S, XL, 2X) BOTTOM AND COLLAR EDGING

Join MC with sl st to RS of back panel at any trefoil after joining motif. Place m at center back neck and at top of hip opening at side seam.

RND 1 (RS): Ch 1, sc in same trefoil, *ch 8, sc in next trefoil, sc evenly across edge of joining motif, sc in next trefoil, rep from * around, placing 3 sc in adjustable ring of each quarter joining motif, place m in center sc, sl st to first sc, do not turn.

RND 2: Ch 1, 8 sc in each ch-8 sp, sc in each sc around to m. Before both back neck and hip opening markers, sc3tog over st before m and next 2 sts, place m. At quarter motif m, 3 sc in marked st, place m in center sc. Sl st to first sc, do not turn.

RNDS 3–4: Ch 1, sc in each sc around to m. Before both back neck and hip opening m, sc3tog over st before m and next 2 sts, place m. At quarter motif m, 3 sc in marked st, place m in center sc. Sl st to first sc, do not turn.

RND 5: Sl st in each sc around, fasten off.

Pin tunic closed with shawl pin or belt.

M (L) BOTTOM AND COLLAR EDGING

Join MC with sl st to RS of back panel at any trefoil after joining motif. Place m at center back neck and at top of hip opening at side seam.

RND 1 (RS): Ch 1, sc in same trefoil, *ch 8, sc in next trefoil, sc evenly across edge of joining motif, sc in next trefoil, rep from * around to front panel placing 3 sc in adjustable ring of each quarter joining motif, place m in center sc, **sc evenly across half snowflake, ch 4; rep from ** around front panel opening; rep from * around bottom edge, sl st to first sc, do not turn.

RND 2: Ch 1, 8 sc in each ch-8 sp, 4 sc in ea ch-4 sp, sc in each sc around to m. Before both back neck and hip opening markers, sc3tog over st before m and next 2 sts, place m. At quarter motif m, 3 sc in marked st, place m in center sc. Sl st to first sc, do not turn.

RNDS 3–5: Rep Rnds 3–5 of XS (S, XL, 2X) bottom and collar edging.

Layout Key

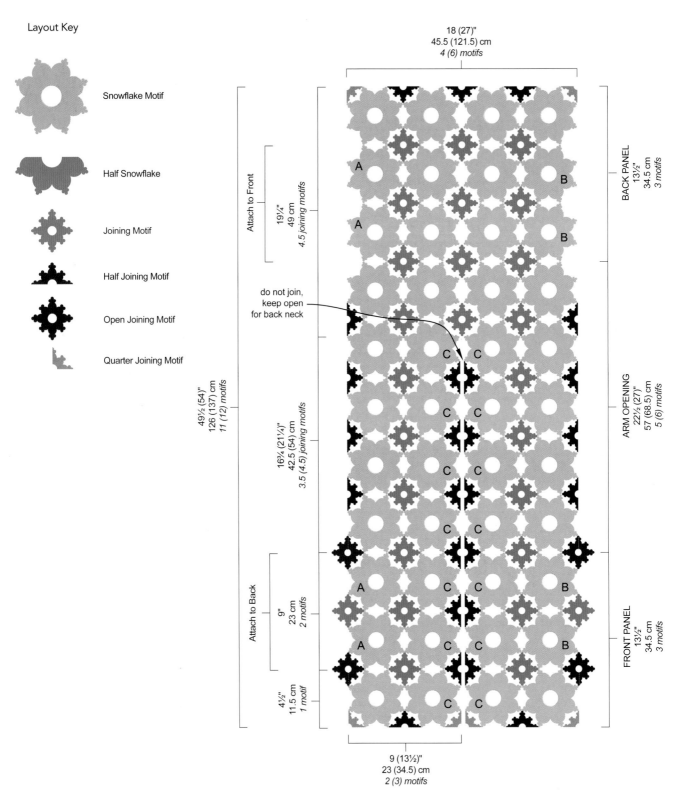

Snowflake Motif

Half Snowflake

Joining Motif

Half Joining Motif

Open Joining Motif

Quarter Joining Motif

18 (27)"
45.5 (121.5) cm
4 (6) motifs

Attach to Front

19¼"
49 cm
4.5 joining motifs

BACK PANEL
13½"
34.5 cm
3 motifs

do not join,
keep open
for back neck

ARM OPENING
22½ (27)"
57 (68.5) cm
5 (6) motifs

49½ (54)"
126 (137) cm
11 (12) motifs

16¾ (21¼)"
42.5 (54) cm
3.5 (4.5) joining motifs

Attach to Back

9"
23 cm
2 motifs

FRONT PANEL
13½"
34.5 cm
3 motifs

4½"
11.5 cm
1 motif

9 (13½)"
23 (34.5) cm
2 (3) motifs

Small/2X Layout

16 (24)"
40.5 (61) cm
4 (6) motifs

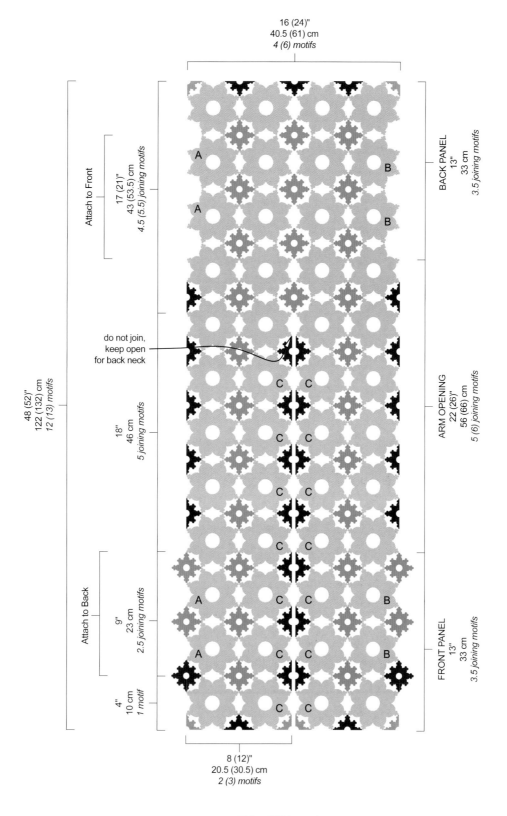

Attach to Front

17 (21)"
43 (53.5) cm
4.5 (5.5) joining motifs

BACK PANEL
13"
33 cm
3.5 joining motifs

A

A

B

B

do not join,
keep open
for back neck

18"
46 cm
5 joining motifs

ARM OPENING
22 (26)"
56 (66) cm
5 (6) joining motifs

C   C

C   C

C   C

C   C

48 (52)"
122 (132) cm
12 (13) motifs

Attach to Back

9"
23 cm
2.5 joining motifs

A   C   C   B

A   C   C   B

FRONT PANEL
13"
33 cm
3.5 joining motifs

4"
10 cm
1 motif

C   C

8 (12)"
20.5 (30.5) cm
2 (3) motifs

X-Small/X-Large Layout

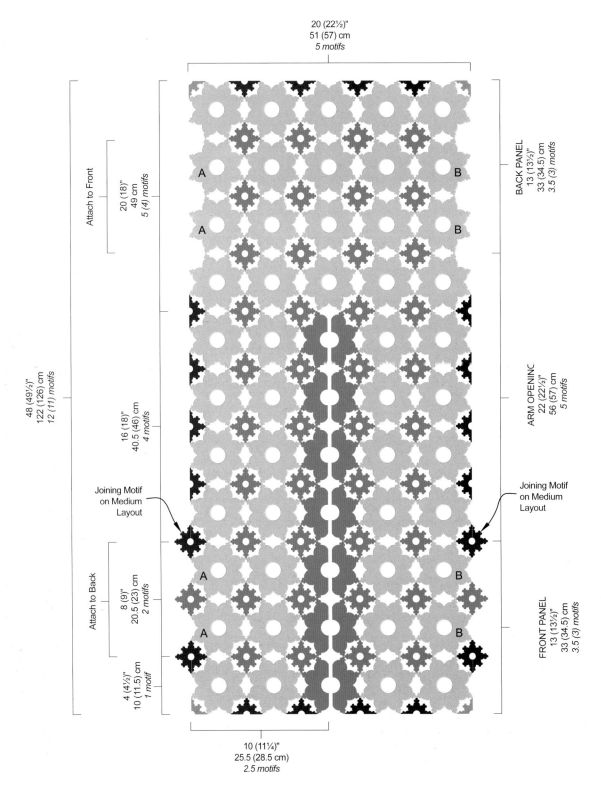

20 (22½)"
51 (57) cm
5 motifs

Attach to Front

20 (18)"
49 cm
5 (4) motifs

48 (49½)"
122 (126) cm
12 (11) motifs

16 (18)"
40.5 (46) cm
4 motifs

Joining Motif
on Medium
Layout

Attach to Back

8 (9)"
20.5 (23) cm
2 motifs

4 (4½)"
10 (11.5) cm
1 motif

A
A

A

A

B
B

B

B

BACK PANEL
13 (13½)"
33 (34.5) cm
3.5 (3) motifs

ARM OPENING
22 (22½)"
56 (57) cm
5 motifs

Joining Motif
on Medium
Layout

FRONT PANEL
13 (13½)"
33 (34.5) cm
3.5 (3) motifs

10 (11¼)"
25.5 (28.5 cm)
2.5 motifs

Medium/Large Layout

Layout Key

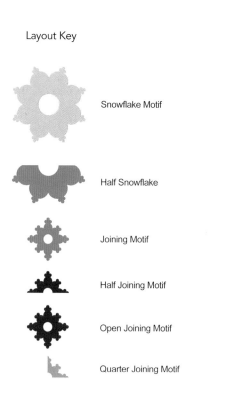

Snowflake Motif

Half Snowflake

Joining Motif

Half Joining Motif

Open Joining Motif

Quarter Joining Motif

Seams to Me...

The beauty of this project is that the fabric looks seamless. Here's the good news: achieving that look is really quite simple in a motif project with chain spaces in the last round. It's as easy as using a slip stitch instead of a chain. In crochet, chains and slip stitches are actually the same stitch, with the latter being connected to something and the former being worked "in the air." Switching a slip stitch for a chain lets you connect adjoining motifs without pausing or adding any bulk. Because a slip stitch and a chain look exactly the same, your project becomes seamless since there will be no ugly seam lines marring the beautiful fabric.

ruby
CROPPED CARDI

This cardigan is perfect for spring when you need just a little cover over your favorite light dress. The motifs are connected while you crochet for a seamless look. The waistband cinches in while the collar can be adjusted to your V-neck depth preference.

Designed by MARLIANA BIRD

Materials

YARN

Sportweight (#3 light).

SHOWN: Bijou Basin Ranch Bijou Spun Lhasa Wilderness (75% yak, 25% bamboo; 180 yd [165 m]/2 oz [56 g]): Ruby (MC), 3 (4, 5, 6) balls.

HOOK

Size H/8 (5 mm) and size F/5 (3.75 mm) or hook needed to obtain gauge.

NOTIONS

Tapestry needle for weaving in ends; five ⅝" (1.5 cm) diameter buttons; spray bottle with water; straight pins for blocking

Gauge

4" × 4" (10 × 10 cm) = motif with larger hook.

3" × 3" (7.5 × 7.5 cm) = motif with smaller hook.

Finished Size

Bust measurement is 32–34 (36–38, 42–44, 48–50)" (81.5–86.5 [91.5–96.5, 106.5–112, 122–127] cm). Sized for Small, (Medium, Large, X-Large). Size shown is Small with negative ease.

Notes

Work motifs for Small and Large sizes with the smaller hook. Work Medium and X-Large sizes with the larger hook. Work the first motif completely, then join the following motifs on the last round.

Special Stitches

SHELL (SH)

Work (sc, hdc, 3 dc, hdc, sc) in st indicated.

CH-5 JOIN

Ch 2, sl st to adjoining motif's ch-5 sp, ch 2.

DC JOIN

Dc in same ch-sp, sl st to center dc on adjoining motif's corner shell.

Castaneda Motif

See Castenada motif diagram (page 102) for assistance.

Make 1. Make an adjustable ring.

RND 1 (RS): Ch 1, 12 sc in ring, sl st in first sc, pull ring closed, do not turn—12 sc.

RND 2: Ch 1, sc in 1st sc, *ch 5, sk 2 sc, sc in next sc; rep from * around, ch 5, sl st in first sc, do not turn—4 ch-5 sps.

RND 3: Ch 1, sh in each ch-5 sp around, sl st in first sc, do not turn.

RND 4: Ch 1, sc in first sc, *ch 3, sk 2 sts, sc in next dc, ch 3, sk 2 sts, sc in next sc, ch 5, sc in next sc; rep from * around omitting last ch 5 and sc, ch 2, dc in first sc (counts as ch-5 sp), do not turn—12 ch-sps.

RND 5: Ch 3 (counts as dc), (dc, hdc, sc) around post of dc, *ch 3, sc in next ch-3 sp, ch 5, sc in next ch-3 sp, ch 3, sh in next ch-5 sp; rep from * around omitting last sh, (sc, hdc, dc) in last ch-sp, sl st to top of tch, fasten off, weave in ends.

Joining

Connecting Castaneda Motifs

Join 39 (43, 39, 43) motifs by following the directions for a Castaneda motif through Rnd 4. In Rnd 5, when next to an adjoining motif, substitute a CH-5 JOIN for a ch-5 and substitute a DC JOIN for the center dc in the corner shell (see Diagram A on page 102), thus seamlessly connecting the two. When

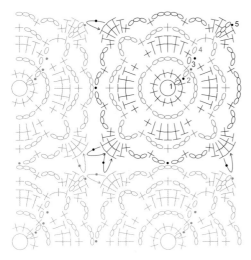

a. Joining Motifs

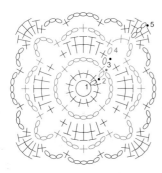

Castaneda Motif

RND 2: Ch 1, sc in 1st sc, *ch 5, sk 2 sc, sc in next sc; rep from * one more time, turn—2 ch-5 sps.

RND 3: Ch 1, sh in each ch-5 sp around, sl st in first sc, turn.

RND 4: Ch 7, sc in first sc, ch 3, sk 2 sts, sc in next dc, ch 3, sk 2 sts, sc in next sc, ch 5, sc in next sc, ch 3, sk 2 sts, sc in next dc, ch 3, sk 2 sts, sc in next sc, ch 2, trtr in last sc on Rnd 2—7 ch-sps.

RND 5: Ch 3 (counts as dc), sl st to center dc on adjoining motif's corner sh, (dc, hdc, sc) in ch-2 sp, ch 3, sc in next ch-3 sp, ch-5 join, sc in next ch-3 sp, ch 3, (sc, hdc, dc join, dc join, dc, hdc, sc) in next ch-5 sp, ch 3, sc in next ch-3 sp, ch-5 join, sc in next ch-3 sp, ch 3, (sc, hdc, dc join, dc) in ch-7 sp, fasten off.

Connecting Half Motifs

Join 0 (14, 0, 14). Follow the sweater layout diagrams (pages 104–105) for the location of adjoining motifs. See Diagram C for assistance.

Make an adjustable ring.

RND 1 (RS): Ch 1, 8 sc in ring, turn—8 sc.

RND 2: Ch 1, sc in first sc, ch 2, sk 1 sc, sc in next sc, ch 5, sk 2 sc, sc in next sc, ch 2, sk 1 sc, sc in last sc, turn—3 ch-sps.

RND 3: Ch 3 (counts as dc), (dc, hdc, sc) in ch-2 sp, sh in next ch-5 sp, (sc, hdc, dc) in last ch-2 sp, dc in last sc, turn.

RND 4: Ch 1, sc in first dc, ch 3, sk 2 sts, sc in next sc, ch 5, sc in next sc, ch 3, sk 2 sts, sc in next dc, ch 3, sk 2 sts, sc in next sc, ch 5, sc in next sc, ch 3, sc in top of tch—6 ch-sps.

RND 5: Ch 4 (or ch 1, sl st to adjoining motif's ch-sp, ch 2), sc in next ch-3 sp, ch 3, (sc, hdc, dc, dc join, dc, hdc, sc) in next ch-5 sp, ch 3, sc in next ch-3 sp, ch-5 join, sc in next ch-3 sp, ch 3, (sc, hdc, dc, dc join, dc, hdc, sc) in next ch-5 sp, ch 3, sc in next ch-3 sp, ch 4 (or ch 2, sl st to adjoining motif, ch 1), sl st to last sc, fasten off.

Connecting Quarter Motifs

Join 0 (2, 0, 2). Follow the sweater layout diagrams (pages 104–105) for the location of adjoining motifs. See Diagram C for assistance.

Make an adjustable ring.

RND 1 (RS): Ch 1, 5 sc in ring, turn—5 sc.

RND 2: Ch 1, sc in first sc, ch 2, sk 1 sc, sc in next sc, ch 2, sk 1 sc, sc in last sc, turn—2 ch-sps.

RND 3: Ch 3 (counts as dc), (dc, hdc, sc) in ch-2 sp, (sc, hdc, dc) in last ch-2 sp, dc in last sc, turn.

RND 4: Ch 1, sc in first dc, ch 3, sk 2 sts, sc in next sc, ch 5, sc in next sc, ch 3, sk 2 sts, sc in top of tch—3 ch-sps.

RND 5: Ch 1, sl st to adjoining motif's ch-sp, ch 2, sc in next ch-3 sp, ch 3, (sc, hdc, dc join, dc join, dc, hdc, sc) in next ch-5 sp, ch 3, sc in next ch-3 sp, ch 2, sl st to adjoining motif, ch 1, sl st to last sc, fasten off.

connecting three motifs together at once, substitute a DC JOIN for the first and second dc in the corner shell. Follow the sweater's layout diagrams (pages 104–105) for the location of adjoining motifs. Note that motifs labeled A connect to adjoining A motifs at the underside of the arm. B motifs connect to B motifs, and C motifs connect to C motifs on the side seam. See Diagram A (above) for assistance.

Connecting Triangle Motifs

Join 2 (0, 2, 0). Follow the sweater layout diagrams (pages 104–105) for the location of adjoining motifs. See Diagram B for assistance.

Make an adjustable ring.

RND 1 (RS): Ch 1, 7 sc in ring, turn—7 sc.

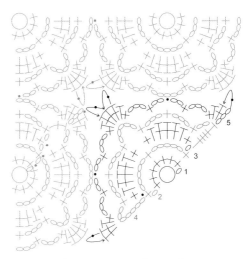

b. Joining Triangle Motif

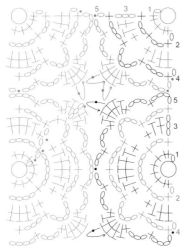

c. Joining Half and Quarter Motifs

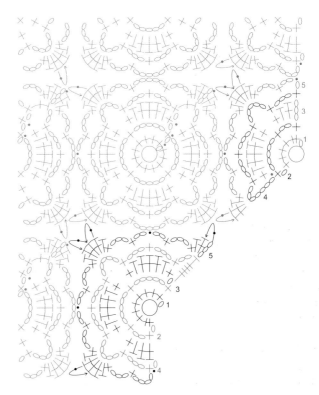

d. Joining Neck and Partial Motifs

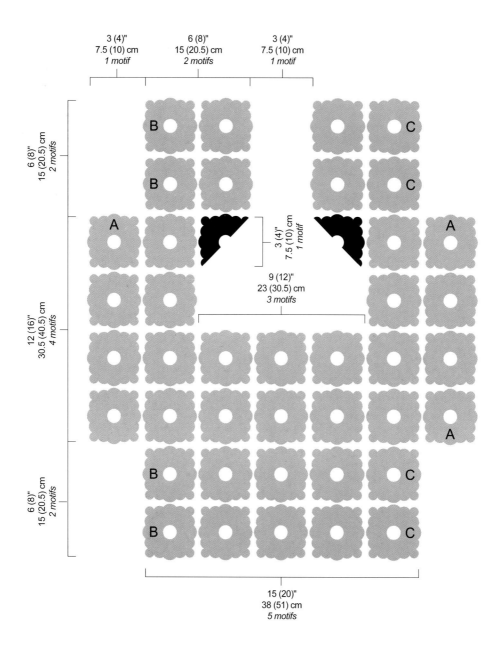

3 (4)"
7.5 (10) cm
1 motif

6 (8)"
15 (20.5) cm
2 motifs

3 (4)"
7.5 (10) cm
1 motif

6 (8)"
15 (20.5) cm
2 motifs

B

B

A

C

C

A

3 (4)"
7.5 (10) cm
1 motif

9 (12)"
23 (30.5) cm
3 motifs

12 (16)"
30.5 (40.5) cm
4 motifs

A

A

6 (8)"
15 (20.5) cm
2 motifs

B

B

C

C

15 (20)"
38 (51) cm
5 motifs

Small/Large Layout

Connecting Neck Motifs

Join 0 (2, 0, 2). Follow the sweater layout diagrams for the location of adjoining motifs. See Diagram D (page 103) for assistance.

Make an adjustable ring.

RND 1 (RS): Ch 1, 9 sc in ring, turn—9 sc.

RND 2: Ch 1, sc in first sc, ch 2, sk 1 sc, *sc in next sc, ch 5, sk 2 sc; rep from * once more, sc in last sc, turn—3 ch-sps.

RND 3: Ch 1, sh in next 2 ch-5 sp, (sc, hdc, dc) in last ch-2 sp, dc in last sc, turn.

RND 4: Ch 1, sc in first dc, ch 3, sk 2 sts, *sc in next sc, ch 5, sc in next sc, ch 3, sk 2 sts, sc in next dc, ch 3, sk 2 sts; rep from * once, sc in next sc, ch 2, trtr in sc in Rnd 2—8 ch-sps.

RND 5: Ch 3 (counts as dc), sl st to center dc of adjoining motif, (dc, hdc, sc) in ch-2 sp, *ch 3, sc in next ch-3 sp, ch-5 join, sc in next ch-3 sp, ch 3, (sc, hdc, dc join, dc join, dc, hdc, sc) in next ch-5 sp, ch 3, sc in next ch-3 sp, ch-5 join, sc in next ch-3 sp, ch

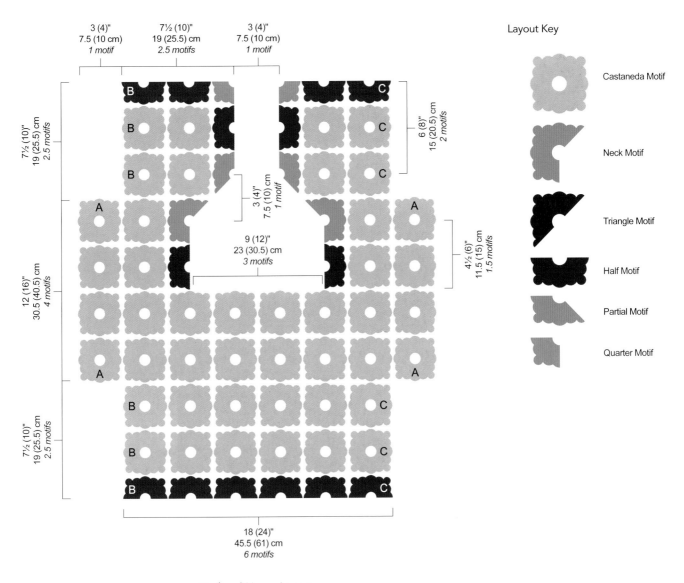

Layout Key

Castaneda Motif

Neck Motif

Triangle Motif

Half Motif

Partial Motif

Quarter Motif

3 (4)"
7.5 (10 cm)
1 motif

7½ (10)"
19 (25.5) cm
2.5 motifs

3 (4)"
7.5 (10 cm)
1 motif

7½ (10)"
19 (25.5) cm
2.5 motifs

6 (8)"
15 (20.5) cm
2 motifs

3 (4)"
7.5 (10) cm
1 motif

9 (12)"
23 (30.5) cm
3 motifs

4½ (6)"
11.5 (15) cm
1.5 motifs

12 (16)"
30.5 (40.5) cm
4 motifs

7½ (10)"
19 (25.5) cm
2.5 motifs

18 (24)"
45.5 (61) cm
6 motifs

Medium/X-Large Layout

3, (sc, hdc, dc join, dc, hdc, sc) in next ch-5 sp, ch 3, sc in next ch-3 sp, ch 4 (or ch 2, sl st to adjoining motif, ch 1), sl st to last sc, fasten off.

Connecting Partial Motifs

Join 0 (2, 0, 2). Follow the sweater layout diagrams for the location of adjoining motifs. See Diagram D for assistance.

Make an adjustable ring.

RND 1 (RS): Ch 1, 6 sc in ring, turn—6 sc.

RND 2: Ch 1, sc in first sc, ch 5, sk 2 sc, sc in next sc, ch 2, sk 1 sc, sc in last sc, turn—2 ch-sps.

RND 3: Ch 3 (counts as dc), (dc, hdc, sc) in ch-2 sp, sh in next ch-5 sp, sl st in last sc, turn.

RND 4: Ch 7, sc in first sc, ch 3, sk 2 sts, sc in next dc, ch 3, sk 2 sts, sc in next sc, ch 5, sc in next sc, ch 3, sc in top of tch—5 ch-sps.

RND 5: Ch 1, sl st to adjoining motif's ch-sp, ch 2, sc in next ch-3 sp, ch 3, (sc, hdc, dc join, dc join, dc, hdc, sc) in next ch-5 sp, ch 3, sc in next ch-3 sp, ch-5 join, sc in next ch-3 sp, ch 3, (sc, hdc, dc join, dc) in last ch-7 sp, fasten off.

Finishing

BLOCKING AND EDGING

Pin cardigan to schematic size and spray with water. Allow to dry.

Body Edge

Join yarn with sl st and smaller hook to right-side bottom edge of body in corner shell st.

ROW 1: Ch 1, sc evenly around front edge to left side bottom edge of body, turn.

ROW 2: Ch 1, sc in each sc around, turn.

RND 3: Ch 1, sc in each of next 2 sts, ch 2, sk 2 sc, *sc in each of next 4 sts, ch 2, sk 2 sc; repeat from * 3 times more; sc in each sc to end, turn—5 buttonholes.

RND 4: Ch 1, sc in each sc and 2 sc in each ch-2 sp around, turn.

RND 5: Ch 1, sc in each sc to end. Finish off.

Arm Edge

With the smaller hook, join yarn with sl st to right-side corner shell st of motif.

RND 1: Ch 1, sc evenly around arm edge, sl st to first sc to join, turn.

RND 2: Ch 1, sc in each sc around, sl st to first sc, turn.

RND 3: Repeat Row 2. Finish off.

Bottom Edge

With the smaller hook, join yarn with sl st to last row of sc on right front edge of body edging.

Ch 15.

ROW 1: Sc in 2nd ch from hook and each sc across, sl st to fabric twice (first sl st joins ribbing to motifs, second counts as a tch), turn—14 sc.

ROW 2: Skip both sl sts, sc-blp in each sc across, turn.

ROW 3: Ch 1, sc-blp in each sc across, sl st to fabric twice, turn.

ROWS 4–6: Rep Rows 2–3, then rep Row 2.

ROW 7: Ch 3, dc-blp in each sc across, sl st to fabric twice, turn.

Repeat Rows 2–7 around bottom edge. Finish off.

Sew buttons in place.

Think Outside the Box

Motif garments are notorious for their boxy, non-form-fitting shapes, but they certainly don't have to be that way. Sure, a number of motifs are squares, but luckily you can convert square motifs into many other schematic shapes. However, at times, not even those changes are enough to overcome the boxy nature of a garment. Here is when a good waistband or collar comes into play. By adding a thick edging, you can not only smooth out tough angles but also add dimension to your garment's shape. In this cardigan, the waistline could easily become too loose to be flattering. But by using a wide edging, you can close the bottom of the cardigan for a tight waistline while letting the upper bust portion have its full circumference.

calypso
KIMONO

This gorgeous tunic turns heads with its beautiful lace fabric and bold waistband. It was designed to show off the waistline, but if you don't wish to do so, simply increase the length of the waistband by 2" (5 cm) and choose complementary secondary colors, rather than contrasting ones. When you increase the length of the waistband, the tunic will flow instead of cinch beneath the bustline.

Materials

YARN

Fingering Weight (#2 Fine).

SHOWN: Universal Yarn Nazli Gelin Garden 5 (100% Egyptian Giza mercerized cotton; 174 yd [160 m]/1.75 oz [50 g]): #500-62 Deep Blue 8 (8, 10, 10, 12, 13) balls (MC), #500-64 Medium Green 2 (2, 2, 3, 3, 3) balls (A), #500-67 Fern 1 (1, 1, 2, 2, 2) balls (B), #500-70 Caramel 1 (1, 1, 1, 1, 1) ball (C).

HOOKS

(XS, M, XL) Size C/2 (2.75 mm) and size D/3 (3.25 mm); **(S, L, 2X)** size D/3 (3.25 mm) and size F/5 (3.75 mm), or hooks needed to obtain gauge.

NOTIONS

Tapestry needle for weaving in ends; spray bottle with water; straight pins for blocking; 9 (9, 14, 15, 14, 15)" (23 [23, 35.5, 38, 35.5, 38] cm) matching invisible zipper and sewing thread; stitch markers.

Gauge

Diagonally across motif ch-5 sp to ch-5 sp = 5½" (14 cm) with size C/2 (2.75 mm) hook, 6" (15 cm) with size D/3 (3.25 mm) hook, 6½" (16.5 cm) with size F/5 (3.75 mm) hook.

24 dc = 4" (10 cm) with size D/3 (3.25 mm) hook.

Finished Size

Bust measurement is 33 (36, 39, 42, 44, 48)" (84 [91.5, 99, 106.5, 112, 122] cm). Sized for X-Small (Small, Medium, Large, X-Large, and 2X). Sweater is close-fitting. Size shown is Small.

Notes

For XS, M, XL sizes, small hook is size C/2 (2.75 mm) and large hook is size D/3 (3.25 mm). For S, L, 2X sizes, small hook is size D/3 (3.25 mm) and large hook is size F/5 (3.75 mm).

Special Stitches

PICOT

Ch 3, sl st in flp of prev st.

CH-5 JOIN

Ch 2, sl st to adjoining motif's corner ch-5 sp, ch 2.

CH-2 JOIN

Sl st to adjoining motif's ch-2 sp, ch 1.

TRIPLE TREBLE CROCHET (TRTR)

Yo 4 times, insert hook in indicated st or sp, yo, pull through, (yo, pull through 2 lps on hook) 5 times.

Sachem Blossom Motif

Sachem Blossom Motif

See Sachem Blossom Motif diagram. Make 2 with small hook (one for top, one for skirt).

Ch 10, sl st to first ch to form ring.

RND 1 (RS): Ch 1, 24 sc in ring, sl st to first sc, do not turn—24 sc.

RND 2: Ch 2, 2 dc-cl in first sc, *[ch 3, sk 1 sc, 3 dc-cl in next sc] twice, ch 5, sk 1 sc, 3 dc-cl in next sc, rep from * twice more, [ch 3, sk 1 sc, 3 dc-cl in next sc] twice, ch 2, dc in top of 2 dc-cl, do not turn—12 dc-cl.

RND 3: Ch 5 (counts as tr, ch-sp), (tr, picot, tr, ch 1, tr, picot, tr) around post of dc, *ch 2, sk 1 dc-cl, sc in next dc-cl, ch 2, ([tr, picot, tr, ch 1] 4 times, tr, picot, tr) in next ch-5 sp; rep from * twice, ch 2, sk 1 dc-cl, sc in next dc-cl, ch 2, ([tr, picot, tr, ch 1] twice, tr, picot) in next ch-2 sp, sl st to 4th ch of tch, do not turn—40 tr.

RND 4: Ch 1, sc in next ch, ch 5, sc in next ch-1 sp, *ch 5, dc2tog in next 2 ch-2 sps, [ch 5, sc in next ch-1 sp] 4 times; rep from * twice, ch 5, dc2tog in next 2 ch-2 sps, [ch 5, sc in next ch-1 sp] twice, ch 2, dc in first sc, do not turn—20 ch-sp.

RND 5: Ch 1, 3 sc around post of dc, *(3 sc, ch 2, 3 sc) in next 4 ch-5 sp, (3 sc, ch 5, 3 sc) in next ch-5 sp; rep from * around omitting last ch-5 sp, 3 sc in last ch-sp, ch 5, sl st in first sc, fasten off—120 sc.

Joining Sachem Blossom Motifs

Join 41 (41, 51, 51, 71, 71) motifs with the small hook and join 12 (12, 14, 14, 16, 16) motifs with the large hook by following the directions for a Sachem Blossom motif (left) through Rnd 4. In Rnd 5, when next to an adjoining motif, substitute a ch-2 join for a ch 2 and a ch-5 join for a ch-5 (see Diagram A on page 110), thus seamlessly connecting the two. Follow the tunic's layout diagrams (pages 112–114) for the location of adjoining motifs on both the top and skirt. *Note: Layouts show the top and skirt as a flat piece, but they are actually seamless. Note that motifs labeled A, B, C, and D connect to adjoining A, B, C, and D motifs, respectively. A motifs connect the side seams together. B motifs connect at the underside of the arm. The opposite sides of the top do not connect for zipper (see connecting half and quarter motifs). C and D on the skirt connect it together on the back side.*

Joining Half Motifs

See Diagram B (page 110). Join 16 (16, 27, 27, 27, 27) with small hook. Join 6 (6, 7, 7, 8, 8) with large hook. Follow tunic layout diagrams (pages 112–114) for the location of adjoining motifs.

Ch 10, sl st to first ch to form ring.

RND 1 (RS): Ch 1, 13 sc in ring, turn—13 sc.

RND 2: Ch 8, sk first sc, 3 dc-cl in next sc, [ch 3, sk 1 sc, 3 dc-cl

in next sc] twice, ch 5, sk 1 sc, 3 dc-cl in next sc, [ch 3, sk 1 sc, 3 dc-cl in next sc] twice, ch 2, trtr in last sc, turn—6 dc-cl.

RND 3: Ch 4 (counts as tr), ([tr, ch 1, tr, picot] twice, tr) in next ch-2 sp, ch 2, sk 1 dc-cl, sc in next dc-cl, ch 2, ([tr, picot, tr, ch 1] 4 times, tr, picot, tr) in next ch-5 sp, ch 2, sk 1 dc-cl, sc in next dc-cl, ch 2, ([tr, picot, tr, ch 1] twice, 2 tr) in tch sp, turn—21 tr.

RND 4: Ch 6,*[sc in next ch-1 sp, ch 5] twice, dc2tog in next 2 ch-2 sps, ch5, [sc in next ch-1 sp, ch 5] twice; rep from * once, omitting last ch-5 sp, ch 2, tr in top of tch, turn—9 ch-5 sp.

RND 5: Ch 1, ch-5 join, 3 sc in ch-2 sp, *(3 sc, ch-2 join, 3 sc) in next 4 ch-5 sp, (3 sc, ch-5 join, 3 sc) in next ch-5 sp; rep from * around omitting last 3 sc, ch 1, sl st to 4th ch of tch, fasten off—60 sc.

Joining Quarter Motifs

See Diagram C (page 111). Join 4 (4, 2, 2, 4, 4) with small hook.

Ch 8, sl st to first ch to form ring.

RND 1 (RS): Ch 1, 7 sc in ring, turn—7 sc.

RND 2: Ch 8, sk first sc, 3 dc-cl in next sc, [ch 3, sk 1 sc, 3 dc-cl in next sc] twice, ch 2, trtr in last sc, turn—3 dc-cl.

RND 3: Ch 4 (counts as tr), ([tr, ch 1, tr, picot] twice, tr) in next ch-2 sp, ch 2, sk 1 dc-cl, sc in next dc-cl, ch 2, ([tr, picot, tr, ch 1] twice, 2 tr) in tch sp, turn—12 tr.

RND 4: Ch 6, [sc in next ch-1 sp, ch 5] twice, dc2tog in next 2 ch-2 sps, ch 5, sc in next ch-1 sp, ch 5, sc in next ch-1 sp, ch 2, tr in top of tch, turn—4 ch-5 sp.

RND 5: Ch 1, ch-5 join, 3 sc in ch-2 sp, *(3 sc, ch-2 join, 3 sc) in next 4 ch-5 sp, (3 sc, ch-5 join) in tch sp, ch 1, sl st to 4th ch of tch, fasten off—30 sc.

(XS, S)
Joining Collar Motifs

See Diagram D. Join 2 (2) with small hook.

Join 1 on the RS and 1 on the WS.

Ch 10, sl st to first ch to form ring.

RND 1 (RS): Ch 1, 16 sc in ring, turn—16 sc.

RND 2: Ch 8, sk first sc, *3 dc-cl in next sc, [ch 3, sk 1 sc, 3 dc-cl in next sc] twice, ch 5, sk 1 sc; rep from * once, 3 dc-cl in next sc, ch 3, sk 1 sc, 2 dc-cl in last sc, turn—7 3dc-cl.

RND 3: Ch 1, *sc in next dc-cl, ch 2, ([tr, picot, tr, ch 1] 4 times, tr, picot, tr) in next ch-5 sp, ch 2; rep from * once, sc in next dc-cl, ch 2, ([tr, picot, tr, ch 1] twice, 2 tr) in tch sp, turn—26 tr.

RND 4: Ch 6,*[sc in next ch-1 sp, ch 5] twice, dc2tog in next 2 ch-2 sps, ch 5, [sc in next ch-1 sp, ch 5] twice; rep from * once, [sc in next ch-1 sp, ch 5] twice, dc2tog in last ch-2 sp and sc, turn—12 ch-5 sp.

RND 5: Ch 1, (3 sc, ch 2, 3 sc) in next 2 ch-5 sp, (3 sc, ch-5 join, 3 sc) in next ch-5 sp, *(3 sc, ch-2 join, 3 sc) in next 4 ch-5 sp, (3 sc, ch-5 join, 3 sc) in next ch-5 sp; rep from * around omitting last 3 sc. Ch 1, sl st to 4th ch of tch, fasten off—75 sc.

a. Joining Sachem Blossom Motifs

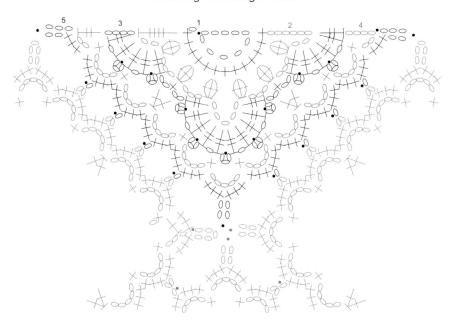

b. Joining Half Triangle Motifs

c. Joining Quarter Motifs

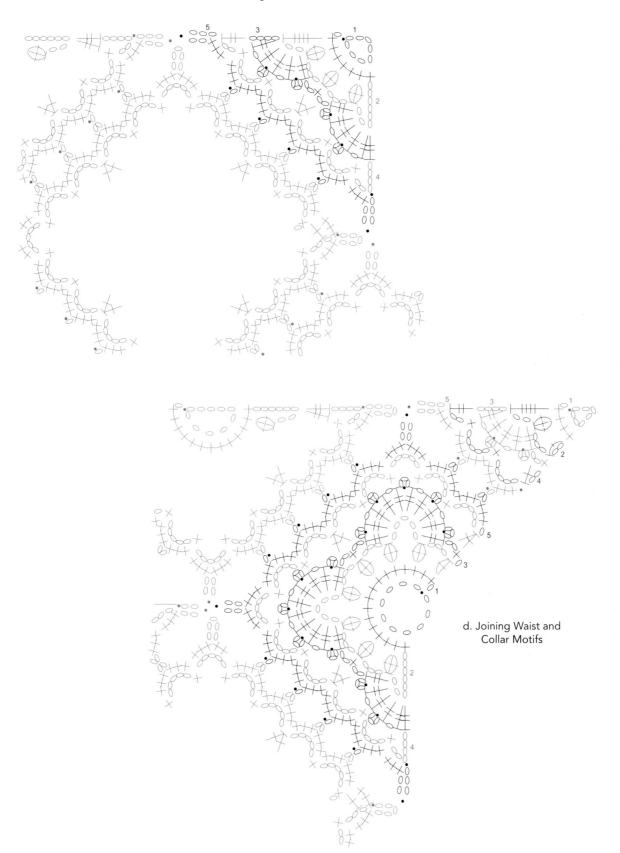

d. Joining Waist and
Collar Motifs

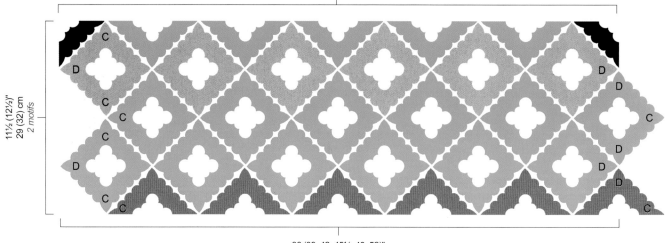

33 (36, 38½, 42, 44, 48)"
84 (91.5, 98, 106.5, 112, 122) cm
6 (6, 7, 7, 8, 8) motifs

11½ (12½)"
29 (32) cm
2 motifs

36 (39, 42, 45½, 48, 52)"
91.5 (99, 106.5, 115.5, 122, 132) cm
6 (6, 7, 7, 8, 8) motifs

Skirt Layout

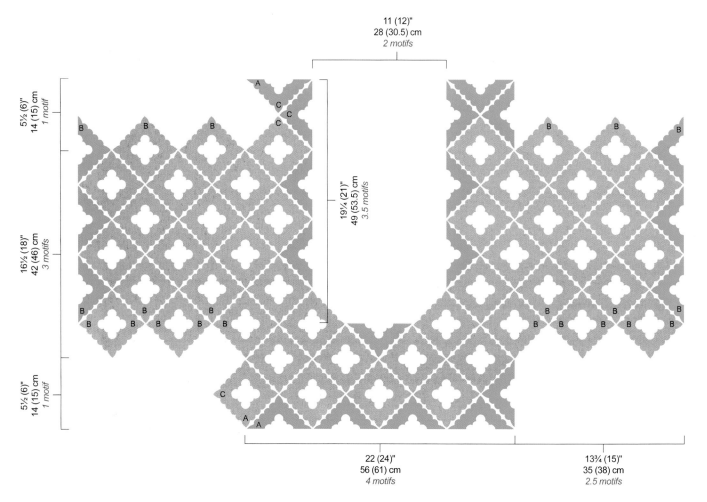

11 (12)"
28 (30.5) cm
2 motifs

5½ (6)"
14 (15) cm
1 motif

16½ (18)"
42 (46) cm
3 motifs

5½ (6)"
14 (15) cm
1 motif

19¼ (21)"
49 (53.5) cm
3.5 motifs

22 (24)"
56 (61) cm
4 motifs

13¾ (15)"
35 (38) cm
2.5 motifs

Medium/Large Layout

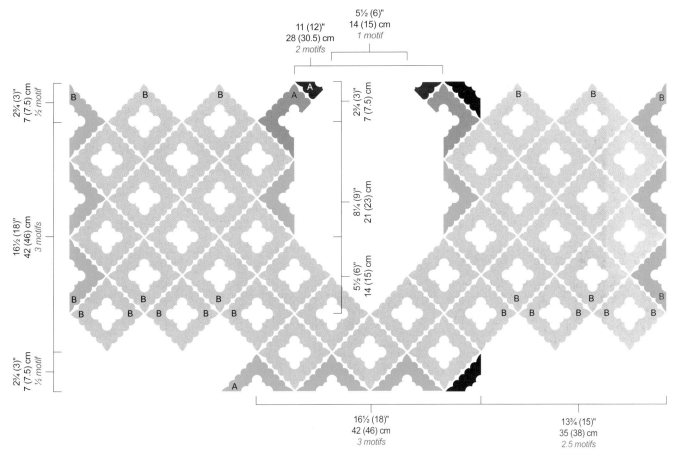

5½ (6)"
14 (15) cm
1 motif

11 (12)"
28 (30.5) cm
2 motifs

2¾ (3)"
7 (7.5) cm
½ motif

2¾ (3)"
7 (7.5) cm

8¼ (9)"
21 (23) cm

5½ (6)"
14 (15) cm

16½ (18)"
42 (46) cm
3 motifs

2¾ (3)"
7 (7.5) cm
½ motif

16½ (18)"
42 (46) cm
3 motifs

13¾ (15)"
35 (38) cm
2.5 motifs

X-Small/Small Layout

Layout Key

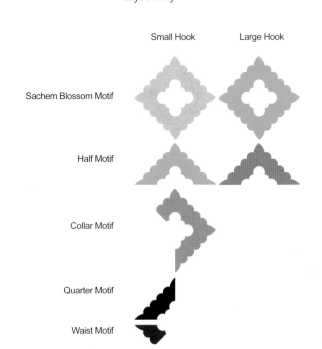

	Small Hook	Large Hook
Sachem Blossom Motif		
Half Motif		
Collar Motif		
Quarter Motif		
Waist Motif		

(XS, S)

Joining Waist Motifs

See Diagram D (page 111). Join 2 (2, 0, 0, 0, 0) with small hook.

Join 1 on the RS and 1 on the WS.

Ch 7, sl st to first ch to form ring.

RND 1 (RS): Ch 1, 4 sc in ring, turn—4 sc.

RND 2: Ch 2, dc in first sc, ch 3, sk next sc, 3 dc-cl in next sc, ch 2, trtr in last sc, turn—1 dc-cl.

RND 3: Ch 4 (counts as tr), ([tr, ch 1, tr, picot] twice, tr) in next ch-2 sp, ch 2, sk 1 dc-cl, sc in last dc, turn—6 tr.

RND 4: Ch 2, dc in ch-2 sp, ch 5, sc in next ch-1 sp, ch 5, sc in next ch-1 sp, ch 2, tr in top of tch, turn—2 ch-5 sp.

RND 5: Ch 1, ch-5 join, 3 sc in ch-2 sp, (3 sc, ch-2 join, 3 sc) in next 2 ch-5 sp, sl st in dc, fasten off—15 sc.

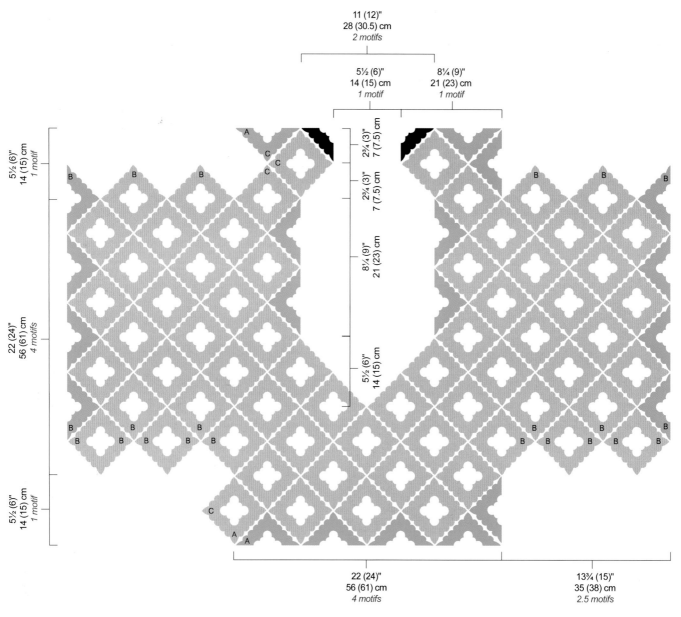

11 (12)"
28 (30.5) cm
2 motifs

5½ (6)"
14 (15) cm
1 motif

8¼ (9)"
21 (23) cm
1 motif

2¾ (3)"
7 (7.5) cm

2¾ (3)"
7 (7.5) cm

8¼ (9)"
21 (23) cm

5½ (6)"
14 (15) cm

5½ (6)"
14 (15) cm
1 motif

22 (24)"
56 (61) cm
4 motifs

5½ (6)"
14 (15) cm
1 motif

22 (24)"
56 (61) cm
4 motifs

13¾ (15)"
35 (38) cm
2.5 motifs

X-Large/2X Layout

Finishing

Blocking and Edging

Pin to schematic measurements and spray with water. Allow to dry. Join MC to bottom edge of skirt. Ch 1, sc around edge of skirt, sl st to first sc, fasten off. Repeat on edge of sleeve, top of skirt, side seam, and waist edge.

Waistband and Zipper

With size D/3 hook and A, ch 176 (194, 206, 230, 242, 266).

ROW 1 (RS): Dc in 4th ch from hk, dc in each ch across, turn—174 (192, 204, 228, 240, 264) dc.

ROWS 2–8: Ch 3 (counts as dc), dc in each dc across, turn, fasten off A.

RND 9: Join B, sc across edge of waistband, 3 sc in last st, sc down edge (in ends of rows), 3 sc in first sc; rep from * around, sl st to first sc to join, turn.

RNDS 10–11: Ch 1, *sc in each sc across edge, 3 sc in last sc; rep from * around, sl st to first sc to join, turn, fasten off B.

Join C to foundation ch, sl st across foundation ch (inserting hook from front to back of fabric), down short edge (in Rnd 9), across Row 8, and up short edge, fasten off, weave in ends.

Waistband measures 29.5 (32.5, 34.5, 38.5, 40.5, 44.5)" (75 [82.5, 86.5, 103, 113] cm) across. Pin waistband to top, gathering waist edge of top as needed. Straight stitch waistband to waist edge. Repeat on top edge of skirt.

Pin zipper to side seam, and backstitch zipper to seam.

COLLAR EDGING

With size D/3 hook, join MC to a ch-2 sp on back neck edge with sl st.

RND 1 (RS): Ch 1, sc in same ch-2 sp, [ch 3, sc in next ch-sp] rep across sachem blossom motifs, sc evenly around collar to waistband, sc blp in each waistband st, sc evenly up collar to back neck, [ch 3, sc in next ch-2 sp] across sachem blossom motifs, **(M/L)** sc evenly across back neck, **(ALL)** sl st to first sc, fasten off MC.

Place stitch markers in all inside corners.

RNDS 2–3: Join B, sc in each st across to m, sc2tog over next 2 sts, move m; rep from * around, sl st to first sc, turn.

RNDS 4–9: Join A, ch 3, dc in each st across to 1 st before m, dc2tog over front panel m and dc3tog over back neck m, move m; rep from * around, sl st to top of tch, turn.

RND 10: Ch 1, sc in each st around, sl st to first sc, turn.

RND 11: Sl st in each sc around, fasten off.

Motif Magic

Motif projects are great for garments because they create fascinating and truly original fabrics. They also are incredibly challenging, especially when you shape a neckline. I have a few tricks to avoid the overly boxy neckline that can result when your stitches get unwieldy. Try these tips for success: First, add large collars that smooth out the rough corners. Let the simple rounds of sc or dc turn a box into an oval. Second, use symbols to divide motifs. Dividing a motif into a partial motif can help avoid a boxy look by adding diagonals you might not have had. I like to limit my partial motifs to multiples of 45 degrees, meaning those which can be cut in half diagonally, vertically, or horizontally to create the partial motif I need.

Unique
CONSTRUCTION

The best part of crochet is that it's simple to work in any direction, vertically, horizontally, diagonally, or sculptural. I use these out-of-the-box shapes when I want either the body or the stitch pattern (but not the seams) to take center stage. In the Stormy Lace Tunic (page 130), the shape is a Roman-style tunic that just cries out to be draped on the body. Although classic-construction panels can't create this shaping, overlapping parallelogram-shaped panels can. If you have ever wondered how to easily shape a cape sweater, check out Veronica Pullover (page 138) to see how our expert does it. Whether it's lace, as in the Walnut Berry V-Neck (page 142), or cables, as in the Clover Car Coat (page 118), I use single-panel construction most often when I want the stitch pattern to sing. The projects shown are just the tip of the crochet iceberg; I hope they inspire you to transform your crochet with but a simple twist of your wrist!

clover
CAR COAT

The standout part of this car coat is by far the stitch pattern. Combining cables and filet lace creates texture and depth within a basic rectangle shape. This stitch pattern would be dreadful in traditional panels with the seams imposing on the design. However, when you use the one-piece method, the eye is drawn not to the seams but rather to the collar and upward to your face, which is, of course, where the proper attention should be!

Materials

YARN

DK weight (#3 Light)

SHOWN: Universal Yarn Blossom Street Collection Rosebud (100% superwash extrafine merino; 137 yd [125 m]/1.75 oz [50 g]): #507 Clover, 9 (10, 12, 14, 16) balls.

HOOK

Size I/8 (5.5 mm) or hook needed to obtain gauge.

NOTIONS

Size I/8 (5.5 mm) or hook needed to obtain gauge.

Gauge

24 sts (2 SR) by 14 rows (1 RR) = 5¾" × 6" (14.5 × 15 cm) in stitch pattern.

Finished Size

Bust measurement is 35 (41, 46½, 50½, 58)" (89 [104, 118, 128.5, 147.5] cm) with an oversized fit. Sized for X-Small (Small, Medium, Large, X-Large). Size shown is Small.

Notes

Coat is worked from the bottom edge up to and over the shoulders down to the front-panel edge.

Special Stitches

RIGHT DOUBLE CROCHET DECREASE (RT DC DEC)

Yo, insert hook into next indicated st, yo and pull up lp, yo and draw through 2 lps on hook, yo, insert hook around post of next indicated st from back to front to back, yo and pull up a lp, yo and draw through 2 lps on hook, yo and draw through 3 lps on hook.

LEFT DOUBLE CROCHET DECREASE (LF DC DEC)

Yo, insert hook around post of next indicated st from back to front to back, yo and pull up a lp, yo and draw through 2 lps on hook, yo, insert hook into next indicated st, yo and pull up lp, yo and draw through 2 lps on hook, yo and draw through 3 lps on hook.

RIGHT TREBLE CROCHET DECEASE (RT TR DEC)

Yo, insert hook into next indicated st, yo and pull up lp, yo and draw through 2 lps on hook, yo twice, insert hook around post of next indicated st from front to back to front, yo and pull up a lp, (yo and draw through 2 lps on hook) twice, yo and draw through 3 lps on hook.

LEFT TREBLE CROCHET DECREASE (LF TR DEC)

Yo twice, insert hook around post of next indicated st from front to back to front, yo and pull up a lp, (yo and draw through 2 lps on hook) twice, yo, insert hook into next indictaed st, yo and pull up lp, yo and draw through 2 lps on hook, yo and draw through 3 lps on hook.

FILET DIAMOND CABLE STITCH PATTERN (FDSP)

See File Diamond Cable diagram for assistance.

Chain a multiple of 12 plus 4.

ROW 1 (RS): Dc in 4th ch from hook (sk ch count as dc), dc in next ch, *ch 1, sk next ch, dc in next 6 ch, ch 1, sk next ch, dc in next 4 ch; rep from * across, end dc in last 3 chs, turn.

ROW 2: Ch 3 (counts as dc here and throughout), dc in next 2 dc, *ch 1, dc in next dc, sk 2 dc, BPtr in next 2 dc, BPtr in previous 2 skipped dc (in front of other BPtr), dc in next dc, ch 1, dc in next 4 dc; rep from * across, dc in top of tch, turn.

ROW 3: Ch 3, *dc in next dc, ch 1, dc in ch-1 sp, rt tr dec over next 2 sts, (FPtr, dc) in next st, (dc, FPtr) in next st, lf tr dec over next 2 sts, dc in ch-1 sp, ch 1, sk 1 dc, dc in next dc; rep from * across, dc in top of tch, turn.

ROW 4: Ch 4 (counts as dc, ch-1 sp), *dc in ch-1 sp, lf dc dec over next 2 sts, (BPdc, dc) in next st, ch 1, dc bet next 2 dc, ch 1, (dc, BPdc) in next tr, rt dc dec over next 2 sts, dc in next ch-1 sp, ch 1; rep from * across to top of tch, dc in top of tch, turn.

ROW 5: Ch 3, dc in ch-1 sp, *rt tr dec over next 2 sts, (FPtr, dc) in next st, ch 1, dc in next 2 ch-1 sps, ch 1, (dc, FPtr) in next st, rt tr dec over next 2 sts, 2 dc in next ch-1 sp; rep from * across omitting 2 dc in last ch-sp, dc in 4th ch of tch, dc in 3rd ch of tch, turn.

ROW 6: Ch 3, *lf dc dec over next 2 sts, (BPdc, dc) in next st, ch 1, dc in ch-1 sp, dc in next 2 dc, dc in next ch-1 sp, ch 1, sk 1 dc, (dc, BPdc) in next st, rt dc dec over next 2 sts; rep from * across, dc in top of tch, turn.

ROW 7: Ch 3, FPdc in next 2 sts, *dc in next dc, ch 1, dc in next 4 dc, ch 1, dc in next dc, sk 2 sts, FPtr around next 2 sts, FPtr around previous 2 skipped sts (in front of previous FPtr); rep from * across to last 3 sts omitting cable, FPdc in next 2 sts, dc in top of tch, turn.

ROW 8: Ch 3, *BPdc around next 2 sts, dc in next dc, ch 1, dc in next 4 dc, ch 1, dc in next dc, BPdc around next 2 sts; rep from * across, dc in top of tch, turn.

ROW 9: Rep Row 7.

ROW 10: Ch 3, *(dc, BPdc) in next st, rt dc dec over next 2 sts, dc in ch-1 sp, ch 1, sk 1 dc, dc in next 2 dc, ch 1, dc in ch-1 sp, lf dc dec, (BPdc, dc) in next st; rep from * across, dc in top of tch, turn.

ROW 11: Ch 4 (counts as dc, ch-1 sp), *(dc, FPtr) in next st, lf tr dec over next 2 sts, dc in ch-1 sp, ch 1, dc in ch-1 sp, rt tr dec over next 2 sts, (FPtr, dc) in next st, ch 1, dc bet next 2 dc, ch 1; rep from * across omitting last 2 sts, dc in top of tch, turn.

ROW 12: Ch 3, *dc in next ch-1 sp, ch 1, sk next dc, (dc, BPdc) in next st, rt dc dec over next 2 sts, 2 dc in ch-1 sp, lf dc dec over next 2 sts, (BPdc, dc) in next st, ch 1, dc in ch-1 sp; rep from * across, dc in 3rd ch of tch, turn.

ROW 13: Ch 3, *dc in next dc, dc in ch-1 sp, ch 1, sk 1 dc, (dc, FPtr) in next st, lf tr dec over next 2 sts, rt tr dec over next 2 sts, (FPtr, dc) in next st, ch 1, dc in ch-1 sp, dc in next dc; rep from * across, dc in top of tch, turn.

ROW 14: Rep Row 2.

ROW 15: Ch 3, *dc in next 2 dc, ch 1, dc in next dc, BPdc in next 4 sts, dc in next dc, ch 1, dc in next 2 dc; rep from * across, dc in top of tch, turn.

Rep Rows 2–15 for pattern.

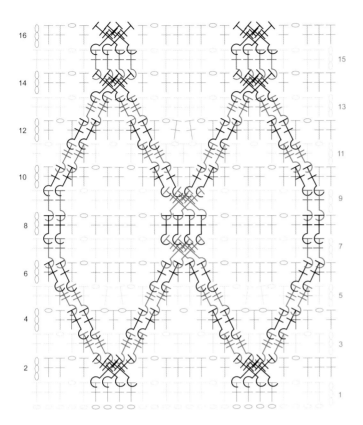

Filet Diamond Cable Stitch Pattern

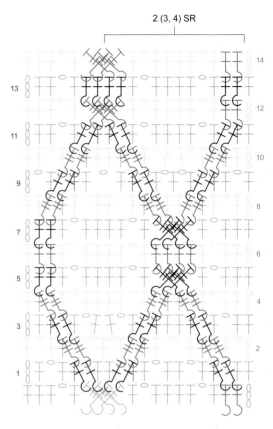

e. X-Small/Medium/X-Large Front Panel

Back

Ch 76 (88, 100, 112, 124).

(XS, S, M)

ROW 1 (RS): Dc in 4th ch from hook (sk ch count as dc), dc in next ch, *ch 1, sk next ch, dc in next 6 ch, ch 1, sk next ch, dc in next 4 ch; rep from * across, turn—12 (14, 16) ch-1 sps and 6 (7, 8) SR.

ROW 2: Rep Row 2 of FDSP.

(M ONLY)

ROWS 3–6: [Rep Row 15 of FDSP. Rep Row 2 of FDSP] twice.

(L, XL)

ROW 1 (RS): Dc in 4th ch from hook (sk ch count as dc), * dc in next 2 ch, ch 1, sk next ch, dc in next 4 ch, ch 1, sk next ch, dc in next 4 ch; rep from * across, turn—19 (20) ch-1 sps and 9 (10) SR.

ROWS 2–8: Rep Rows 8–14 of FDSP.

(ALL)

Rep Row 15 of FDSP. Rep Rows 2–15 of FDSP 3 times, rep Rows 2–12 of FDSP.

X-Small Neck Shaping

See Diagram A (page 124) for assistance.

ROW 1A: Ch 3, dc in next dc, dc in ch-1 sp, ch 1, sk 1 dc, (dc, FPtr) in next st, lf tr dec over next 2 sts, rt tr dec over next 2 sts, (FPtr, dc) in next st, ch 1, dc in ch-1 sp, dc in next 2 dc, dc in ch-1 sp, ch 1, sk 1 dc, (dc, FPtr) in next st, lf tr dec over next 2 sts, rt tr dec over next 2 sts, (FPtr, dc) in next st, dc in next dc, dc2tog over ch-1 sp and next dc, leave remaining sts unworked, turn.

ROW 2A: Ch 2, sk dc2tog, dc in next 2 dc, cont in Row 14 of FDSP across, turn—1 less st.

ROW 3A: Cont in Row 15 of FDSP across to last 2 dc, dc in last 2 dc, turn.

ROW 4A: Ch 3, dc in next dc, cont in Row 2 of FDSP across, turn.

ROW 2A: Ch 2, sk dc2tog, dc in next dc, ch 1, dc in next 2 dc, cont in Row 14 of FDSP across, turn—1 less st.

ROW 3A: Cont in Row 15 of FDSP across to last 4 sts, dc in next 2 dc, ch 1, dc in last dc, turn.

ROW 4A: Ch 4 (counts as dc, ch-1 sp), dc in next 2 dc, cont in Row 2 of FDSP across, turn.

ROW 5A: Cont in Row 3 of FDSP across to last 4 sc, dc in next dc, ch 1, sk 1 dc, dc in 4th ch and 3rd ch of tch, turn.

ROW 6A: Ch 3, dc in next dc, dc in ch-1 sp, ch 1, sk 2 dc, cont in Row 4 of FDSP across, turn.

ROW 7A: Cont in Row 5 of FDSP across to last ch-1 sp, 2 dc in last ch-1 sp, rt tr dec over next 2 sts, (FPtr, 2 dc) in tch, turn—1 add'l st.

ROW 8A: Ch 3, dc in first dc, ch 1, sk 1 dc, cont in Row 6 of FDSP of across, turn—2 add'l sts.

ROW 9A: Cont in Row 7 of FDSP across to tch, 2 dc in top of tch, turn—3 add'l sts.

ROW 10A: Ch 8, dc in 4th ch from hook, dc in next 2 ch, ch 1, sk 1 ch, dc in last ch, dc in next 3 dc, cont in Row 8 of FDSP across, turn—9 add'l sts.

ROW 11A: Cont in Row 9 of FDSP across, turn—3 SR.

Medium/X-Large Neck Shaping

See Diagram C (page 125) for assistance.

ROW 1A: Cont in Row 13 of FDSP for 2 (3) SR, dc in next dc, dc in ch-1 sp, ch 1, sk 1 dc, (dc, FPtr) in next st, lf tr dec over next 2 sts, rt tr dec over next 2 sts, FPtr in next st, dc2tog in previous and next dc, leave remaining sts unworked, turn

ROW 2A: Ch 2, sk dc2tog, dc in next 2 sts, BPdc around next 2 sts, dc in next dc, cont in Row 14 of FDSP across, turn—1 less st.

ROW 3A: Cont in Row 15 of FDSP across to last 2 sts, dc in last 2 sts, turn.

ROW 4A: Ch 3, dc in next dc, BPdc around next 2 sts, dc in next dc, cont in Row 2 of FDSP across, turn.

ROW 5A: Cont in Row 3 of FDSP across to last 2 sts, dc in last 2 sts, turn.

ROW 6A: Ch 4 (counts as dc, ch-1 sp), sk first dc, dc bet next 2 dc, ch 1, sk next dc, (dc, BPdc) in next st, cont in Row 4 of FDSP across, turn.

ROW 7A: Cont in Row 5 of FDSP across to tch, dc in 4th ch of tch, 2 dc in 3rd ch of tch, turn—1 add'l st.

ROW 8A: Ch 3, dc in first dc, dc in next 3 dc, dc in next ch-1 sp, ch 1, sk next dc, cont in Row 6 of FDSP across, turn—2 add'l sts.

ROW 9A: Cont in Row 7 of FDSP across to last 2 sts, dc in next dc, 2 dc in top of tch, turn—3 add'l sts.

ROW 10A: Ch 10, dc in 4th ch from hook, dc in next ch, ch 1, sk next ch, dc in next 4 ch, dc in next 2 dc, ch 1, sk 1 dc, dc in next 4 dc, cont in Row 8 of FDSP across, turn—11 add'l sts.

ROW 5A: Cont in Row 3 of FDSP across to tch, dc in top of tch, turn.

ROW 6A: Ch 2, sk first dc, BPdc around next st, (BPdc, dc) in next st, cont in Row 4 of FDSP across, turn.

ROW 7A: Cont in Row 5 of FDSP across to last 2 sts, (dc, FPtr) in next st, dc in last dc, turn—1 add'l st.

ROW 8A: Ch 3, dc in first dc, dc in next tr, cont in Row 6 of FDSP across, turn—2 add'l sts.

ROW 9A: Cont in Row 7 of FDSP across to last 3 sts, dc in next 2 dc, 2 dc in top of tch, turn—3 add'l sts.

ROW 10A: Ch 8, dc in 4th ch from hook, dc in next ch, ch 1, sk 1 ch, dc in next 2 ch, dc in next 4 dc, cont in Row 8 of FDSP across, turn—9 add'l sts.

ROW 11A: Cont in Row 9 of FDSP across to tch, dc in top of tch, turn—2.5 SR.

Small Neck Shaping

See Diagram B (page 124) for assistance.

ROW 1A: Cont in Row 13 of FDSP for 2 SR, dc in next dc, dc in ch-1 sp, ch 1, sk 1 dc, dc in next dc, dc2tog in next 2 sts, turn.

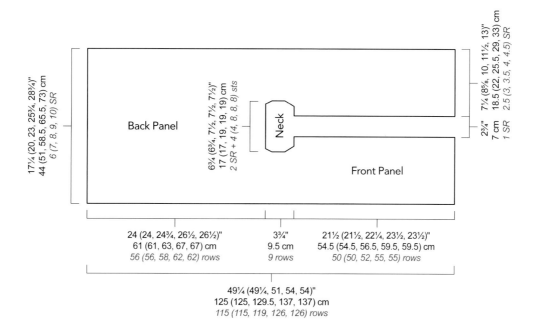

Back Panel

17¼ (20, 23, 25¾, 28¾)"
44 (51, 58.5, 65.5, 73) cm
6 (7, 8, 9, 10) SR

6¾ (6¾, 7½, 7½, 7½)"
17 (17, 19, 19, 19) cm
2 SR + 4 (4, 8, 8, 8) sts

Neck

Front Panel

7¼ (8⅝, 10, 11½, 13)"
18.5 (22, 25.5, 29, 33) cm
2.5 (3, 3.5, 4, 4.5) SR

2¾"
7 cm
1 SR

24 (24, 24¾, 26½, 26½)"
61 (61, 63, 67, 67) cm
56 (56, 58, 62, 62) rows

3¾"
9.5 cm
9 rows

21½ (21½, 22¼, 23½, 23½)"
54.5 (54.5, 56.5, 59.5, 59.5) cm
50 (50, 52, 55, 55) rows

49¼ (49¼, 51, 54, 54)"
125 (125, 129.5, 137, 137) cm
115 (115, 119, 126, 126) rows

ROW 11A: Cont in Row 9 of FDSP across to tch, dc in top of tch, turn—3.5 (4.5) SR.

Large Neck Shaping

See Diagram D (page 125) for assistance.

ROW 1A: Cont in Row 13 of FDSP for 3 SR, dc in next dc, dc in ch-1 sp, dc2tog in next 2 sts, turn.

ROW 2A: Ch 2, sk dc2tog, dc in next 2 dc, cont in Row 14 of FDSP across, turn—1 less st.

ROW 3A: Cont in Row 15 of FDSP across to last 2 sts, dc in next 2 dc, turn.

ROW 4A: Ch 3, dc in next dc, cont in Row 2 of FDSP across, turn.

ROW 5A: Cont in Row 3 of FDSP across to last 2 sts, dc in next dc, dc in top of tch, turn.

ROW 6A: Ch 4, sk 3 dc, dc in ch-1 sp, cont in Row 4 of FDSP across, turn.

ROW 7A: Cont in Row 5 of FDSP across to tch, 2 dc in 4th ch of tch, 2 dc in 3rd ch of tch, turn—1 add'l st.

ROW 8A: Ch 3, dc in first dc, dc in next 2 dc, cont in Row 6 of FDSP of across, turn—2 add'l sts.

ROW 9A: Cont in Row 7 of FDSP across to tch, 2 dc in top of tch, turn—3 add'l sts.

ROW 10A: Ch 10, dc in 4th ch from hook, dc in next 2 ch, ch 1, sk 1 ch, dc in last 3 ch, dc in next dc, ch 1, sk 1 dc, dc in next dc, BPdc in next 2 sts, cont in Row 8 of FDSP across, turn—11 add'l sts.

ROW 11A: Cont in Row 9 of FDSP across, turn—4 SR.

SMALL/LARGE FRONT PANEL

Rep Rows 10–15 of FDSP once, rep Rows 2–15 of FDSP three times, rep Row 2 of FDSP, (S) rep Row 15 of FDSP, fasten off, (L) Rep Rows 3–8 of FDSP, fasten off.

X-SMALL/MEDIUM/X-LARGE FRONT PANEL

See Diagram E (page 121).

ROW 1: Ch 3, dc in next dc, ch 1, sk 1 dc, dc in next ch-1 sp, lf dc dec over next 2 sts, (BPdc, dc) in next st, cont in Row 10 of FDSP across, turn—2 (3, 4) SR.

ROW 2: Cont in Row 11 of FDSP across to last ch-1 sp, dc in next ch-1 sp, ch 1, dc in top of tch, turn.

ROW 3: Ch 3, dc in next ch-1 sp, lf dc dec over next 2 sts, (BPdc, dc) in next st, ch 1, sk 1 dc, dc in next ch-1 sp, cont in Row 12 of FDSP across, turn.

ROW 4: Cont in Row 13 of FDSP across to tch, dc in top of tch, turn.

ROW 5: Ch 3, sk first dc, BPdc around next 2 sts, dc in next dc, ch 1, dc in next 4 dc, cont in Row 14 of FDSP across, turn.

ROW 6: Cont in Row 15 of FDSP across to last 4 sts, dc in next dc, FPdc around next 2 dc, dc in top of tch, turn.

ROW 7: Ch 3, sk first dc, BPdc around next 2 sts, dc in next dc, ch 1, dc in next 4 dc, cont in Row 2 of FDSP across, turn.

ROW 8: Cont in Row 3 of FDSP across to tch, dc in top of tch, turn.

ROW 9: Ch 4, sk first 2 dc, (dc, BPdc) in next st, rt dc dec over next 2 sts, dc in next ch-1 sp, ch 1, sk 2 dc, cont in Row 4 of FDSP across, turn.

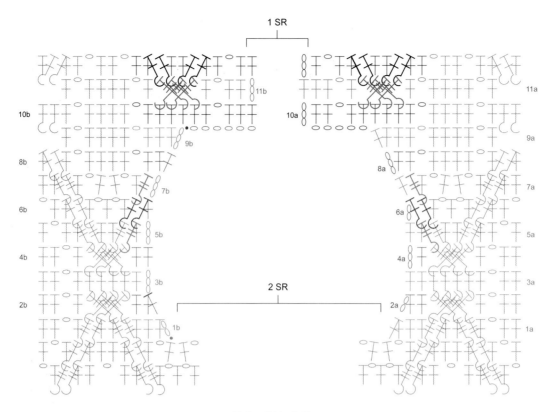

a. X-Small Neck Shaping

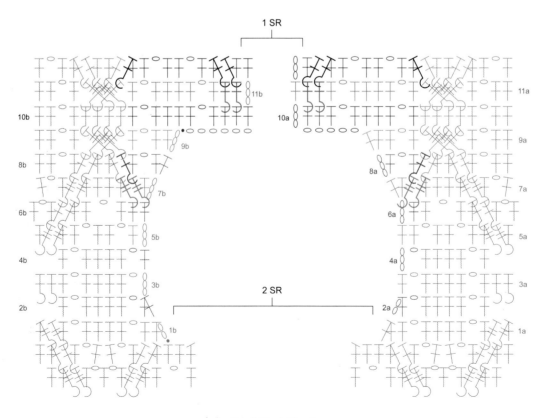

b. Small Neck Shaping

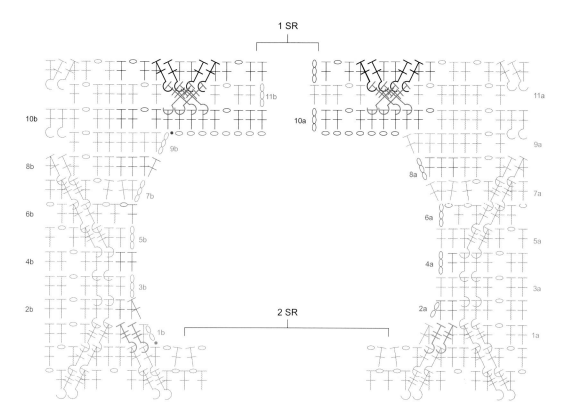

c. Medium/X-Large Neck Shaping

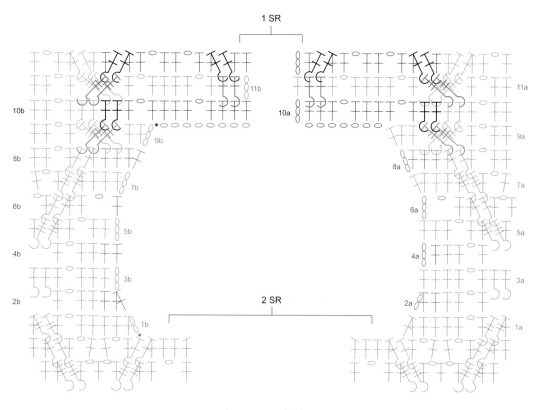

d. Large Neck Shaping

ROW 10: Cont in Row 5 of FDSP across to tch, dc in 4th ch of tch, dc in 3rd ch of tch, turn.

ROW 11: Ch 3, dc in next dc, dc in next ch-1 sp, ch 1, sk next dc, (dc, BPdc) in next dc, rt dc dec over next 2 sts, cont in Row 6 of FDSP across, turn.

ROW 12: Cont in Row 7 of FDSP across to tch, dc in top of tch, turn.

ROW 13: Ch 3, dc in next 2 dc, ch 1, dc in next dc, cont in Row 8 of FDSP across, turn.

ROW 14: Cont in Row 9 of FDSP across to tch, dc in top of tch, turn.

Rep Rows 1–14 of front panel twice more,

(XS)

Rep Rows 1–7 and Row 6 of front panel, fasten off.

(M)

Rep Rows 1–7 of front panel, rep Rows 6–7 once, rep Row 6 once more, fasten off.

(XL)

Rep Rows 1–13 once, fasten off.

Opposite X-Small Neck Shaping

See Diagram A (page 124) for assistance. Sk 24 sts from end of 1a, join to next st with sl st.

ROW 1B: Ch 2, dc in ch-1 sp, dc in next dc, (dc, FPtr) in next st, lf tr dec over next 2 sts, rt tr dec over next 2 sts, (FPtr, dc) in next st, cont in Row 13 of FDSP, turn.

ROW 2B: Cont in Row 14 of FDSP across to last 2 dc, dc2tog over last 2 dc, turn—1 less st.

ROW 3B: Ch 3, dc in next dc, FPdc in next 4 sts, cont in Row 15 of FDSP across, turn.

ROW 4B: Cont in Row 2 of FDSP across to tch, dc in top of tch, turn.

ROW 5B: Ch 3, rt tr dec over next 2 sts, (FPtr, dc) in next st, cont in Row 3 of FDSP across to tch, turn.

ROW 6B: Cont in Row 4 of FDSP across to last 3 sts, (dc, BPdc) in next st, rt dc dec over last st and tch, turn.

ROW 7B: Ch 3, sk first st, (FPtr, dc) in next st, ch 1, sk 1 dc, dc in next ch-1 sp, cont in Row 5 of FDSP across, turn—1 add'l st.

ROW 8B: Cont in Row 6 of FDSP across to last 2 sts, dc in next st, 2 dc in top of tch, turn—2 add'l sts.

ROW 9B: Ch 3, dc in first dc, dc in next 2 dc, ch 1, cont in Row 7 of FDSP across, turn. Join new ball of yarn to top of tch at beg of row with sl st, ch 6, fasten off—3 add'l sts.

ROW 10B: Cont in Row 8 of FDSP across to last 4 dc, dc in next 3 dc, dc in top of tch, dc in next 2 ch, ch 1, sk 1 ch, dc in next 3 ch, turn—9 add'l sts.

ROW 11B: Ch 3, dc in next 2 dc, ch 1, dc in next dc, sk 2 sts, FPtr around next 2 sts, FPtr around previous 2 skipped sts (in front of previous FPtr), cont in Row 9 of FDSP across, turn—2.5 SR.

Opposite Small Neck Shaping

See Diagram B (page 124) for assistance. Sk 24 sts from end of Row 1a, join to next st with sl st.

ROW 1B: Ch 2, dc in next 2 dc, ch 1, sk 1 dc, dc in next ch-1 sp, dc in next 2 dc, cont in Row 13 of FDSP across, turn—2.5 SR.

ROW 2B: Cont in Row 14 of FDSP across to last ch-1 sp, ch 1, dc2tog over last 2 dc, turn—1 less st.

ROW 3B: Ch 4 (counts as dc, ch-1 sp), dc in next 4 dc, cont in Row 15 of FDSP across, turn.

ROW 4B: Cont in Row 2 of FDSP across to tch, ch 1, dc in 3rd ch of tch, turn.

ROW 5B: Ch 3, dc in next ch-1 sp, ch 1, sk 1 dc, dc in next dc, cont in Row 3 of FDSP across, turn.

ROW 6B: Cont in Row 4 of FDSP across to last ch-1 sp, dc in last ch-1 sp, dc in next dc, dc in top of tch, turn.

ROW 7B: Ch 3, (dc, FPdc) in first dc, lf tr dec over next 2 sts, cont in Row 5 of FDSP across, turn—1 add'l st.

ROW 8B: Cont in Row 6 of FDSP across to last 2 sts, ch 1, sk 1 dc, 2 dc in top of tch, turn—2 add'l sts.

ROW 9B: Ch 3, dc in first dc, dc in next dc, ch 1, dc in next dc, cont in Row 7 of FDSP across, turn. Join new ball of yarn to top of tch at beg of row with sl st, ch 6, fasten off—3 add'l sts.

ROW 10B: Cont in Row 8 of FDSP across to last ch-1 sp, ch 1, dc in next 2 dc, dc in top of tch, dc in next ch, ch 1, sk 1 ch, dc in next 4 ch, turn—9 add'l sts.

ROW 11B: Cont in Row 9 of FDSP across, turn—3 SR.

Opposite Medium/X-Large Neck Shaping

See Diagram C (page 125) for assistance. Sk 28 sts from end of 1a, join to next st with sl st.

ROW 1B: Ch 2, (dc, FPtr) in next st, lf tr dec over next 2 sts, rt tr dec over next 2 sts, (FPtr, dc) in next st, cont in Row 13 of FDSP, turn.

ROW 2B: Cont in Row 14 of FDSP across to last 6 sts, dc in next dc, BPdc in next 2 sts, dc in next st, dc2tog over next 2 sts, turn—1 less st.

ROW 3B: Ch 3, sk dc2tog, dc in next dc, FPdc around next 2 dc, dc in next dc, cont in Row 15 of FDSP across, turn.

ROW 4B: Cont in Row 2 of FDSP across to last 5 sts, dc in next dc, BPdc in next 2 dc, dc in next dc, dc in top of tch, turn.

ROW 5B: Ch 3, dc in next dc, (dc, FPtr) in next dc, lf tr dec over next 2 sts, cont in Row 3 of FDSP across, turn.

ROW 6B: Cont in Row 4 of FDSP across to last 3 sts, ch 1, dc bet next 2 dc, ch 1, dc in top of tch, turn.

ROW 7B: Ch 3, dc in first dc, dc in next 2 ch-1 sps, ch 1, sk 1 dc, cont in Row 5 of FDSP across, turn—1 add'l st.

ROW 8B: Cont in Row 6 of FDSP across to last 3 sts, dc in next 2 dc, 2 dc in top of tch, turn—2 add'l sts.

ROW 9B: Ch 3, dc in first dc, dc in next 5 dc, cont in Row 7 of FDSP across, turn. Join new ball of yarn to top of tch at beg of row with sl st, ch 8, fasten off—3 add'l sts.

ROW 10B: Cont in Row 8 of FDSP across to last dc, dc in last dc, dc in top of tch, dc in next 4 ch, ch 1, sk 1 ch, dc in next 3 ch, turn—11 add'l sts.

ROW 11B: Ch 3, dc in next 2 dc, ch 1, dc in next dc, sk 2 sts, FPtr around next 2 sts, FPtr around previous 2 skipped sts (in front of previous FPtr), cont in Row 9 of FDSP across, turn—3.5 (4.5) SR.

Opposite Large Neck Shaping

See Diagram D (page 125) for assistance. Sk 28 sts from end of Row 1a, join to next st with sl st.

ROW 1B: Ch 2, dc in next dc, dc in next ch-1 sp, dc in next 2 dc, cont in Row 13 of FDSP across, turn—3.5 SR.

ROW 2B: Cont in Row 14 of FDSP across to last 2 dc, dc2tog over last 2 dc, turn—1 less st.

ROW 3B: Ch 3, dc in next 3 dc, cont in Row 15 of FDSP across, turn.

ROW 4B: Cont in Row 2 of FDSP across to tch, ch 1, dc in 3rd ch of tch, turn.

ROW 5B: Ch 3, dc in next 2 dc, cont in Row 3 of FDSP across, turn.

ROW 6B: Cont in Row 4 of FDSP across to last ch-1 sp, dc in last ch-1 sp, ch 1, dc in top of tch, turn.

ROW 7B: Ch 3, dc in first dc, 2 dc in next ch-1 sp, cont in Row 5 of FDSP across, turn—1 add'l st.

ROW 8B: Cont in Row 6 of FDSP of across to last 2 sts, dc in next dc, 2 dc in top of tch, turn—2 add'l sts.

ROW 9B: Ch 3, dc in first dc, dc in next dc, cont in Row 7 of FDSP across, turn. Join new ball of yarn to top of tch at beg of row with sl st, ch 8, fasten off—3 add'l sts.

ROW 10B: Cont in Row 8 of FDSP across to last 3 sts, dc in next dc, ch 1, sk 1 dc, dc in top of tch, dc in next 3 ch, ch 1, sk 1 ch, dc in next 4 ch, turn—9 add'l sts.

ROW 11B: Cont in Row 9 of FDSP across, turn—3 SR.

OPPOSITE SMALL/ LARGE FRONT PANEL

Rep directions of small/large front panel, fasten off.

OPPOSITE X-SMALL/MEDIUM/X-LARGE FRONT PANEL

ROW 1: Cont in Row 10 of FDSP across to last 7 sts, (dc, BPdc) in next st, lf dc dec over next 2 sts, dc in next ch-1 sp, ch 1, sk 1 dc, dc in next dc, dc in top of tch, turn—2 (3, 4) SR.

ROW 2: Ch 4 (counts as dc, ch-1 sp), dc in next ch-1 sp, lf tr dec over next 2 sts, (FPtr, dc) over next st, ch 1, dc bet next 2 dc, ch 1, cont in Row 11 of FDSP across, turn.

ROW 3: Cont in Row 12 of FDSP across to tch, dc in 4th ch of tch, dc in 3rd ch of tch, turn.

ROW 4: Ch 3, sk first dc, lf tr dec over next 2 sts, (FPtr, dc) in next st, ch 1, sk 1 dc, dc in next ch-1 sp, dc in next dc, cont in Row 13 of FDSP across, turn.

ROW 5: Cont in Row 14 of FDSP across to last 4 sts, dc in next dc, BPdc around next 2 dc, dc in top of tch, turn.

ROW 6: Ch 3, FPdc around next 2 dc, dc in next dc, cont in Row 15 of FDSP across, turn.

ROW 7: Cont in Row 2 of FDSP across to last 4 sts, dc in next dc, BPdc around next 2 dc, dc in top of tch, turn.

ROW 8: Ch 3, (dc, FPtr) in next st, rt tr dec over next 2 sts, dc in ch-1 sp, cont in Row 3 of FDSP across, turn.

ROW 9: Cont in Row 4 of FDSP across to last 2 sts, ch 1, dc in top of tch, turn.

ROW 10: Ch 3, dc in ch-1 sp, ch 1, sk 1 dc, (dc, FPtr) in next st, rt tr dec over next 2 sts, 2 dc in next ch-1 sp, cont in Row 5 of FDSP, turn.

ROW 11: Cont in Row 6 of FDSP across to last ch-1 sp, dc in last ch-1 sp, dc in next dc, dc in top of tch, turn.

ROW 12: Ch 3, dc in next 2 dc, ch 1, dc in next dc, cont in Row 7 of FDSP across, turn.

Repeats Simplified

For challenging stitch patterns, it's critical to have a good grasp on the term "stitch repeat" (SR). An SR is simply the stitches you repeat across the row. In this pattern, 12 stitches make up the repeat. By recognizing that each row has a repeat and a flow, you can avoid the pitfalls of counting stitches. Look at your diagram; you can keep track simply by counting the cabling diamond shapes. It's so much easier to count 7 SRs than 84 stitches. SRs also come in handy during shaping. This sweater is a rectangle with shaping only at the neckline. Use this structure to your advantage. Don't worry about the ends and beginnings of the rows along the side-seam edge. They'll be straight and worked in the same method as always. The only part you need to pay attention to is the neckline—and then to only a few stitches. It will take a bit of faith to believe you're doing it right. In any case, if you're getting cabled diamonds in a rectangle shape, you have the pattern down pat!

ROW 13: Cont in Row 8 of FDSP across to tch, dc in top of tch, turn.

ROW 14: Ch 3, dc in next 2 dc, ch 1, dc in next dc, cont in Row 9 of FDSP across, turn.

Rep Rows 1–14 of opposite front panel twice more.

(XS)

Rep Rows 1–7 and Row 6 of opposite front panel, fasten off.

(M)

Rep Rows 1–7 of opposite front panel, rep Rows 6–7 once, rep Row 6 once more, fasten off.

(XL)

Rep Rows 1–13 of opposite front panel once, fasten off.

Finishing

BLOCKING AND SEAMING

Pin body to schematic size and spray with water. Allow to dry. Fold body in half at shoulder seam with RS facing. Whipstitch side seam from bottom edge to shoulder for 16" (40.5 cm) on each side. Turn RS out.

ARM EDGING

Join yarn with sl st to RS edge of armhole at side seam, ch 1.

RND 1: Sc an even number of sts around edge of armhole, sl st to first sc, do not turn.

RND 2: Ch 1, *sc in next sc, ch 1, sk 1 sc; rep from * around, sl st to first sc, do not turn.

RND 3: Ch 1, *sc in next ch-1 sp, ch 1, sk next sc; rep from * around, sl st to first sc, do not turn.

RNDS 4–8: Rep Rnd 3 five more times. Fasten off.

BOTTOM EDGING

Join yarn to RS edge of front panel with sl st, ch 1.

ROW 1: Sc in each st across, turn.

ROW 2: Ch 1, sc in each sc across, turn.

ROW 3: Sl st in each sc across. Fasten off.

FRONT PANEL RIBBING

Join yarn to top of front panel at neck shaping with sl st, ch 14.

ROW 1: Sc in 2nd ch from hook, sc in each ch across, sl st to edge of front panel twice (once to join row to edge, one for tch); turn—13 sc.

ROW 2: Sk both sl st, sc blp in each sc across, turn.

ROW 3: Ch 1, sc blp in each sc across, sl st to edge of front panel twice, turn.

Rep Rows 2–3 once.

BUTTONHOLE ROW 1: Sk both sl st, sc blp in next 7sc, ch 3, sk 3 sc, sc blp in last 3 sc, turn.

BUTTONHOLE ROW 2: Ch 1, sc blp in next 3 sc, 3 sc in ch-3 sp, sc blp in last 7 sc, sl st twice to edge, turn.

[Rep Rows 2–3 six times, Buttonhole Rows 1–2 once] 5 times, rep Rows 2–3 to end of front panel. Fasten off.

Rep directions on opposite front panel without buttonhole rows.

COLLAR RIBBING

Join yarn to top of front panel at ribbing with sl st, ch 18.

ROW 1: Sc in 2nd ch from hook, sc in each ch across, sl st to edge of front panel twice (once to join row to edge, one for turning ch), turn—17 sc.

ROWS 2–5: Rep Rows 2–3 of front panel ribbing twice.

BUTTONHOLE ROW 1: Sk both sl st, sc blp in next 7sc, ch 3, sk 3 sc, sc blp in last 7 sc, turn.

BUTTONHOLE ROW 2: Ch 1, sc blp in next 7 sc, 3 sc in ch-3 sp, sc blp in last 7 sc, sl st twice to edge, turn.

Rep Rows 2–3 around collar, fasten off.

stormy
LACE TUNIC

Crocheted lace can make the most beautiful fabric, but figuring out the shaping can be a challenge. Instead of getting tangled in the stitches, I use crochet diagrams to mark my path. In these diagrams you'll notice that the shaping is in color and the stitch pattern is in gray. That way, you can focus on the shaping, knowing that the rest of the stitch pattern isn't changing.

Materials

YARN

DK weight (#3 Light)

SHOWN: Caron International Naturally Caron Spa (75% microdenier acrylic, 25% rayon from bamboo; 251 yd [230m]/3 oz [85 g]): #0010 Stormy Blue (MC), 5 (5, 6, 7, 8) balls.

HOOK

Size H/8 (5.0 mm) or hook needed to obtain gauge.

NOTIONS

Tapestry needle for weaving in ends; one ⅞" (22 mm) button; spray bottle with water; straight pins for blocking, stitch markers, ⅝" (16 mm) wide by 52 (56, 60, 64, 68)" (132 [142, 152, 162.5, 172.5] cm) grosgrain ribbon, tracing paper, 1 (1, 1, 1.5, 1.5) yd (0.9 [0.9, 0.9, 1.5, 1.5] m) of sheer fabric, matching sewing thread and needle, two hook-and-eye closures.

Gauge

2 SR by 10 rows = 5" × 3¾" (12.5 × 9.5 cm) in stitch pattern.

Finished Size

Waist measurement is 28 (32, 36, 40, 44)" (71 [81.5, 91.5, 102, 112] cm). Sized for X-Small (Small, Medium, Large, X-Large). Size shown is Small. Bust measurement varies depending on how open you like the neckline to be when you wear the garment. Wearing the top half lower on the shoulders will accommodate larger busts.

Notes

Top panels are crocheted and blocked, then the bottom skirt is crocheted directly onto the ends of the top-panel rows.

Special Stitches

SHELL (SH)

Work ([dc, ch 1] 4 times, dc) in st indicated.

V-ST

Work (2 dc, ch 1, 2 dc) in st indicated.

BLACKBERRY STORM STITCH PATTERN (BSSP)

See Blackberry Storm Diagram (right) for assistance.

Chain a multiple of 14 plus 2.

ROW 1 (RS): Sc in 2nd ch from hk, *ch 4, sk 6 ch, sh in next ch, ch 4, sk 6 ch, sc in next ch; rep from * across, turn.

ROW 2: Ch 3 (counts as dc), 2 dc in same sc, *ch 2, [sc in next ch-1 sp, ch 3] 3 times, sc in next ch-1 sp, ch 2, V-st in next sc; rep from * to last sc, 3 dc in last sc, turn.

ROW 3: Ch 3 (counts as dc), 2 dc in same dc, *[ch 3, sc in next ch-3 sp] 3 times, ch 3, sk 1 ch-2 sp, V-st in next ch-1 sp; rep from * across to tch, 3 dc in top of tch, turn.

ROW 4: Ch 3 (counts as dc), 2 dc in same dc, *ch 4, sk next ch-3 sp, [sc in next ch-3 sp, ch 4] twice, V-st in next ch-1 sp; rep from * across to tch, 3 dc in top of tch, turn.

ROW 5: Ch 3 (counts as dc), 2 dc in same dc, *ch 5, sk next ch-4 sp, sc in next ch-4 sp, ch 5, V-st in next ch-1 sp; rep from * across to tch, 3 dc in top of tch, turn.

ROW 6: Ch 1, sc in dc, *ch 4, sk next ch-5 sp, sh in next sc, ch 4, sc in next ch-1 sp; rep from * across to tch, sc in top of tch, turn.

Rep Rows 2–6 to desired length.

Body

TOP PANEL

See Diagram A (page 134). Ch 114 (114, 114, 114, 114).

ROW 1 (RS): Sc in 2nd ch from hk, *ch 4, sk 6 ch, sh in next ch, ch 4, sk 6 ch, sc in next ch; rep from * across, turn—8 sh or SR.

ROW 2: Ch 3 (counts as dc), (dc, ch 1, 2 dc) in same sc, cont in Row 2 of BSSP to last sc, V-st in last sc, turn—8 V-sts.

ROW 3: Ch 5 (counts as tr, ch-1 sp), V-st in next ch-1 sp, cont in Row 3 of BSSP to last ch-1 sp, V-st in last ch-1 sp, ch 1, tr in top of tch, turn—9 V-sts.

ROW 4: Ch 8 (counts as dtr, ch-3 sp), V-st in next v-st, cont in Row 4 of BSSP to last V-st, V-st in last V-st, ch 3, dtr in 4th ch of tch, turn—9 V-sts.

ROW 5: Ch 8 (counts as tr, ch-4 sp), V-st in next V-st, cont in Row 5 of BSSP to last V-st, V-st in last v-st, ch 4, tr in 5th ch of tch, turn—9 V-sts.

ROW 6: Ch 3 (counts as dc), ([dc, ch 1] twice, dc) in tr, ch 4, sc in first ch-1 sp, cont in Row 6 of BSSP to last V-st, sc in last ch-1 sp, ch 4, ([dc, ch 1] twice, 2 dc) in 4th ch of tch, turn—8 sh.

ROW 7: Ch 4 (counts as dc, ch-1 sp), sc bet first and next dc, [ch 3, sc in next ch-1 sp] twice, ch 2, V-st in next sc, cont in Row 2 of BSSP to last sc, V-st in last sc, ch 2, [sc in next ch-1 sp, ch 3] twice, sc bet tch and dc, ch 1, dc in top of tch, turn—9 V-sts.

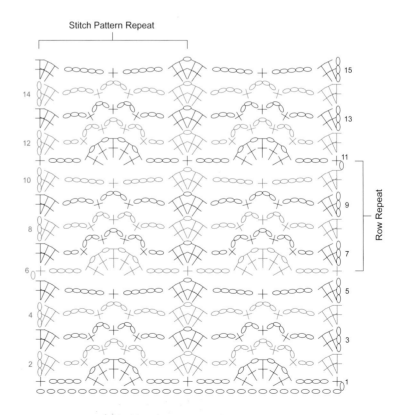

Blackberry Storm Stitch Pattern

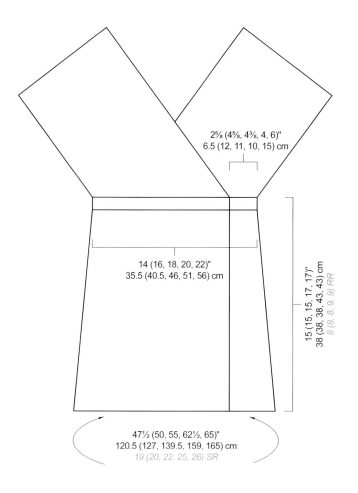

2⅝ (4⅝, 4⅜, 4, 6)"
6.5 (12, 11, 10, 15) cm

14 (16, 18, 20, 22)"
35.5 (40.5, 46, 51, 56) cm

15 (15, 15, 17, 17)"
38 (38, 38, 43, 43) cm
8 (8, 8, 9, 9) RR

47½ (50, 55, 62½, 65)"
120.5 (127, 139.5, 159, 165) cm
19 (20, 22, 25, 26) SR

ROW 8: Ch 1, sc in dc, [ch 3, sc in next ch-3 sp] twice, ch 3, V-st in next ch-1 sp, cont in Row 3 of BSSP to last ch-1 sp, V-st in last ch-1 sp, [ch 3, sc in next ch-3 sp] 3 times, turn—9 V-sts.

ROW 9: Ch 9 (counts as dtr, ch-3 sp), [sc in next ch-3 sp, ch 4] twice, V-st in next v-st, cont in Row 4 of BSSP to last V-st, V-st in last V-st, ch 4, sk ch-3 sp, [sc in next ch-3 sp, ch 4] twice, dtr in last sc, turn—9 V-sts.

ROW 10: Ch 10 (counts as dtr, ch-5 sp), sk ch-4 sp, sc in next ch-4 sp, ch 5, V-st in next V-st, cont in Row 5 of BSSP to last V-st, V-st in last V-st, ch 5, sk next ch-4 sp, sc in next ch-4 sp, ch 5, dtr in 5th ch of tch, turn—9 V-sts.

ROW 11: Ch 1, sc in dtr, cont in Row 6 of BSSP to tch, ch 4, sc in 5th ch of tch, turn—10 sh.

ROWS 12–21 (21, 31, 31, 31): Rep Rows 2–11 of top panel 1 (1, 2, 2, 2) times.

(XS, S, L, XL)

ROWS 22 (22, 32, 32)–25 (25, 35, 35): Rep Rows 2–5 of top panel once more.

(ALL)

Fasten off—13 (13, 14, 14, 15) SR.

Pin top panels to schematic size and spray with water. Allow to dry before continuing.

WAISTBAND

Lay top panels down on a table with the WS facing up. The angled edge (the row-end side) should be at the bottom in a straight line. This will be the back of the tunic. The foundation chain should be on the left and right sides (they will be the armholes). The last row should be on the inside (it will form the neckline). Overlap panels 8¾ (6¾ 9¼, 12, 10)" (22 [17, 23.5, 30.5, 25.5] cm) at the bottom edge and pin in place. Fold panels so the top edge is over the bottom edge. Join yarn to RS edge of front panel (the top one) at the angled edge.

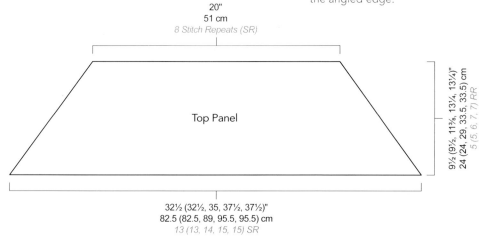

20"
51 cm
8 Stitch Repeats (SR)

Top Panel

9½ (9½, 11⅜, 13¼, 13¼)"
24 (24, 29, 33.5, 33.5) cm
5 (5, 6, 7, 7) RR

32½ (32½, 35, 37½, 37½)"
82.5 (82.5, 89, 95.5, 95.5) cm
13 (13, 14, 15, 15) SR

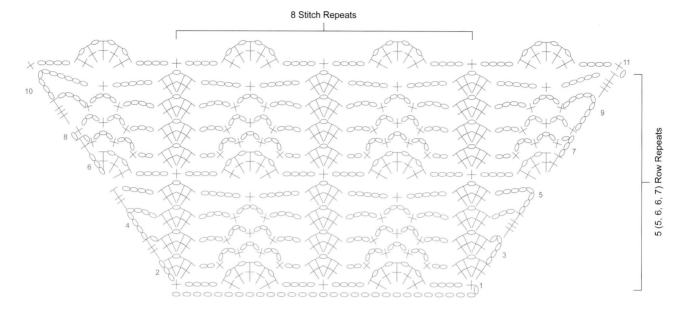

8 Stitch Repeats

5 (5, 6, 6, 7) Row Repeats

a. Top Panel Stitch Diagram

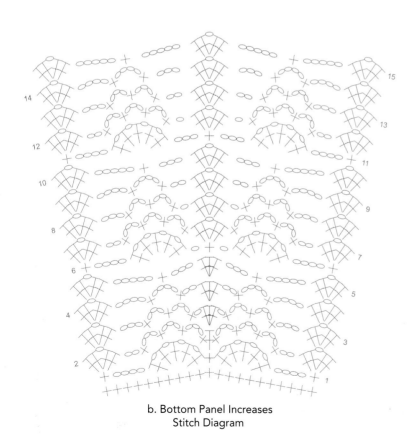

b. Bottom Panel Increases
Stitch Diagram

ROW 1: Ch 1, 64 (64, 73, 89, 89) sc evenly across front panel, 75 (89, 99, 109, 123) sc evenly across back panel (working through both thicknesses of fabric at overlapped area on back panels), and 64 (64, 73, 89, 89) sc evenly across opposite front panel, turn. *Note: Sc across front panel to back panel to join front and back together, forming the sleeves—203 (217, 245, 287, 301) sc.*

ROWS 2–4: Ch 1, sc in each sc across, turn. Do not fasten off.

Place stitch markers at following sc from both edges for a total of 8 markers: (**XS, S**) 25 (45, 65, 85). (**M, L, XL**) 39 (59, 79, 99).

SKIRT

See Diagram B.

ROW 1 (RS): Ch 1, sc in first sc, *ch 4, sk 6 ch, sh in next ch, ch 4, sk 6 ch, sc in next ch*; rep from * to 10 sc before first m, **ch 4, sk 6 ch, sh in next sc, sk 2 sc, sc in next sc, move m to sc just made, sk 2 sc, sh in next sc, ch 4, sk 6 sc, sc in next sc**; rep from ** 3 times, rep from * to * 1 (2, 2, 4, 5) times, rep from ** to ** 4 times, rep from * to * 1 (1, 2, 2, 2) times, turn—19 (20, 22, 25, 26) sh.

ROW 2: *Cont in Row 2 of BSSP to m, dc in next sc, move m to dc just made; rep from * across, cont in Row 2 of BSSP to end, turn.

ROW 3: *Cont in Row 3 of BSSP to ch-3 sp before m, sc in ch-3 sp, ch 1, 3 dc in next dc, move m to middle dc of dc group just made, ch 1, sc in next ch-3 sp; rep from * across, cont in Row 3 of BSSP to end, turn.

ROW 4: *Cont in Row 4 of BSSP to ch-3 sp before m, sc in next ch-3 sp, ch 2, 3 dc in marked dc, move m to middle dc of dc group just made, ch 2, sc in next ch-3 sp; rep from * across, cont in Row 4 of BSSP to end, turn.

ROW 5: *Cont in Row 5 of BSSP to ch-4 sp before m, sc in next ch-4 sp, ch 3, 3 dc in marked dc, move m to middle dc of dc group just made, ch 3, sc in next ch-4 sp; rep from * across, cont in Row 5 of BSSP to end, turn.

ROW 6: *Cont in Row 6 of BSSP to sc before m, ch 4, sh in next sc, ch 1, sc in marked dc, move m to sc just made, ch 1, sh in next sc; rep from * across, cont in Row 6 of BSSP to end, turn.

ROW 7: *Cont in Row 2 of BSSP to m, V-st in next sc, move m to V-st just made; rep from * across, cont in Row 2 of BSSP to end, turn—18 (19, 21, 24, 25) V-sts.

ROW 8: *Cont in Row 3 of BSSP to ch-3 sp before m, sc in ch-3 sp, ch 1, V-st in next V-st, move m to V-st just made, ch 1, sc in next ch-3 sp; rep from * across, cont in Row 3 of BSSP to end, turn.

ROW 9: *Cont in Row 4 of BSSP to ch-3 sp before m, sc in next ch-3 sp, ch 2, V-st in next V-st, move m to V-st just made, ch 2, sc in next ch-3 sp; rep from * across, cont in Row 4 of BSSP to end, turn.

ROW 10: *Cont in Row 5 of BSSP to ch-4 sp before m, sc in next ch-4 sp, ch 3, V-st in next V-st, move m to V-st just made, ch 3, sc in next ch-4 sp; rep from * across, cont in Row 5 of BSSP to end, turn.

ROW 11: *Cont in Row 6 of BSSP to sc before m, sh in next sc, ch 3, sc in ch-1 sp of next V-st, move m to sc just made, ch 3, sh in next sc; rep from * across, cont in Row 6 of BSSP to end, turn.

ROW 12: *Cont in Row 2 of BSSP to last ch-1 sp before m, sc in ch-1 sp, ch 1, V-st in next sc, move m to V-st just made, ch 1, sc in next ch-1 sp; rep from * across, cont in Row 2 of BSSP to end, turn.

ROW 13: *Cont in Row 3 of BSSP to ch-3 sp before m, sc in ch-3 sp, ch 2, V-st in next V-st, move m to V-st just made, ch 2, sc in next ch-3 sp; rep from * across, cont in Row 3 of BSSP to end, turn.

ROW 14: *Cont in Row 4 of BSSP to ch-3 sp before m, sc in next ch-3 sp, ch 3, V-st in next V-st, move m to V-st just made, ch 3, sc in next ch-3 sp; rep from * across, cont in Row 4 of BSSP to end, turn—19 (20, 22, 25, 26) SR.

ROW 15: Cont in Row 5 of BSSP, turn.

ROW 16: Cont in Row 6 of BSSP, turn.

ROW 17–36 (36, 36, 41, 41): Cont Rows 2–6 of BSSP 4 (4, 4, 5, 5) times.

ROWS 37 (37, 37, 42, 42)–40 (40, 40, 45, 45): Cont Rows 2–5 of BSSP once.

ROW 41 (41, 41, 46, 46): Ch 1, sc in next 3 dc, *5 sc in ch-5 sp, sk sc, 5 sc in ch-5 sp, 4 sc in ch-1 sp of V-st; rep from * across to last 3 sts, sc in each st to end, fasten off.

Finishing

EDGING

Join yarn to RS of armhole opening, *6 sc in ch-6 sp, sc in same ch as sh, 6 sc in ch-6 sp, sc in same ch as sc; rep from * across, sl st to first sc, fasten off, weave in ends.

Join yarn to RS bottom edge of front panel, sc evenly up front panel edge over row ends of skirt, *5 sc in ch-sp, sk sc, 5 sc in ch-sp, sc in next 2 dc, (sc, ch 1, sc) in ch-1 sp, sc in next 2 dc; rep from * across, sl st to last st of top panel. Fasten off. Join yarn to RS edge of opposite front panel, *5 sc in ch-sp, sk sc, 5 sc in ch-sp, sc in next 2 dc, (sc, ch 1, sc) in ch-1 sp, sc in next 2 dc; rep from * across, sc evenly down opposite front panel skirt, fasten off.

BLOCKING

Pin skirt to schematic size and spray with water. Allow to dry.

LINING

Sketch schematic size of top panel on tracing paper. Add ¾" (2 cm) to all dimensions and cut out. Pin tracing paper to sheer fabric and cut out. Press edges ⅜" (1 cm) down, and then ⅜" (1 cm) again. Pin fabric lining to inside of top panel. Straight-stitch lining to top panel.

RIBBON

Mark ribbon 12" (30.5 cm) in from the edge, pin ribbon to waistband starting at edge of right side across to opposite end, do not attach last 12" (30.5 cm) of ribbon. Straight-stitch ribbon to waistband with sewing thread.

CLOSURES

Sew hook closures to end of front panels at each end of waistband. Sew opposite hook to inside fabric with sewing thread.

Stretch (The Truth)

One little-known secret of crochet is how to make garments stop draping. We're usually trying to get them to drape, but every now and then drape goes awry. Fiber that has natural drape (such as silk or bamboo) will often drape too much when combined with lace crochet stitches and fabric on the bias. In such cases, if left untreated, the waistband will sink to the top of your hips. The solution? Lining. Adding a lining works perfectly to keep the top lacy but still strong enough to support the weight of the skirt. If you substitute yarns when you make this tunic, try it on before you line it. If the weight of the skirt doesn't bring down the waistband, then you don't have to line it.

veronica
PULLOVER

The loveliest quality of crochet is that it can be worked in any direction without fuss. This dolman-sleeved pullover isn't built with classic-construction panels, but rather with wedges. The overall effect creates a stunning top that's as much fun to wear as it is to crochet.

Designed by KRISTIN OMDAHL

Materials

YARN

DK weight (#3 Light)

SHOWN: Lion Brand Microspun (100% micro-fiber acrylic; 168 yd [154 m]/2.5 oz [71 g]): #910-147 Purple, 5 (5, 6, 7) skeins.

HOOK

Size G/6 (4.0 mm) or hook needed to obtain gauge.

NOTIONS

Tapestry needle for weaving in ends; spray bottle with water; straight pins for blocking.

Gauge

5 SR by 14 rows = 4" × 4" (10 × 10 cm) in stitch pattern.

Finished Size

Pullover fits 34 (38, 42, 46)" (86.5 [96.5, 106.5, 117] cm). Sized for Small (Medium, Large, X-Large). Fit is relaxed through the bust and fitted in the waist. Size shown is Medium.

Notes

Pullover is worked in sections. Strips are crocheted first, then the lace wedges are crocheted directly onto a strip. The last row of each wedge joins a new strip to the wedge.

Pattern

STRIPS

Make 9 (10, 11, 12).

ROW 1: Ch 4 (counts as tr), 3 tr in 4th ch from hook, turn—4 tr.

ROW 2: Sl st into sp bet 2nd and 3rd sts, ch 4 (counts as tr), 3 tr in same sp, turn.

ROWS 3–32: Rep Row 2. At end of last row, sl st into sp bet 2nd and 3rd sts. Fasten off.

FIRST WEDGE

See Lace Wedge Diagram (page 140) for assistance.

ROW 1: Working along the side edge of any strip, join with sl st to side of first tr on first row, ch 5, sc in same sp, *ch 5, skip next end of row, sc in next end of row. Rep from * 14 more times, ch 2, dc in last end of row (counts as ch-5 sp), turn—17 ch-5 sps.

ROW 2: *Ch 5, sc in next ch-5 sp. Rep from * fifteen more times, turn—16 ch-5 sps.

ROW 3: Ch 5, sc in same ch-5 sp, *ch 5, sc in next ch-5 sp. Rep from * to last ch-5 sp, ch 2, dc in last ch-5 sp, turn—16 ch-5 sps.

ROW 4: *Ch 5, sc in next ch-5 sp. Rep from * to last ch-5 sp, turn—15 ch-5 sps.

ROW 5: Ch 5, sc in same ch-5 sp *ch 5, sc in next ch-5 sp. Rep from * to last ch-5 sp. Ch 2, dc in last ch-5 sp, turn—15 ch-5 sps.

ROWS 6–17: Rep Rows 4–5 six more times. At end of Row 17, you will have 9 ch-5 sps.

ROW 18: Rep Row 4—8 ch-5 sps.

ROW 19: Ch 5, sc in same ch-5 sp, *ch 5, sc in next ch-5 sp. Rep from * to last ch-5 sp. Working along diagonal, *ch 5, skip next end of row, sc in next end of row. Rep from * to last end of row, turn—18 ch-5 sps.

Joining row:

Note: On this row, each ch-5 sp is replaced with a ch 2, sl st in adjacent strips every other end of row to join.

ROW 20: *Ch 2, sl st into end of first row of next strip, ch 2, sc in next ch-5 sp on prev row (Row 19). Rep from * to last ch-5 sp. Fasten off.

NEXT WEDGE

Note: All following wedges will be worked onto the last strip joined to create a seamless fabric.

ROW 1: Working into free side end of rows of strip (currently joined to the prev wedge), join with sl st to the side of the first dc on first row, ch 5, sc in same sp, *ch 5, skip next end of row, sc in next end of row. Rep from * 14 more times, ch 2, dc in last end of row—17 ch-5 sps.

ROWS 2–20: Rep Rows 2–20 of first wedge.

Rep directions for 9 (10, 11, 12) wedges total, joining last wedge to first strip.

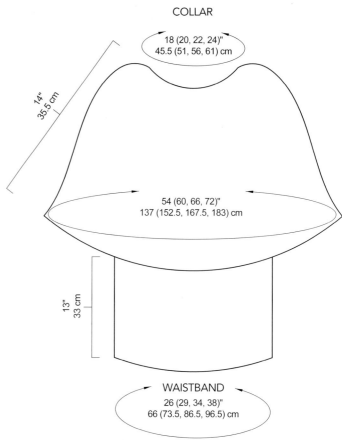

COLLAR

18 (20, 22, 24)"
45.5 (51, 56, 61) cm

14"
35.5 cm

54 (60, 66, 72)"
137 (152.5, 167.5, 183) cm

13"
33 cm

WAISTBAND

26 (29, 34, 38)"
66 (73.5, 86.5, 96.5) cm

Dazzling Dolmans

Classic dolman or "batwing" sleeves start at the waistline and taper to the cuff. The style was very popular in the 1990s, but isn't as popular now. The trick to elevating dolman sleeves to the current fashion lies in the cape! Circular cape shapes with a cinching waist are extremely popular. They're also great fun to crochet. Working from the top down is an easy choice for a cape, increasing evenly for a circular shape. Or you can combine circular motifs and increase the hook size or quantity on each row for a different cape shape. You can, of course, think outside the box, like our expert Kristin Omdahl did, and work vertically up the cape in wedge shapes. This construction creates a flattering and stylish shape for a skirt, with wedges added at the hemline for flare. Just think of the styles made possible by using the wedges from another skirt design and adding the waistband from this one. My fingers are just itching to crochet!

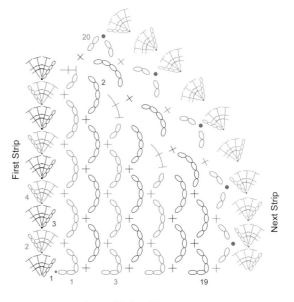

First Strip

Next Strip

20

2

4

3

2

1

1

3

19

Lace Wedge Diagram

Finishing

BLOCKING

Pin body to schematic size and spray with water. Allow to dry.

WAISTBAND

ROW 1: Join yarn with sl st to center of any lower end of strip. Ch 50, hdc in 3rd ch from hook and each ch across—49 hdc, sl st in next ch-5 sp, turn.

ROW 2: Hdc blp in each st across, turn—49 hdc.

ROW 3: Ch 2 (counts as hdc), hdc blp in each st across, sl st in next ch-5 sp (or strip), turn.

**Rep Rows 2–3 until you have worked across the lower edge for 10 (13, 13, 16)" (25.5 [33, 33, 40.5] cm). End with a Row 3.

SIDE SEAM ROWS 1–9 (5, 13, 9): Ch 2, hdc blp in each st across, turn.

JOINING ROW 10 (6, 14, 10): Repeat Row 3. Skip next 17 (17, 20, 20)" (43 [43, 51, 51] cm) on edge, sl st in next ch-5 sp, turn.**

Rep from ** to ** once more.

Join last row to beg chain as follows to turn lower body into a tube: ch1, insert hook into back loop only of last row and into first of beg ch, yo, pull though all loops (double thickness slip stitch). *Insert hook into back loop only of next st and next beg ch, yo, pull through all loops. Rep from * across. Fasten off.

SLEEVE EDGING

Join with sl st to underarm, *ch 4, dc2tog in 4th ch from hook, sc in next ch-5 sp along sleeve edging. Rep from * around. Fasten off.

Rep for second sleeve.

NECK EDGING

Join with sl st to any ch-5 sp on neck. *ch 4, dc2tog in 4th ch from hook, sc in next ch-5 sp of neck opening. Rep from * around. Sl st to first sc at beg of round. Fasten off.

walnut berry
V-NECK

Classic style and fit are two of my favorite qualities in fashion. Modern looks are great for now, but my crocheted sweaters usually outlast the trends. The stitch pattern for the Walnut Berry Cardigan is a classic berry stitch, updated only by the weight of the yarn. Because the cardigan is crocheted in one piece from bottom edge to front edge, the stitch pattern shines throughout.

Materials

YARN

DK weight (#3 Light)

SHOWN: Cascade Yarn 220 Superwash (100% superwash wool; 220 yd [200 m]/3.5 oz [100 g]): #862 Walnut Heather (MC) 4 (5, 6, 7, 8) balls; #875 Feather Gray (CC) 1 (1, 1, 1, 1) ball.

HOOK

Size H/8 (5.0 mm) for S, L, 2X; size I/9 (5.5 mm) for M, XL; or hook needed to obtain gauge.

NOTIONS

Tapestry needle for weaving in ends; spray bottle with water; straight pins for blocking; one 1⅛" (28 mm) diameter button.

Gauge

1 SR by 8 rows = 3⅝" × 3¾" (9.25 × 9.5 cm) in berry lace stitch pattern with size H/8 hook.

1 SR by 8 rows= 3⅞" × 4" (9.75 × 10 cm) in berry lace stitch pattern with size I/9 hook.

Finished Size

Bust measurement is 35¾ (38½, 43, 46, 50)" (90.5 [98, 109, 117, 127] cm). Sized for Small (Medium, Large, X-Large, 2X). Size shown is Small.

Notes

M, XL use the larger hook size throughout; S, L, 2X use the smaller hook size throughout.

Cardigan is worked from the back bottom edge up to the neck and down to the front edge. Arms are added by crocheting on a foundation chain that's added at the beginning and end of the indicated row.

Special Stitches

SHELL (SH)

Work (ch 1, [dc, ch 1] 6 times) in st indicated.

HALF SHELL (HALF SH)

Work ([dc, ch 1] twice, dc) in st indicated.

V-ST

Work (dc, ch 3, dc) in st indicated.

DCDTRTOG

Yo, insert hook into st indicated and draw up lp, yo and pull through 2 lps on hook, yo 3 times, insert hook into next st indicated and draw up a lp, [yo and pull through 2 lps on hook] 3 times, yo and pull through last 3 lps on hook.

BERRY LACE STITCH PATTERN (BLSP)

See Berry Lace Diagram (page 144) for assistance.

Ch a mult of 17 sts plus 4.

ROW 1 (RS): Sc in 5th ch from hook, ch 3, sk 2 ch, sc in next ch, *sk 3 ch, sh in next ch, sk 3 ch, [sc in next ch, ch 3, sk 2 ch] 3 times, sc in next ch; rep from * across to last 13 ch, sk 3 ch, sh in next ch, sk 3 ch, sc in next ch, ch 3, sk 2 ch, sc in next ch, ch 1, sk 1 ch, hdc in last ch, turn.

ROW 2: Ch 4 (counts as dc, ch 1), dc in hdc, ch 3, *sk 1st dc on sh, [sc in next ch-1 sp, ch 3] 4 times, sc in next ch-1 sp, ch 3, sk 1st ch-3 sp, V-st in next ch-3 sp, ch 3, sk last ch-3 sp; rep from * across to last sh, sk 1 ch-1 sp on sh, [sc in next ch-1 sp, ch 3] 4 times, sc in next ch-1 sp, ch 3, sk next ch-3 sp, [dc, ch 1, dc] in 2nd ch of tch, turn.

ROW 3: Ch 3 (counts as dc), (half sh, ch 1) in ch-1 sp, sk next ch-3 sp, *[sc in next ch-3 sp, ch 3] 3 times, sc in next ch-3 sp, sk next ch-3 sp, sh in next ch-3 sp, sk next ch-3 sp; rep from * across to last 5 ch-3 sps, [sc in next ch-3 sp, ch 3] 3 times, sc in next ch-3 sp, sk next ch-3 sp, (ch 1, half sh, dc) in tch sp, turn.

ROW 4: Ch 1, sc in 1st dc, [ch 3, sc in next ch-1 sp] twice, *ch 3, sk next ch-3 sp, V-st in next ch-3 sp, ch 3, sk last ch-3 sp, sk 1st dc on sh, [sc in next ch-1 sp, ch 3] 4 times, sc in next ch-1 sp; rep from * across to last sh, ch 3, sk next ch-3 sp, V-st in next ch-3 sp, ch 3, sk last ch-3 sp, sk 1st dc on sh, [sc in next ch-1 sp, ch 3] twice, sc in top of tch, turn.

ROW 5: Ch 3 (counts as hdc, ch-1 sp), sc in next ch-3 sp, ch 3, sc in next ch-3 sp, *sk next ch-3 sp, sh in next ch-3 sp, sk next ch-3 sp, [sc in next ch-3 sp, ch 3] 3 times, sc in next ch-3 sp; rep from * across to last 5 ch-3 sps, sk next ch-3 sp, sh in next ch-3 sp, sk next ch-3 sp, sc in next ch-3 sp, ch 3, sc in next ch-3 sp, ch 1, hdc in last sc, turn.

Rep Rows 2–5 for pattern.

Pattern

BACK

Ch 89 (89, 106, 106, 123) with MC.

ROW 1 (RS): Cont in Row 1 of BLSP 5 (5, 6, 6, 7) sh or SR.

ROWS 2–29 (29, 33, 33, 33): Rep Rows 2–5 of BLSP 7 (7, 8, 8, 8) times.

ROWS 30 (30, 34, 34, 34)–32 (32, 36, 36, 36): Rep Rows 2–4 of BLSP once.

ARMS

See Diagram A (page 146) for assistance.

ROW 1 (RS): Join new ball of yarn to first sc of last row with sl st, ch 35, fasten off. Ch 37 (at end of last row), cont with Row 1 of BLSP to last ch, sk last ch, ch 3, sc in next ch-3 sp, cont in Row 5 of BLSP across to last ch-3 sp, sc in last ch-3 sp, ch 3, sk 1 ch, sc in next ch, cont in Row 1 of BLSP across to end, turn—9 (9, 10, 10, 11) SR.

ROWS 2–5 (5, 5, 5, 9): Rep Rows 2–5 of BLSP 1 (1,1,1,2) times,

(S, M, 2X)

ROW 6 (6,10): Rep Row 2 of BLSP.

(L, XL)

ROWS 6–8: Rep Rows 2–4 of BLSP.

NECK OPENING

See Diagram B (page 146) for assistance.

ROW 1 (RS): Cont in Row 3 (3, 5, 5, 3) of BLSP across to 3rd (3rd, 4th, 4th, 4th) V-st, (ch 1, half sh, dc) in V-st, leave remaining sts unworked, turn. 3 (3, 3.5, 3.5, 4) SR.

ROW 2: Cont in Row 4 of BLSP to end (end, tch, tch, end), **(L, XL)** (dc, ch 1, dc) in tch sp, turn.

ROW 3: **(S, M, 2X)** Ch 3, sc in next ch-3 sp, ch 3, sc in next ch-3 sp, **(L, XL)** ch 3, (half sh, ch 1) in ch-1 sp, [sc in next ch-3 sp, ch 3] 3 times, sc in next ch-3 sp, **(ALL)** cont in Row 5 of BLSP across, turn.

ROW 4: Cont in Row 2 of BLSP to end (end, half sh, half sh, end), **(L, XL)** [sc in next ch-1 sp, ch 3] twice, sc in top of tch, turn.

ROW 5: **(L, XL)** Ch 3, sc in next ch-3 sp, ch 3, sc in next ch-3 sp, **(S, M, 2X)** ch 3, (half sh, ch 1) in ch-1 sp, [sc in next ch-3 sp, ch 3] 3 times, sc in next ch-3 sp, **(ALL)** cont in Row 3 of BLSP across, turn.

ROWS 6–17 (17, 21, 21, 21): Rep Rows 2–5 of neck opening 3 (3, 4, 4, 4) times.

ROW 18 (18, 22, 22, 22): Rep Row 2 of neck opening.

Neck Shaping

See Diagram C (page 147) for assistance.

ROW 1 (RS): **(S, M, 2X)** Ch 3, sc in next ch-3 sp, ch 3, sc in next ch-3 sp, **(L, XL)** ch 3, (half sh, ch 1) in ch-1 sp, [sc in next ch-3 sp, ch 3] 3 times, sc in next ch-3 sp, **(ALL)** cont in Row 5 of BLSP across to last ch-3 sp, sc in last ch-3 sp, ch 3, hdc in last sc, turn.

ROW 2: Ch 3, V-st in first ch-3 sp, ch 3, cont in Row 2 of BLSP to end (end, half sh, half sh, end), **(L, XL)** [sc in next ch-1 sp, ch 3] twice, sc in top of tch, turn.

(S, M, 2X)

ROW 3: Cont in Row 3 of BLSP across to last V-st, ([ch 1, dc] 5 times, ch 1] in last V-st, dc2tog over last V-st and tch, turn—1 add'l sh.

ROW 4: Ch 4, [sc in next ch-1 sp, ch 3] 4 times, sc in next ch-1 sp, cont in Row 4 of BLSP to end, turn.

Fastening Off Arms

See Diagram D (page 147) for assistance.

ROW 1 (RS): Ch 3, *sc in next ch-3 sp, ch 2, dc in next ch-3 sp, ch 2, (hdc, ch 2, hdc) in V-st, ch 2, dc in next ch-3 sp, ch 2, sc in next ch-3 sp, ch 2; rep from * once, sc in next ch-3 sp, ch 3, sc in next ch-3 sp, sh in next V-st, cont in BLSP to tch (tch, last V-st, last V-st, tch), **(S, M, 2X)** ch 1, dtr in

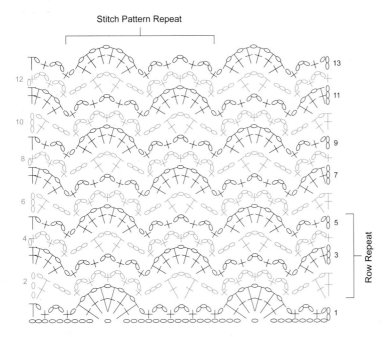

Berry Lace Stitch Pattern

Stitch Pattern Repeat

Row Repeat

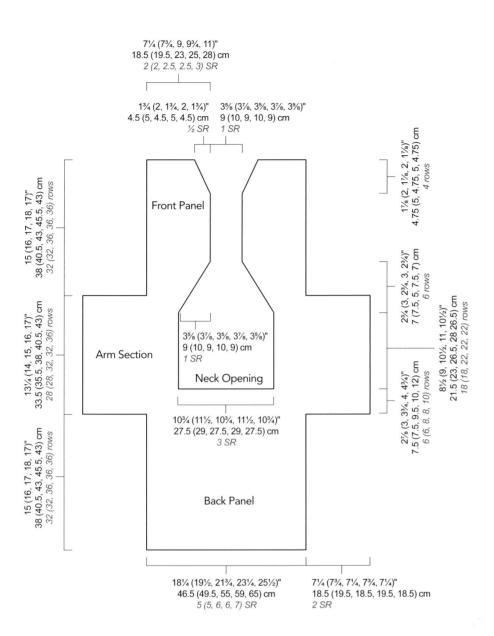

Front Panel

Arm Section

Neck Opening

Back Panel

7¼ (7¾, 9, 9¾, 11)"
18.5 (19.5, 23, 25, 28) cm
2 (2, 2.5, 2.5, 3) SR

1¾ (2, 1¾, 2, 1¾)"
4.5 (5, 4.5, 5, 4.5) cm
½ SR

3⅝ (3⅞, 3⅝, 3⅞, 3⅝)"
9 (10, 9, 10, 9) cm
1 SR

1⅞ (2, 1⅞, 2, 1⅞)"
4.75 (5, 4.75, 5, 4.75) cm
4 rows

15 (16, 17, 18, 17)"
38 (40.5, 43, 45.5, 43) cm
32 (32, 36, 36, 36) rows

13¼ (14, 15, 16, 17)"
33.5 (35.5, 38, 40.5, 43) cm
28 (28, 32, 32, 36) rows

2¾ (3, 2¾, 3, 2¾)"
7 (7.5, 7, 7.5, 7) cm
6 rows

2⅞ (3, 3¾, 4, 4¾)"
7.5 (7.5, 9.5, 10, 12) cm
6 (6, 8, 8, 10) rows

8½ (9, 10½, 11, 10½)"
21.5 (23, 26.5, 28 26.5) cm
18 (18, 22, 22, 22) rows

3⅝ (3⅞, 3⅝, 3⅞, 3⅝)"
9 (10, 9, 10, 9) cm
1 SR

10¾ (11½, 10¾, 11½, 10¾)"
27.5 (29, 27.5, 29, 27.5) cm
3 SR

15 (16, 17, 18, 17)"
38 (40.5, 43, 45.5, 43) cm
32 (32, 36, 36, 36) rows

18¼ (19½, 21¾, 23¼, 25½)"
46.5 (49.5, 55, 59, 65) cm
5 (5, 6, 6, 7) SR

7¼ (7¾, 7¼, 7¾, 7¼)"
18.5 (19.5, 18.5, 19.5, 18.5) cm
2 SR

ROW 4: Ch 1, sc in dc, ch 3, sc in ch-1 sp, ch 3, sc in next ch-1 sp, cont in Row 4 of BLSP across, turn.

(ALL)

ROW 3 (3, 5, 5, 3): Cont in Row 3 (3, 5, 5, 3) of BLSP across to last ch-3 sp, sc in last ch-3 sp, ch 3, hdc in last sc, turn.

ROW 4 (4, 6, 6, 4): Ch 3, V-st in next ch-3 sp, ch 3, cont in Row 4 (4, 2, 2, 4) of BLSP across, turn.

ROW 5 (5, 7, 7, 5): Cont in Row 5 (5, 3, 3, 5) of BLSP to last V-st, ([ch 1, dc] 5 times, ch 1] in last V-st, dc2tog over last V-st and tch, turn—1 add'l sh.

ROW 6 (6, 8, 8, 6): Ch 4, [sc in next ch-1 sp, ch 3] 4 times, sc in next ch-1 sp, cont in Row 2 (2, 4, 4, 2) of BLSP to end, turn.

ROW 7 (7, 9, 9, 7): Cont in Row 3 (3, 5, 5, 3) of BLSP to tch, ch 1, dtr in tch sp, (ch 1, hdc, ch 1, dc) in post of dtr just made, turn.

ROW 8 (8, 10, 10, 8): Ch 1, sc in dc, ch 3, sc in ch-1 sp, ch 3, sc in next ch-1 sp, cont in Row 4 (4, 2, 2, 4) of BLSP across, turn—2 (2, 2.5, 2.5, 3) SR.

FRONT PANEL

ROW 1 (RS): (S, M, 2X) Ch 3, sc in next ch-3 sp, ch 3, sc in next ch-3 sp, (L, XL) ch 3, (half sh, ch 1) in ch-1 sp, [sc in next ch-3 sp, ch 3] 3 times, sc in next ch-3 sp, (ALL) cont in Row 5 of BLSP across, turn.

ROW 2: Cont in Row 2 of BLSP to end (end, half sh, half sh, end), (L, XL) [sc in next ch-1 sp, ch 3] twice, sc in top of tch, turn.

ROW 3: (L, XL) Ch 3, sc in next ch-3 sp, ch 3, sc in next ch-3 sp, (S, M, 2X) ch 3, (half sh, ch 1) in ch-1 sp, [sc in next ch-3 sp, ch 3] 3 times, sc in next ch-3 sp, (ALL) cont in Row 3 of BLSP across, turn.

ROW 4: Cont in Row 4 of BLSP to end (end, tch, tch, end), (L, XL) (dc, ch 1, dc) in tch sp, turn.

ROW 5–20 (20, 20, 20, 24): Rep Rows 1–4 of front panel 4 (4, 4, 4, 5) times.

tch sp, (ch 1, hdc, ch 1, dc) in post of dtr just made (insert hook into center of st at middle horizontal bar created by yo), turn; (L, XL) ([ch 1, dc] 5 times, ch 1] in last V-st, dc2tog over last V-st and tch, turn—2 (2, 1, 1, 2) less sh.

ROW 2: (S, M, 2X) Ch 1, sc in dc, ch 3, sc in ch-1 sp, ch 3, sc in next ch-1 sp, (L, XL) ch 4, [sc in next ch-1 sp, ch 3] 4 times, sc in next ch-1 sp, (ALL) cont in BLSP to first ch-2 sp, (dc, ch 1, dc) in ch-2 sp, turn, leave remaining sts unworked.

(L, XL)

ROW 3: Cont in Row 3 of BLSP to tch, ch 1, dtr in tch sp, (ch 1, hdc, ch 1, dc) in post of dtr just made (insert hook into center of st at middle horizontal bar created by yo), turn.

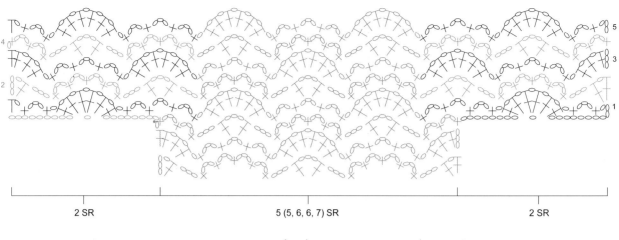

2 SR | 5 (5, 6, 6, 7) SR | 2 SR

a. Arm Increase

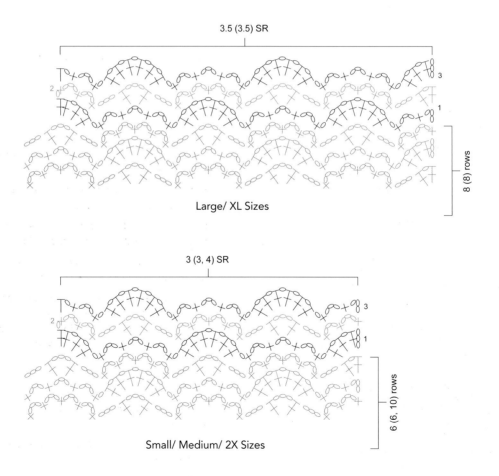

3.5 (3.5) SR

8 (8) rows

Large/ XL Sizes

3 (3, 4) SR

6 (6, 10) rows

Small/ Medium/ 2X Sizes

b. Neck Opening

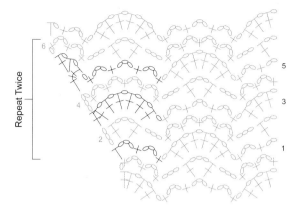

c. Neck Shaping

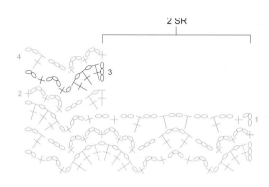

d. Fastening Off Arm Section

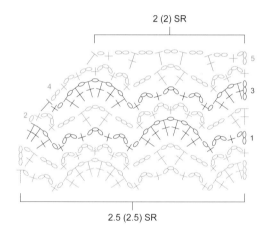

Large/XL Sizes

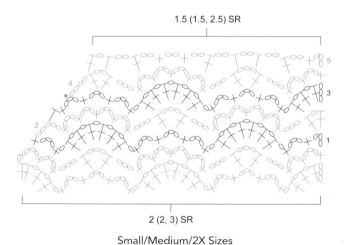

Small/Medium/2X Sizes

e. Bottom Edge Shaping

(L, XL)

ROWS 21–22: Rep Rows 1–2 once more.

Bottom Edge Shaping

See Diagram E for assistance.

(S, M, 2X)

ROW 1 (RS): Cont in Row 5 of BLSP across to last ch-3 sp, sc in last ch-3 sp, turn.

ROW 2: Ch 5, sk ch-3 sp, sk ch-1 sp, sc in next ch-1 sp, cont in Row 2 of BLSP across, turn.

ROW 3: Cont in Row 3 of BLSP across to last ch-3 sp, sc in last ch-3 sp, hdc in ch-5 sp, fasten off. Turn.

ROW 4: Join w sl st to first ch-3 sp, ch 4, V-st in next ch-3 sp, cont in Row 4 of BLSP across, turn.

ROW 5: Ch 3, * sc in next ch-3 sp, ch 2, dc in next ch-3 sp, ch 2, (hdc, ch 2, hdc) in V-st, ch 2, dc in next ch-3 sp, ch 2, sc in next ch-3 sp, ch 2; rep from * 0 (0, 1) time(s), sc in next ch-3 sp, ch 2, dc in next ch-3 sp, ch 2, hdc in V-st, ch 1, dc bet tch and V-st, fasten off.

(L, XL)

ROW 1 (RS): Cont in Row 5 of BLSP across to tch, (dc, ch 1, 2 dc) in tch sp, turn.

ROW 2: Ch 1, sc in dc, ch 3, sc in ch-1 sp, cont in Row 2 of BLSP across, turn.

ROW 3: Cont in Row 3 of BLSP across to last ch-3 sp, sc in last ch-3 sp, hdc in last sc, turn.

ROW 4: Ch 2, sk ch-1 sp, [sc in next ch-1 sp, ch 2] twice, [sc in next ch-1 sp, ch 3] twice, sc in next ch-1 sp, cont in Row 4 of BLSP across, turn.

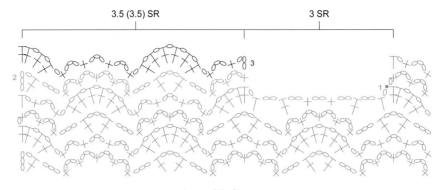

3.5 (3.5) SR   3 SR

Large/XL Sizes

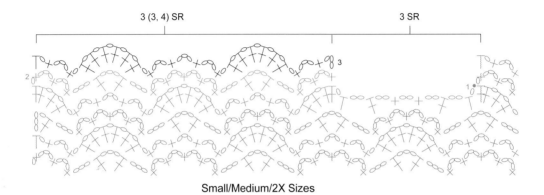

3 (3, 4) SR   3 SR

Small/Medium/2X Sizes

f. Opposite Neck Opening

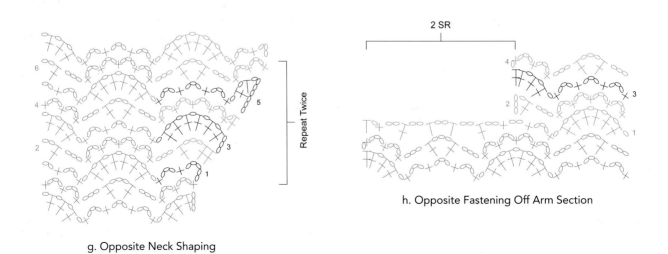

g. Opposite Neck Shaping

2 SR

h. Opposite Fastening Off Arm Section

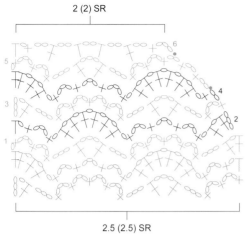

2 (2) SR

2.5 (2.5) SR

Large/XL Sizes

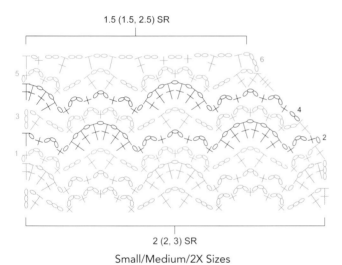

1.5 (1.5, 2.5) SR

2 (2, 3) SR

Small/Medium/2X Sizes

j. Opposite Bottom Edge Shaping

ROW 5: Ch 3, sc in next ch-3 sp, ch 2, dc in next ch-3 sp, ch 2, (hdc, ch 2, hdc) in V-st, ch 2, dc in next ch-3 sp, [ch 2, sc in next ch-3 sp] twice, ch 2, dc in next ch-3 sp, ch 2, (hdc, ch 2, hdc) in V-st, ch 2, dc in next ch-3 sp, ch 2, sc in next ch-3 sp, ch 1, hdc in next ch-2 sp, fasten off.

Opposite Neck Shaping

See Diagram F for assistance.

ROW 1 (RS): Join yarn with sl st to top of last dc in Row 1 of neck shaping. Ch 1, hdc in same V-st as half sh, *ch 2, sk ch-3 sp, dc in next ch-3 sp, [ch 2, sc in next ch-3 sp] twice, ch 2, dc in next ch-3 sp, ch 2, (hdc, ch 2, hdc) in V-st; rep from * once, ch 2, sk ch-3 sp, dc in next ch-3 sp, [ch 2, sc in next ch-3 sp]

twice, ch 2, dc in next ch-3 sp, ch 2, (hdc, ch 1, dc, half sh, ch 1) in V-st, cont in Row 3 (3, 5, 5, 3) of BLSP across, turn—3 (3, 3.5, 3.5, 4) SR.

ROW 2: (L, XL) Ch 4, dc in hdc, ch 3, sk ch-3 sp, sk ch-1 sp [sc in next ch-1 sp, ch 3] 5 times, (**ALL**) cont in Row 4 of BLSP across, turn.

ROW 3: Cont in Row 5 of BLSP across to end (end, tch, tch, end), (**L/XL**) (ch 1, half sh, dc) in tch sp, turn.

ROW 4: (L/ XL) Ch 1, sc in dc, [ch 3, sc in ch-1 sp] twice, (**ALL**) cont in Row 2 of BLSP across, turn.

ROW 5: Cont in Row 3 of BLSP to end (end, last ch-3 sp, last ch-3 sp, end), (**L, XL**) sc in last ch-3 sp, ch 1, hdc in last sc, turn.

ROWS 6–17 (17, 21, 21, 21): Rep Rows 2–5 of opposite neck opening 3 (3, 4, 4, 4) times.

ROW 18 (18, 22, 22, 22): Rep Row 2 of neck opening.

Neck Shaping

See Diagram G for assistance.

ROW 1 (RS): Ch 5, sc in next ch-3 sp, ch 3, sc in next ch-3 sp, cont in Row 5 of BLSP across to end (end, tch, tch, end), (**L/XL**) (ch 1, half sh, dc) in tch sp, turn.

ROW 2: (L/ XL) Ch 1, sc in dc, [ch 3, sc in ch-1 sp] twice, (**ALL**) cont in Row 2 of BLSP across to tch, (V-st, dc) in tch sp, turn.

ROW 3: Ch 3, ([dc, ch 1] 6 times) in V-st, cont in Row 3 of BLSP to end, turn—1 add'l sh.

ROW 4: Cont in Row 4 of BLSP to last ch-1 sp, sc in ch-1 sp, ch 1, dc in top of tch, turn.

Opposite Fastening Off

See Diagram H (page 148) for assistance.

ROW 1 (RS): (S, M, 2X) Ch 7, (hdc, ch 1, dc) in 5th ch from hook, ch 1, sc in next ch-3 sp, (L, XL) ch 3, ([dc, ch 1] 6 times) in V-st, (ALL) cont in BLSP to last 14 ch-3 sps, *ch 2, sc in next ch-3 sp, ch 2, dc in next ch-3 sp, ch 2, (hdc, ch 2, hdc) in V-st, ch 2, dc in next ch-3 sp, ch 2, sc in next ch-3 sp, rep from * once, ch 1, hdc in last sc, fasten off—2 (2, 1, 1, 2) less sh.

ROW 2: Join with sl st to last ch-2 sp, ch 4, dc in same ch-2 sp, ch 3, cont in BLSP across to last ch-1 sp, (S, M, 2X) sc in last ch-1 sp, ch 3, (sc, ch 3, sc) in tch sp, turn; (L, XL) sc in last ch-1 sp, ch 1, dc in top of tch, turn.

(L, XL)

ROW 3: Ch 7, (hdc, ch 1, dc) in 5th ch from hook, ch 1, sc in next ch-3 sp, cont in Row 3 of BLSP across, turn.

ROW 4: Cont in Row 4 of BLSP across to last ch-1 sp, sc in last ch-1 sp, ch 3, (sc, ch 3, sc) in tch sp, turn.

(ALL)

ROW 3 (3, 5, 5, 3): Ch 5, sc in next ch-3 sp, ch 3, sc in next ch-3 sp, cont in Row 3 (3, 5, 5, 3) of BLSP across to end, turn.

One-Piece Wonderful

Because crochet can go in any direction at any time, garments don't require classic panels. Many beautiful silhouettes can be achieved by simply removing the seams. This cardigan has neither shoulder nor armhole seams. It hides the seams on the underarms and sides to let the beauty of the stitch pattern continue uninterrupted through the shoulders and arms. This method isn't ideal for truly fitted sleeves (because there's no cap shaping to remove bulk), but it works very well for oversized or batwing sleeves. Sweaters can be fitted in the waist just as classic panels are fitted. Sweaters can overlap, wrap, float open, or be buttoned closed; there are no limits to the front-panel styles. The only caveat of this style is that you need to use a lace-stitch pattern or a less dense yarn. Without shoulder seams, there is no reinforcement to help take the weight of the garment. Make sure that patterns are lacy and/or that yarn isn't heavy so your garment won't stretch over time.

ROW 4 (4, 6, 6, 4): Cont in Row 4 (4, 2, 2, 4) of BLSP across to tch, (V-st, dc) in tch sp, turn.

ROW 5 (5, 7, 7, 5): Ch 3, ([dc, ch 1] 6 times) in V-st, cont in Row 5 (5, 3, 3, 5) of BLSP to end, turn—1 add'l sh.

ROW 6 (6, 8, 8, 6): Cont in Row 2 (2, 4, 4, 2) of BLSP to last ch-1 sp, sc in ch-1 sp, ch 1, dc in top of tch, turn.

ROW 7 (7, 9, 9, 7): Ch 7, (hdc, ch 1, dc) in 5th ch from hook, ch 1, sc in next ch-3 sp, cont in Row 3 (3, 5, 5, 3) of BLSP across, turn.

ROW 8 (8, 10, 10, 8): Cont in Row 4 (4, 2, 2, 4) of BLSP across to last ch-1 sp, sc in last ch-1 sp, ch 3, (sc, ch 3, sc) in tch sp, turn—2 (2, 2.5, 2.5, 3) SR.

OPPOSITE FRONT PANEL

ROW 1: Cont in Row 5 of BLSP across to end (end, tch, tch, end), (L/XL) (ch 1, half sh, dc) in tch sp, turn.

ROW 2: (L/ XL) Ch 1, sc in dc, [ch 3, sc in ch-1 sp] twice, (ALL) cont in Row 2 of BLSP across, turn.

ROW 3: Cont in Row 3 of BLSP to end (end, last ch-3 sp, last ch-3 sp, end), (L, XL) sc in last ch-3 sp, ch 1, hdc in last sc, turn.

ROW 4: (L, XL) Ch 4, dc in hdc, ch 3, sk ch-3 sp, sk ch-1 sp [sc in next ch-1 sp, ch 3] 5 times, (ALL) cont in Row 4 of BLSP across, turn.

ROWS 5–16 (16, 16, 16, 20): Rep Rows 1–4 of opposite front panel 3 (3, 3, 3, 4) times.

ROWS 17 (17, 17, 17, 21)–19 (19, 19, 19, 23): Rep Rows 1–3 once more.

(L/ XL)

ROWS 20 (20)–21 (21): Rep Row 4 and Row 1 once more.

Opposite Bottom Edge Shaping

See Diagram J (page 149) for assistance.

(S, M, 2X)

ROW 1: Cont in Row 4 of BLSP across to last ch-1 sp, sc in last ch-1 sp, ch 1, dc in top of tch, turn.

ROW 2: Ch 1, sc in dc, ch 3, sc in ch-3 sp, cont in Row 5 of BLSP across, turn.

ROW 3: Cont in Row 2 of BLSP across to last 2 ch-1 sps, sc in next ch-1 sp, ch 2, dc in last sc, turn.

ROW 4: Ch 2, [sc in next ch-3 sp, ch 3] 3 times, cont in Row 3 of BLSP across, turn.

ROW 5: Cont in Row 4 of BLSP across to last 2 ch-3 sps, dc in next ch-3 sp, ch 2, dcdtrtog over prev and last ch-3 sp, turn.

ROW 6: Ch 4, hdc in ch-2 sp, *ch 2, sk next ch-3 sp, dc in next ch-3 sp, [ch 2, sc in next ch-3 sp] twice, ch 2, dc in next ch-3 sp, ch 2, (hdc, ch 2, hdc) in V-st; rep from * 0 (0, 1) time(s), ch 2, sk next ch-3 sp, dc in next ch-3 sp, ch 2, sc in next ch-3 sp, ch 1, hdc in last sc, fasten off.

(L, XL)

ROW 1: Ch 1, sc in dc, [ch 3, sc in ch-1 sp] twice, cont in Row 2 of BLSP across, turn.

ROW 2: Ch 3, (dc, ch 1, dc) in ch-1 sp, ch 1, sk next ch-3 sp, sc in next ch-3 sp, cont in Row 5 of BLSP across, turn.

ROW 3: Cont in Row 2 of BLSP across to last ch-1 sp, sc in last ch-1 sp, ch 3, sc in top of tch, turn.

ROW 4: Ch 2, sc in ch-3 sp, sh in V-st, cont in Row 3 of BLSP across, turn.

ROW 5: Cont in Row 4 of BLSP across to last 4 ch-1 sps, [sc in next ch-1 sp, ch 2] 3 times, sl st to top of tch, turn, fasten off.

ROW 6: Join with sl st to 3rd ch-2 sp, ch 3, sc in next ch-3 sp, ch 2, dc in next ch-3 sp, ch 2, (hdc, ch 2, hdc) in V-st, ch 2, dc in next ch-3 sp, [ch 2, sc in next ch-3 sp] twice, ch 2, dc in next ch-3 sp, ch 2, (hdc, ch 2, hdc) in V-st, ch 2, dc in next ch-3 sp, ch 2, sc in last ch-3 sp, ch 1, hdc in last sc, fasten off.

Finishing

BLOCKING AND SEAMING

Pin to schematic size and spray with water. Allow to dry. Fold cardigan in half at shoulders with right sides together. Pin in place. Whipstitch underarm and side seam with leftover yarn. Turn right side out.

CUFFS

Join yarn to edge of cuff with sl st, ch 16.

ROW 1: Sc in 2nd ch from hook and each ch across, sl st to edge of cuff twice (once to join, once for tch), turn—15 sc.

ROW 2: Sc blp in each sc across, turn.

ROW 3: Ch 1, sc blp in each sc across, sl st to edge of cuff twice, turn.

Rep Rows 2–3 around cuff. Whipstitch last row to first row.

COLLAR AND EDGE

Place markers at 4 inside corners of neck and 6 outside corners of front panels. Join yarn with sl st to back panel's bottom edge.

RND 1: Ch 1, sc evenly around bottom edge, front edge, collar edge, and neck working around row ends, sl st to first sc, turn.

RNDS 2–4: Ch 3, [dc in each st around to m, 2 dc in outside m corners, place m in first dc] 3 times, dc in each st around to 1 st before m, dc3tog over next 3 sts, place m in dc3tog, [dc in each st across to 2 sts before m, dc5tog over next 5 sts, place m in dc5tog] twice, dc in each st around to 1 st before m, dc-3tog over next 3 sts, place m in dc3tog, [dc in each st around

to m, 2 dc in outside m corners, place m in first dc] 3 times, dc in each st to tch, sl st to top of tch, turn.

RND 5: Ch 1, sc in each dc around, sl st to first sc, fasten off.

Join CC to Rnd 3 using dc as a guide, sl st embroider on top of row around (insert hook from right side to wrong side to pick up a loop). Rep on Rnd 4.

Sew button to cardigan at uppermost outside corner; use space between dc as buttonhole.

Symbol Crochet Basics

The key to understanding crochet symbols is that each symbol represents a crochet stitch. I like to think of the symbols as little stick diagrams of the actual stitch. Let's look at the smallest stitch, the chain. The symbol is an oval. Why an oval? Think about making a chain stitch: It's a simple loop pulled through another loop. Each loop looks like an oval. The international crochet symbols try to mimic the actual stitch as much as they can.

Next is the slip stitch, which is a filled dot. It's small and almost invisible, just like the actual stitch. The single crochet is a squat cross, again just like the stitch. The half double crochet is slightly taller then the single crochet. The double crochet is taller then the half double and has an extra cross in its middle. From the double crochet up, the little cross tells you how many yarnovers you have before you insert your hook. If you make a double crochet, you'll see the little cross in the middle of the stitch. That's why the double crochet symbol has a bar in the middle of its post. The rest of the symbols follow the same reasoning. If the stitch is short, the symbol will be short; if the stitch puffs out, the symbol will as well.

To read **granny square diagrams**, you need to start in the center just as you would to crochet. Following the symbol key, crochet the stitches you see. The numbers on the diagram let you know where the beginning of each round is so you can keep track of where you are. Granny square diagrams feature each round in a new color so it's easy to keep track of which round you're on.

Stitch pattern diagrams aren't much different from granny square diagrams. The key difference is that instead of crocheting in the round, you crochet back and forth in turned rows. Therefore, when you read the diagram, you need to start at the bottom foundation chain. Crochet as many chains as the diagram shows. Then, following the symbol key, crochet the stitches you see for the first row. At the end of the row, turn, and continue crocheting the stitches you see for the following rows. The numbers on the diagram let you know where the beginning of each row is so you can keep track of where you are. Each diagram will have a new color for each row so it's easy to keep track of which row you're on.

Top Six Rules of Symbol Crochet

Remember the following simple rules as you follow the symbol crochet diagrams featured throughout the book. They summarize the crochet symbol basics we just reviewed.

1 Each symbol represents one stitch to crochet. (See below for a list of symbols and their stitches.)

2 Each symbol is a tiny stick diagram of the actual stitch. The taller or fatter the symbol, the taller and fatter the stitch it represents.

3 Each row or round is a different color in the diagrams to help you keep track of which one you're working on.

4 Each row or round has a number next to the beginning turning chain, indicating the start of the row or round and the row or round number.

5 Granny square diagrams start in the center and increase outward, just as you would crochet them.

6 Stitch pattern diagrams work rows back and forth and will indicate in brackets how many stitches to repeat in a design.

Symbol Key

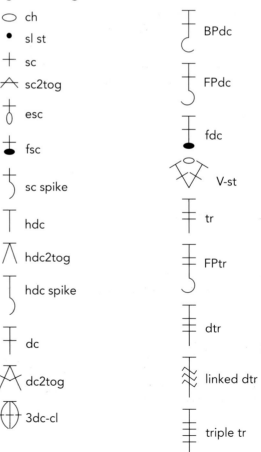

ch	BPdc
sl st	FPdc
sc	fdc
sc2tog	V-st
esc	tr
fsc	FPtr
sc spike	dtr
hdc	linked dtr
hdc2tog	triple tr
hdc spike	
dc	
dc2tog	
3dc-cl	

Abbreviations

BPdc	back post double crochet
beg	begin/beginning
bet	between
blp	through back loop(s) only
BPdc	back post double crochet
BPtr	back post treble crochet
CC	contrasting color
ch	chain
ch-sp	chain space
cm	centimeter(s)
dc	double crochet
dc-cl	double crochet cluster
dec	decrease/decreases/decreasing
dtr	double treble crochet
ea	each
esc	extended single crochet
est	established
fdc	foundation double crochet
flp	through front loop(s) only
foll	follow/follows/following
FPdc	front post double crochet
FPtr	front post treble crochet
fsc	foundation single crochet
g	gram(s)
hdc	half double crochet
incr	increase/increases/increasing
lp(s)	loop(s)
MC	main color
m	marker

opp	opposite
pm	place marker
prev	previous
rem	remain/remaining
rep	repeat(s)
rnd	round
RR	row repeat
RS	right side
sc	single crochet
sh	shell
sk	skip
sl st	slip stitch
SR	stitch repeat
st(s)	stitch(es)
tch	turning chain
tog	together
tr	treble crochet
tr-cl	treble crochet cluster
trtr	triple treble crochet
WS	wrong side
yd	yard(s)
yo	yarn over
*	repeat instructions following asterisk as directed
**	repeat all instructions between asterisks as directed
()	perform stitches in same indicated sts
()	alternate instructions and/or measurements
[]	work bracketed instructions specified number of times

Crochet Stitches

Crochet Chain (ch)

Make a slipknot and place it on crochet hook. *Yarn over hook and draw through loop on hook. Repeat from * for the desired number of stitches.

Slip Stitch (sl st)

*Insert hook into stitch, yarn over hook and draw loop through stitch and loop on hook. Repeat from *.

Single Crochet (sc)

Insert hook into a stitch, yarn over hook and draw up a loop, yarn over hook and draw it through both loops on hook.

Single Crochet 2 Together (sc2tog)

[Insert hook into next indicated stitch, yarn over hook and draw up a loop] x times, yarn over hook, draw through all loops on hook—(x-1) decrease made.

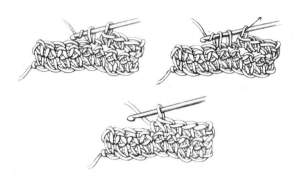

Foundation Single Crochet (fsc)

Ch 2 (does not count as fsc), insert hook in 2nd ch from hook, yo and pull up lp, yo and draw through 1 lp (the "ch"), yo and draw through 2 lps (the "fsc"), * insert hook under 2 lps of the "ch" st of last fsc, yo and pull up lp, yo and draw through 1 lp, yo and draw through 2 lps, rep from * for length of foundation.

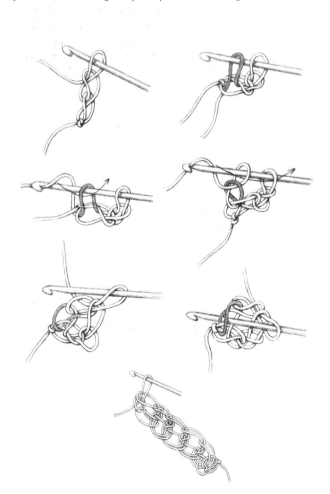

Single Crochet Seaming

To seam with single crochet, make stitches as usual, but insert the hook through both pieces of fabric at the same time.

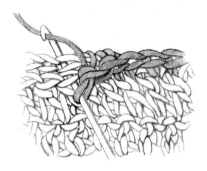

Adjustable Ring

Make a large loop with the yarn. Holding the loop with your fingers, insert hook into loop and pull working yarn through loop. Yarn over hook, pull through loop on hook.

Continue to work indicated number of stitches into loop. Pull on yarn tail to close loop.

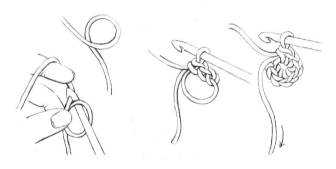

Half Double Crochet (hdc)

*Yarn over hook, insert hook into a stitch, yarn over hook and draw up a loop (3 loops on hook), yarn over hook and draw it through all loops on hook. Repeat from *.

Half Double Crochet x Together (hdcxtog)

[Yarn over hook, insert hook into next indicated stitch, yarn over hook and draw up a loop] x times, yarn over hook and draw yarn through remaining loops on hook—(x-1) decrease made.

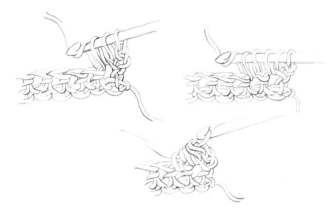

Double Crochet (dc)

*Yarn over hook, insert hook into a stitch, yarn over hook and draw up a loop (3 loops on hook; figure 1), yarn over hook and draw it through 2 loops, yarn over hook and draw it through remaining 2 loops on hook. Repeat from *.

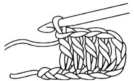

Double Crochet x Together (dcxtog)

[Yarn over hook, insert hook into NEXT indicated stitch, yarn over hook and draw up a loop, yarn over hook and draw yarn through 2 loops] x times, yarn over hook and draw yarn through remaining loops on hook—(x-1) decrease made.

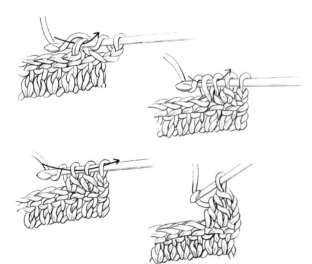

X Double Crochet Cluster (Xdc-cl)

[Yarn over hook, insert hook into indicated stitch, yarn over hook, draw up loop, yarn over hook, draw through 2 loops on hook] x times, yarn over hook, draw through remaining loops on hook.

Front Post double crochet (FPdc)

Yo, insert hook from front to back to front, yo, pull up a lp, yo, draw through 2 lps on hk, yo, draw through last 2 lps on hook.

Back Post double crochet (BPdc)

Yo, insert hook from back to front to back, yo, pull up a lp, yo, draw through 2 lps on hk, yo, draw through last 2 lps on hook.

Treble Crochet (tr)

*Wrap yarn around hook twice, insert hook into next indicated stitch, yarn over hook and draw up a loop (4 loops on hook), yarn over hook and draw it through 2 loops, yarn over hook and draw it through the next 2 loops, yarn over hook and draw it through remaining 2 loops on hook. Repeat from *.

Front Post treble crochet (FPtr)

Yo twice, insert hook from front to back to front around post of stitch indicated, yo and pull up a lp, [yo, draw through 2 lps on hk] twice, yo, draw through last 2 lps on hook.

Back Post treble crochet (BPtr)

Yo twice, insert hook from back to front to back around post of stitch indicated, yo and pull up a lp, [yo, draw through 2 lps on hk] twice, yo, draw through last 2 lps on hook.

Double Treble Crochet (dtr)

*Wrap yarn around hook 3 times, insert hook into stitch, yarn over hook and draw up a loop (5 loops on hook), [yarn over hook and draw it through 2 loops] 4 times. Repeat from *.

Triple Treble Crochet (trtr)

*Wrap yarn around hook 4 times, insert hook into stitch, yarn over hook and draw up a loop (6 loops on hook), [yarn over hook and draw it through 2 loops] 5 times. Repeat from *.

Embroidery Stitches

Backstitch

Working from right to left, bring needle up at 1 and insert behind the starting point at 2. Bring the needle up at 3, repeat by inserting at 1 and bring the needle up at a point that is a stitch length beyond 3.

Whipstitch

With right sides of work facing and working through edge stitches, bring threaded needle out from back to front, along edge of piece.

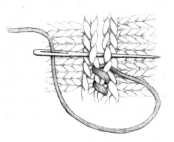

Woven Seam

STEP 1: Secure the seaming yarn on the wrong side of piece A at the start of the seam. Pass the needle through to the right side at the bottom of the first stitch.

STEP 2: Put the needle through the bottom of the first stitch of piece B and pass it up to the right side again at the top of the stitch (or in the stitch above, if you're working in single crochet).

STEP 3: Put the needle through the bottom of the first stitch of piece A, exactly where you previously passed the needle to the right side, and bring the needle to the right side at the top of the stitch.

STEP 4: Put the needle through piece B, where you previously passed the needle to the right side, and bring the needle to the right side at the top of the stitch.

STEP 5: Put the needle through piece A, where you previously passed the needle to the right side, and bring the needle through to the right side at the top of the stitch in the next row.

Repeat Steps 4 and 5, gently tightening the seam as you go, being careful not to distort the fabric. Allow the rows to line up but don't make the seam tighter than the edges themselves. The edges will roll to the wrong side of the work. Secure the end of the seaming yarn.

Piece A   Piece B

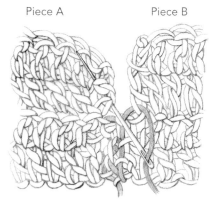

Woven seam applied "row to row."

About the Author

A structural engineer by trade, Robyn Chachula uses her knowledge of building-design processes to create crochet projects in Pittsburgh, Pennsylvania. In her first crochet book, *Blueprint Crochet: Modern Designs for the Visual Crocheter* (Interweave, 2008), she used her engineering background to bring crochet to new learners with the basics of symbol crochet. In her follow-up book, *Baby Blueprint Crochet: Irresistible Projects for Little Ones* (Interweave, 2010), she dove deeper into the mysteries of crochet diagrams through small, parent-friendly baby projects. Robyn is also the author of *Simply Crochet: 22 Stylish Designs for Every Day* (Interweave, 2012), *Unexpected Afghans: Innovative Crochet Designs with Traditional Techniques* (Interweave, 2012), and *Crochet Stitches Visual Encyclopedia* (Wiley, 2011). You can catch Robyn as one of the crochet experts on *Knit and Crochet Now* on public television or in her Interweave Workshop DVDs, *Crochet Sweater Studio*, *Unexpected Crochet Stitches*, *Crocheted Hats*, and *Crochet Baby Sweaters*. Stop by crochetbyfaye.com to see what has inspired her lately.

About the Contributors

MARLAINA BIRD
Ruby Cropped Cardi (page 100)

As a wife and mother, the creative director for Bijou Basin Ranch, a knitting and crochet designer and teacher, and the host of the Yarn Thing Podcast, Marlaina Bird is busy! But Marly wouldn't have it any other way. You can find more of her designs and listen to her show at yarnthing.blogspot.com. Also catch one of her popular classes at craftsy.com.

DREW EMBORSKY
Smoky Cropped Top (page 60)

Drew Emborsky, aka The Crochet Dude®, was taught to crochet at age five by his mother while snowbound in Lake Tahoe. After studying fine art in college and doing the "starving artist" thing for years, he found solace in crocheting for charity while grieving the loss of his mother. During his time with the charity group, he became known as The Crochet Dude, which led to the launch of his wildly popular blog, thecrochetdude.com, in 2005. Since then, Drew has published numerous patterns in magazines and compilations books as well as his own full-length books, and he has appeared as a guest on various TV programs. Drew has teamed up with Boye® brand hooks to launch his own line of kits, hooks, tools, and accessories, called The Crochet Dude® Collection, available nationwide.

SIMONA MERCHANT-DEST
Foliage Shrug (page 30)

Born and raised in the Czech Republic, Simona Merchant-Dest designs knit and crochet patterns for magazines, books, yarn companies, and her own pattern collection. She lives in Maryland with her husband and three daughters. You can read more about Simona and her designs at stylishknits.blogspot.com and simonamerchantdest.com.

KRISTIN OMDAHL
Veronica Pullover (page 138)

Kristin Omdahl is passionate about creating with her hands. She loves coastal tropical living and having fun outside with her son every day. Kristin is the author of *A Finer Edge* (Interweave, 2012), *Wrapped In Crochet: Scarves, Wraps & Shawls* (Interweave, 2008), *Crochet So Fine: Exquisite Designs with Fine Yarns* (Interweave, 2010), *A Knitting Wrapsody: Innovative Designs to Wrap, Drape, and Tie* (Interweave, 2011), and *Seamless Crochet: Techniques and Motifs for Join-As-You-Go Designs* (Interweave 2011). Her latest ventures are "Sweetheart Shawls Workshop" on craftsy.com; "Complements Collection," an eBooklet by Bijou Basin Ranch Yarns; and her YouTube Channel KristinOmdahl. She is the crochet expert on *Knitting Daily TV* and offers several DVD workshops on knitting and crochet. When she isn't running, cooking, and playing guitar and piano, she enjoys knitting and crocheting in her orchid garden in sunny southwest Florida. You can check out what's new with Kristin at styledbykristin.com.

Cranberry Cardigan Diagrams A–H, continued from page 15

36 (40, 44, 50, 54, 58) Stitch Repeats

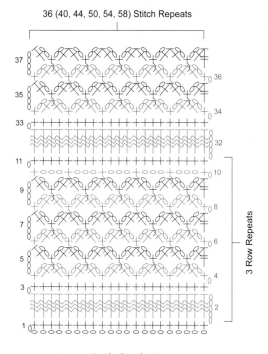

a. Lower Body Stitch Diagram

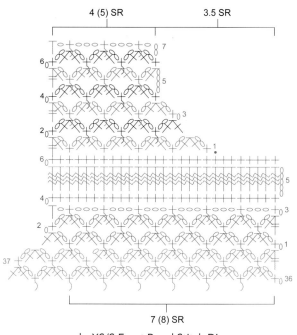

b. XS/S Front Panel Stitch Diagram

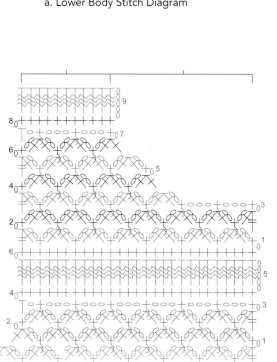

b. M/L Front Panel Stitch Diagram

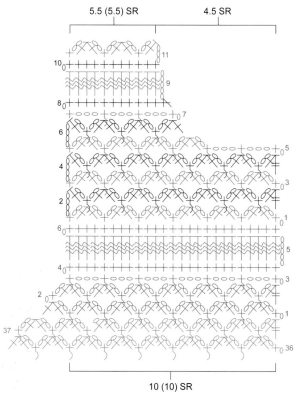

b. XL/2X Front Panel Stitch Diagram

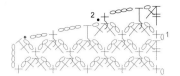

XS Shoulder Stitch Diagram

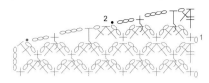

S Shoulder Stitch Diagram

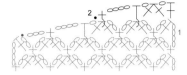

M Shoulder Stitch Diagram

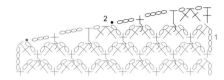

L Shoulder Stitch Diagram

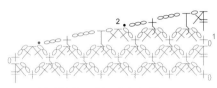

XL/2X Shoulder Stitch Diagram

c. Front Panel Shoulder

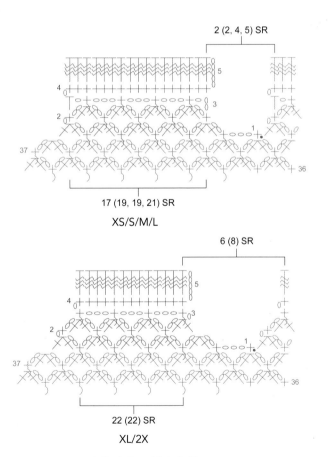

2 (2, 4, 5) SR

17 (19, 19, 21) SR

XS/S/M/L

6 (8) SR

22 (22) SR

XL/2X

d. Back Panel Stitch Diagram

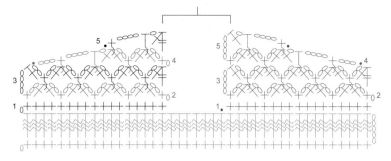

e. X-Small Back Panel Shoulder Stitch Diagram

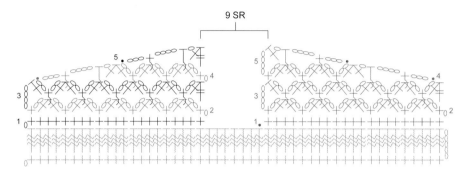

e. Small Back Panel Shoulder Stitch Diagram

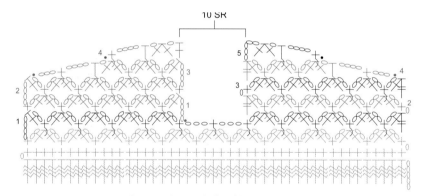

e. Medium Back Panel Shoulder Stitch Diagram

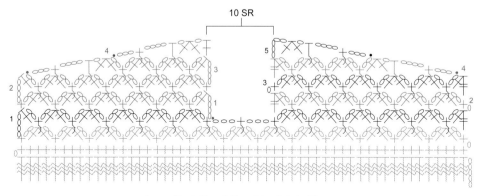

e. Large Back Panel Shoulder Stitch Diagram

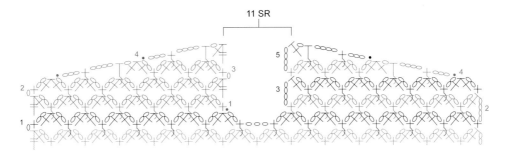

e. XL/2X Back Panel Shoulder Stitch Diagram

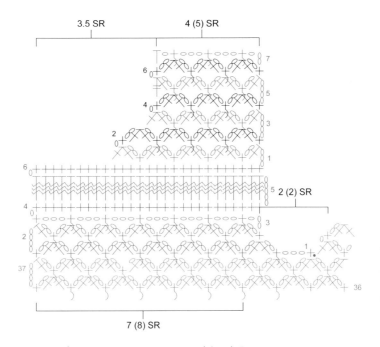

f. XS/S Opposite Front Panel Stitch Diagram

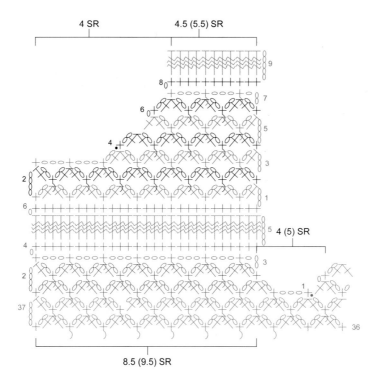

f. M/L Opposite Front Panel Stitch Diagram

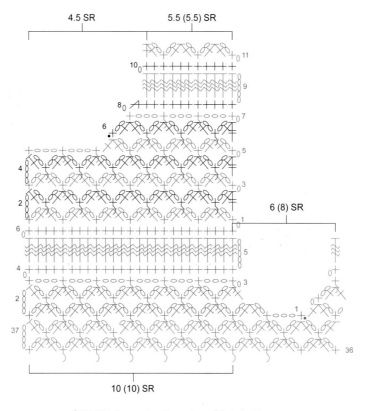

f. XL/2X Opposite Front Panel Stitch Diagram

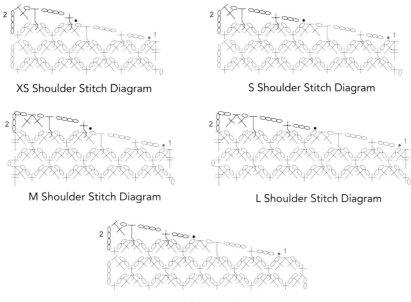

XS Shoulder Stitch Diagram

S Shoulder Stitch Diagram

M Shoulder Stitch Diagram

L Shoulder Stitch Diagram

XL/2X Shoulder Stitch Diagram

g. Opposite Front Panel Shoulder

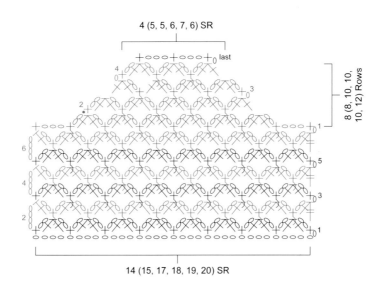

4 (5, 5, 6, 7, 6) SR

8 (8, 10, 10, 10, 12) Rows

14 (15, 17, 18, 19, 20) SR

h. Sleeve Stitch Diagram

Resources

Bijou Basin Ranch

PO Box 154
Elbert, CO
(303) 601-7544
bijoubasinranch.com
Bijou Spun Lhasa Wilderness

Blue Sky Alpacas

PO Box 88
Cedar, MN 55011
(763) 753-5815
blueskyalpacas.com
Spud and Chloe Fine, Suri Merino, Alpaca Silk

Caron International

PO Box 222
Washington, NC 27889
caron.com
Naturally Caron Country; Naturally Caron Spa

Cascade Yarns

1224 Andover Park E.
Tukwila, WA 98188
cascadeyarns.com
Cascade 220 Superwash, Ultra Pima

Lion Brand Yarn

135 Kero Rd.
Carlstadt, NJ 07072
(800) 258-9276
lionbrand.com
MicroSpun; LB Collection Cotton Bamboo

Tahki Stacy Charles

70-30 80th St.
Bldg 36
Ridgewood, NY 11385
(800) 338-9276
tahkistacycharles.com
Filatura Di Crosa Zara

Universal Yarn

284 Ann Street
Concord, NC 28025
(704) 789-Yarn (9276)
universalyarn.com
Blossom Street Collection Rosebud, Garden 5

Index

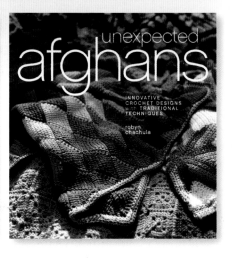